SEE NO EVIL

Robert Baer was a case officer in the Directorate of Operations for the Central Intelligence Agency from 1976 to 1997. He served in places such as Iraq, Dushanbe, Rabat, Beirut, Khartoum, and New Delhi, and received the Career Intelligence Medal in 1997. He now divides his time between Washington DC, and France.

SEE NO EVIL

The true story of a ground soldier in the
CIA's war on terrorism

Robert Baer

ARROW

Published by Arrow Books in 2002

1 3 5 7 9 10 8 6 4 2

Copyright © Robert Baer 2002

Robert Baer has asserted his right under the Copyright, Designs and Patents
Act, 1988 to be identified as the author of this work

CIA's Publications Review Board has reviewed the manuscript for this book
to assist the author in eliminating classified information and poses no
security objection to its publication. This review, however, should not be
construed as an official release of information, confirmation of its accuracy,
or an endorsement of the author's views.

First published in the United Kingdom in 2002 by Arrow

Arrow Books
The Random House Group Limited
20 Vauxhall Bridge Road, London, SW1V 25A

Random House Australia (Pty) Limited
20 Alfred Street, Milsons Point, Sydney,
New South Wales 2061, Australia

Random House New Zealand Limited
18 Poland Road, Glenfield
Auckland 10, New Zealand

Random House (Pty) Limited
Endulini, 5a Jubilee Road, Parktown 2193, South Africa

The Random House Group Ltd Reg. No. 954009

www.randomhouse.co.uk

A CIP catalogue record for this book
is available from the British Library

Papers used by Random House are natural, recyclable
products made from wood grown in sustainable forests.
The manufacturing processes conform to the environmental
regulations of the country of origin.

ISBN 0 09 944554 9

Typeset by MATS, Southend-on-Sea, Essex
Printed and bound in Great Britain by
Bookmarque, Ltd, Croydon, Surrey

TO CHARLOTTE, ROBERT AND JUSTINE.
I hope this goes a little way on explaining where I was for all those years.

ACKNOWLEDGMENTS

I WOULD LIKE TO THANK my former CIA colleagues who devoted their lives to attempting to give America a first-rate intelligence organization, one it now so badly needs. Their many achievements, which can never be made public, are the foundation of everything I managed to accomplish in the CIA. Equally, I thank my many Arab and Iranian agents and friends who patiently walked me through the complexities of the Middle East and provided the raw facts so essential to decoding the place. I am only sorry none of them can be named. Special thanks goes to Rafe Sagalyn, my agent, who was one of the first to see the possibilities of turning my story into a book. Howard Means, Kristin Kiser, and Steve Ross provided the editorial support that turned a rambling CIA story into a book.

CONTENTS

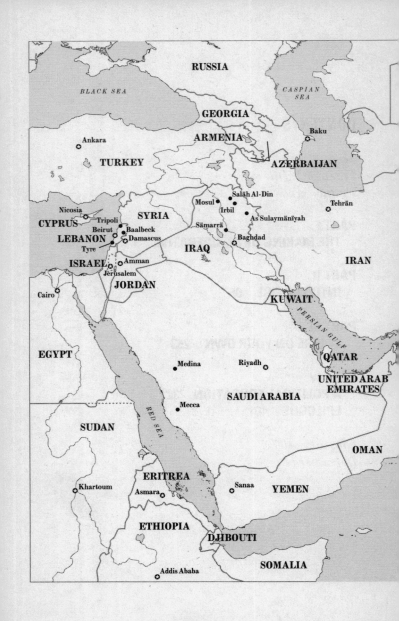

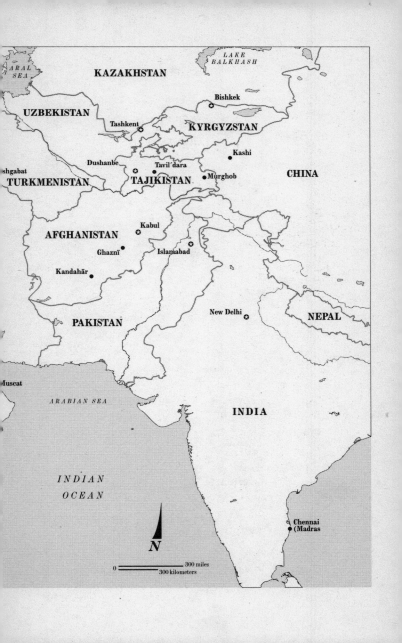

FOREWORD

BOB BAER IS NOT ALONE. Yes, his riveting account of life in the post-cold war CIA is devastating—yet another body blow to the reputation of an intelligence agency that failed to protect America when it needed to be protected. But Baer's account of cowardly bureaucrats and indifferent officials in the White House will ring true to a very special audience—the dozens of distinguished and successful CIA operatives who have taken early retirement in recent years, in lieu of continuing to pretend that they were making a difference. I've talked to many of these men and women in recent months, and they, like Baer, are writhing with pain, anger, and frustration. Like Baer, they weren't allowed to do their job the right way the way it had to be done to be effective.

We've hit intelligence rock bottom in America. As this is being written, nearly three months after the September 11 terrorism attacks, the intelligence community still cannot tell us who was responsible, how the assassins worked, where they trained, which groups they worked for, or whether they will strike again.. Did Osama bin Laden and his Al Qaeda network pull it off by themselves, as the Bush Administration constantly claims, or was at least one other Mideast terrorist group involved, as Bob Baer suggests? We don't know, but I'm betting that the facts, when they emerge, will back up Baer's instinct that the attacks in America were not solely the responsibility of someone operating out of a cave in Afghanistan.

There is another way, too, of looking at *See No Evil*—as a recruiting poster for the spy business. We can identify with Baer's anger at the perceived foolishness and indecisiveness of top management throughout his career, but there are also moments when Baer's brains, energy, and aggressiveness—he was a ski racer as a teenager—led to dramatic break-throughs and deeper understanding of the world of terrorism. Baer was always on the edge in his under-cover work, and his rendition of the risks he took as an undercover CIA operative on mission—some self-assigned—in Lebanon, Tajikistan, Germany, northern Iraq, and inside the White House is the stuff of Clancy thrillers, with the added knowledge that the dangers were real.

Baer tells us, with admiration, about the superb training he received early in his CIA career, and the high standards of those who taught him. "[S]pying wasn't something you learned from a book, a training film, or a lecture," Baer writes. "You learned it by doing it, with someone looking over your shoulder." Once overseas, Baer found that some of the men he worked under weren't up to the job—we all know what that's like—but more often he had superiors who demanded the best from themselves and their staff. He was taught very early in his career as an operative—that is, he was willing to be taught—an enviable lesson: that you can't spy without reading.

Baer tells us how he came to work early and stayed late reading files on terrorists and unpuzzling their connections until he began to see what others who did not could not. In this book, we learn, with Baer, how a good CIA agent goes about his work.

This is the story of one man's disillusionment and anger at an agency whose effectiveness we've come to rely upon. It is also the story of Bob Baer's education and evolution, and his freedom, inside the CIA,to spend the time and have the support necessary to turn himself into an expert. Can one man make a difference, even in a vast, broken agency like the CIA? *See No Evil* tells us yes, he can. This is a memoir that will not win friends and influence on the management floor at CIA headquarters, but it tells us that, with the right leadership, there's still hope for the agency if only it can learn the lessons to be had from this cautionary tale.

Get new managers who see the big picture—and who are willing to take risks—and the Bob Baers will be found. But let's do it before we get hit again.

Seymour M. Hersh
Washington, D.C.
November 24, 2001

PREFACE

IN LATE 1994 I found myself living pretty much on airplanes. I would arrive in Amman, Jordan in the late afternoon, check into a hotel, take a quick shower, and then spend the night talking to one Iraqi dissident or another about what to do with Saddam Hussein. Often I wouldn't crawl into bed until well after midnight, only to get up a few hours later to catch a plane back to Washington and my office at CIA headquarters in Langley, Virginia. It made for a long day. I was used to it, though, having spent nearly twenty years working the streets of the Middle East at the same pace.

Occasionally, in this covert version of shuttle diplomacy, I'd get off the plane in London and just walk around the city so I could catch my breath. I didn't follow a particular route, but often without intending it, I'd end up in the Edgware Road area, a part of central London taken over by Arabs and other Middle Easterners. With the veiled women, and the men walking around in flowing robes, it felt like I'd never left the Middle East, but there was one subtle difference: the Arabic bookstores.

In most parts of the Middle East, bookstores are forbidden from selling radical Islamic tracts that openly advocate violence, but in London's Arabic bookstores there were racks of them. One glance at the bold print and you knew what they were about: a deep, uncompromising hatred for the United States. In the worldview of the people who wrote and published these tracts, a jihad, or holy war, between Islam and America wasn't just a possibility; for them the war was a given, and it was already under way. Having spent so much of my life in the Middle East, I knew that such intense, violent hatred represented an aberration of Islam; but I also knew better than most the human toll that such hatred can take.

Often I would pick up a tract and take a look at the small print. Rarely did the publisher or the editor's name appear on the masthead, and office addresses were never noted. But with few exceptions, they carried a European post-office box, often in Britain or in Germany. It didn't take a sophisticated intelligence organization to figure out that Europe, our traditional ally in the war against the bad guys, had become a hothouse of Islamic fundamentalism.

Curious, I asked my CIA colleagues in London if they knew who was putting this stuff out. They had no idea, but there was really no reason why they should have. Since our London office couldn't claim a single Arabic speaker, it was unlikely that anyone there was going to wander down Edgware Road. Even if someone had, he wouldn't have been able to read the venomous headlines. What's more, the CIA was prohibited by British authorities from recruiting sources, even Islamic fundamentalists, in their country. What was the point, then, in spending time with the Arabs there?

In general, things were no better on the continent.

By the mid-1990s, the CIA was shriveling up everywhere in Europe. Our offices in Bonn, Paris, and Rome were shadows of what they had been during the cold war with the Soviet Union. They lacked the officers to go after Europe's vast Middle Eastern communities, and those they did have too often lacked the inclination, the training, and in some cases the incentive to do so.

Things weren't much better in the Middle East. Often there were only one or two CIA officers assigned to a country. Rather than recruit and run sources—foreign agents—CIA stations in the tinderbox of the world spent most of their time catering to whatever was in fashion in Washington at the time: human rights, economic globalization, the Arab-Israeli conflict. To veterans like me, the CIA seemed to be doing little more than flying the flag.

A LOT OF US who spent time on the ground in the Middle East worried that something big and bad was in the offing. There was too much hatred out there, and too many means of destruction to keep the bubble of American innocence from bursting. But I don't think anyone saw with any precision the September 11 attacks on the World Trade Center and the Pentagon coming. Even by the standards of the terrorists involved, the scale of the assault was almost unimaginable. The point, though, is that we didn't even try to find out what was headed our way.

Like the rest of Washington, the CIA had fallen in love with technology. The theory was that satellites, the Internet, electronic intercepts, even academic publications would tell us all we needed to know about what went on beyond our borders. As for Islamic fundamentalists in particular, the official view had become that our allies in Europe and the Middle East could fill in the missing pieces. Running our own agents—our own foreign human sources—had become too messy. Agents sometimes misbehaved; they caused ugly diplomatic incidents. Worse, they didn't fit America's moral view of the way the world should run.

Not only did the CIA systematically shed many of its agents, it also began to ease out many of their onetime handlers: seasoned officers who had spent their careers overseas in the hellholes of the world. In 1995 the agency handed the title of director of operations—the man officially in charge of spying—to an analyst who had never served overseas. He was followed by a retiree, and the retiree by an officer who had risen through the ranks largely thanks to his political skills. In practical terms, the CIA had taken itself out of the business of spying. No wonder we didn't have a source in Hamburg's mosques to tell us Muhammad Atta, the presumed leader of the hijacking teams on September 11, was recruiting suicide bombers for the biggest attack ever on American soil.

THIS BOOK IS A MEMOIR of one foot soldier's career in the other cold war, the one against terrorist networks that have no intention of collapsing under their own weight as the Soviet Union did. It's a story about places most Americans will never travel to, about people many Americans would prefer to think we don't need to do business with.

It is drawn from memory, investigative notes, and diaries. As the reader will soon figure out, there is too much detail, almost none of which has ever appeared outside of government files, for any one person to remember. All my life I've been a consummate note taker. At the same time, not surprisingly, some of the details simply can't be told. Every CIA employee is required to sign an agreement that allows the agency to review and censor anything written for publication. I've left the censor's blackouts in the text so readers can see how it works. But more than enough detail remains to give the reader an idea just how complicated the problem of terrorism is, and what this life has been like: the highs and lows, the dangerous moments in the field, and the sometimes more dangerous moments around the conference tables of official Washington, often as nasty a snake pit as Lebanon's Biqa' Valley.

I haven't edited out the many mistakes I made in the field. The reader should see how painful the learning curve can be in the spy business. Nor have I hidden that I set out to understand how Washington works, with all of its special interests. I allowed myself to get sucked into the fringes of the Clinton campaign-funding scandal. I have nothing to apologize for—other than maybe my own stupidity— but if my name rings a bell, it's likely to be from that time.

I also intend my story to be a metaphor for what has happened to the CIA that I served for nearly a quarter of a century and for what needs to be done now. September 11 wasn't the result of a single mistake but of a series of them. The Germans failed us, as did the British, French, and Saudis. But most of all, we failed ourselves. We didn't have the intelligence we needed or the means for gathering it. Correcting those mistakes and regaining the upper hand in the long war against terrorism isn't going to be easy, but it can be done. The way to start is by putting CIA officers back on the street, by letting them recruit and run sources in the mosques, the casbahs, or anywhere else we can learn what the bad guys' intentions are before they break into horrible headlines and unbearable film footage.

This memoir, I hope, will show the reader how spying is supposed to work, where the CIA lost its way and how we can bring it back again. But I hope this book will accomplish one more purpose as well: I hope it will show why I am angry about what happened to the CIA. And I want to show why every American and everyone who cares about the preservation of this country should be angry and alarmed, too. In letting the CIA fall into decay we lost a vital shield protecting our national sovereignty.

Americans need to know that what happened to the CIA didn't happen just by chance. The CIA was systematically destroyed by political correctness, by petty Beltway wars, by careerism, and much more. At a time when terrorist threats were compounding globally, the agency that should have been monitoring them was being scrubbed clean instead. Americans were making too much money to bother. Life was good. The oceans on either side of us were all the protection we needed. Afloat on this sea of self-absorption, the White House and the National Security Council became cathedrals of commerce where the interests of big business outweighed the interests of protecting American citizens at home and abroad. Defanged and dispirited, the CIA went along for the ride. And then on September 11, 2001, the reckoning for such vast carelessness was presented for all the world to see.

Even if no one could have foreseen those attacks, it's still inconceivable that so many people had to die in order to wake us up to the fact that we have sacrificed a national resource for greed and convenience and small-minded politics. I'm incensed, and I think we should all be incensed, that the courageous passengers of United Airlines Flight 93 were the White House's first and only line of defense on September 11—not the CIA or the FBI or the Immigration and Naturalization Service or any other office or agency that we pay our taxes to support.

The other day a reporter friend told me that one of the highest-ranking CIA officials had said to him, off the record, that when the dust finally clears, Americans will see that September 11 was a triumph for the intelligence community, not a failure. If that's going to be the official line of thinking at the agency charged with manning the front lines in the war against the Osama bin Ladens of this world, then I am more than angry: I'm scared to death of what lies ahead.

PART I
THE MAKING OF AN OPERATIVE

1

MARCH 15, 1995. LANGLEY, VIRGINIA.

AS INSTRUCTED, I reported to Fred Turco's office right at nine. I had worked for Fred in the CIA's Counterterrorism Center in the mid-1980s. Now he was in charge of some new office set up to tighten up security in the CIA. Why he'd summoned me, I had no idea.

Fred took a good look at me standing in his door and didn't necessarily like what he saw. I'd gotten back from northern Iraq the night before and hadn't had time to get a haircut. Sunburned and wearing a sport coat that had been sitting in the bottom of a duffel bag for the past three months, I must have looked like I'd been in the field for years.

"Sit down," Fred said, pointing at a chair pulled up in front of his desk. When he silently ran his fingers through his shock of prematurely gray hair, I knew it wasn't a morning for pleasantries.

"There are two FBI agents upstairs in the general counsel's office waiting to interview you," he finally said. I didn't have to be told what that meant: The FBI doesn't interview CIA officers returning from an overseas assignment unless a criminal investigation is afoot.

"Why the FBI, Fred?"

Fred moved his in box so he could see me better. As he shifted uneasily in his chair, I knew we hadn't hit bottom yet. He fixed me with a stare he was known for all over the CIA and let me have it: "Tony Lake ordered the FBI to investigate you for trying to assassinate Saddam Hussein."

Assassination? I knew what had happened in Iraq was sure to rattle windows at the White House. I knew Lake, the president's national security adviser, was furious at the CIA. But this was *insane*—turning the FBI loose on the CIA. Not to mention that the accusation wasn't true.

███████████████████████████████████

███████████████████████████████████

███████████████

"He can't be serious," I managed to get out.

Fred shrugged, "You have no idea how this town works. Stay cool, and we'll get you through this."

Rob Davis, a lawyer from the general counsel's office, had been sitting so quietly at the conference table in the back of the room that I'd forgotten about him. Now he joined the party.

"Look, Bob, you've been overseas for almost twenty years. Washington really has changed a lot," Davis said. "These kinds of investigations go on all the time now. Fred's right—you'll get through it. And, by the way, it'll make you a better officer."

He was right about Washington having changed, but the part about the investigation being good for my career was bullshit. I'd worked for the CIA long enough to know that it had long ago stopped backing up its officers in the field. An FBI investigation, no matter how baseless, meant my career was over. In the CIA, as elsewhere in the federal government, you're innocent until you're investigated.

I ignored Davis and turned back to Fred, a former case officer who had survived his own run-in with Washington's new political correctness. Rumor had it that while he was working in counterterrorism, he had a close call with the Department of Justice. Fred was running a source, so the story went—a former terrorist who was helping track Carlos the Jackal. The source let us know when Carlos moved from Damascus to Amman and then to Khartoum, where the French, acting on our information, eventually arrested him. The problem was that the source, many years before, had been involved peripherally in an attack in which an American died. A couple of straight-leg Department of Justice attorneys heard about the source's past and tried to nail Fred's hide to the wall for putting a bad guy on the payroll. They didn't care that our bad guy had helped capture a far worse one: an internationally sought assassin. Fred had lasted, though. He knew how the game was played in Washington, and I was counting on him to give me a few quick lessons.

"I'm going up first," Fred said as he stood to leave. "I'll sit through the interview. So will Davis. But don't forget, he'll be there to represent the CIA—not you. The FBI agents are going to tell you you're entitled to a lawyer. It's your call. But if you ask for one, frankly, it's not going to look good inside this building. See you in five minutes.'"

Maybe I should have paid a little more attention to the irony of it all: I was the one being investigated, but it was the CIA who had a lawyer.

★

THE TWO FBI AGENTS were sitting at the general counsel's oval conference table. They stood up, shook my hand, and showed me their credentials.

I recognized one of them. Mike ██████████ and I had worked together in 1986 in Wiesbaden, Germany, debriefing Father Lawrence Jenco, a Catholic priest serving in Lebanon, a hostage who had just been released by Hizballah. Although Mike had known me by a different name then, he remembered me now. The expression on his face seemed to say, Yeah—I, too, recall better times when we were all on the same side and knew who the enemy was; but his words were all business.

"Mr. Baer, we are conducting a criminal investigation," he said as soon as we sat down. "You have the right to an attorney. Do you wish to consult an attorney at this time?"

I had decided to do without one. For a start, I didn't have a lawyer. And even if I did, there was no way I could afford a protracted investigation on my government salary. What was the alternative? Call up the ACLU and explain that I was an accused CIA assassin who needed pro bono counsel? Besides, I didn't need a lawyer to know that in an investigation like this, the one thing you never do is give up anything freely. I'd conducted enough of my own. Just answer the questions, yes or no.

"We are investigating a conspiracy to commit premeditated murder—the murder of Saddam Hussein," Mike began.

I didn't reply.

"Are you aware Executive Order 12333 prohibits the CIA from conducting assassinations?"

President Reagan had issued 12333 in 1981. Since then every incoming CIA officer was obligated to read and initial it.

"I've read it."

"Did you attempt to assassinate Saddam Hussein?"

"No."

"Did you ever order anyone to assassinate Saddam Hussein?"

"No."

"Did anyone on your team, as far as you know, attempt to assassinate Saddam?"

"No."

"Did you ever use the name Robert Pope?"

I didn't answer.

Mike then turned around a thick manila file so I could read a three-page report he'd marked with his finger. It was about a meeting held in late February 1995 in northern Iraq, between Ahmad Chalabi, the head of an Iraqi dissident group, and two Iranian intelligence officers. According to the report, Chalabi told the Iranians the U.S. finally had decided to get rid of Saddam—to assassinate him. To carry it out, he said, the National Security Council had dispatched an "NSC team" headed by Robert Pope to northern Iraq. The NSC, Chalabi explained, had asked him to contact the Iranian government on its behalf to ask for help. The report went on to say that in the middle of the meeting Chalabi had received a telephone call and left the room, giving the Iranians an opportunity to read a letter left conspicuously in the middle of his desk. Supposedly written on NSC stationery, it asked Chalabi to give Mr. Pope "all assistance requested for his mission."

That's when I stopped reading. I knew Ahmad Chalabi well. I had been in northern Iraq when the meeting took place, and I knew beyond a shadow of a doubt that Chalabi had invented this story from scratch. He must have thought that if he could swindle the Iranians into believing that the NSC and the White House were finally serious about getting rid of Saddam, they would have no choice but to throw their support behind Chalabi and his faction. There were, however, problems. There was no Robert Pope, for one. Nor was there any NSC assassination plan. No one, NSC or otherwise, had asked Chalabi to pass a message to Iran. As for the letter, it was clearly forged. Chalabi left it on his desk knowing the Iranians couldn't resist reading it when he was called out of the room.

So far, so good. But like a lot of traps, Chalabi's had caught the wrong hare—not the Iranians he wanted to buy into it, but the national security adviser to the president of the United States. Tony Lake apparently didn't understand how the Middle East works—how conspiracies, lies, and double-crosses like Chalabi's Pope scam make the place go around. But Lake did know Washington and politics.

He had been had, and someone was going to pay. In the endless Beltway turf wars, that meant the CIA, and since I was the CIA's man in northern Iraq, that meant me.

Never mind that Lake knew Ahmad Chalabi had been tried and convicted for defrauding his own bank. Never mind that we were in the middle of the most important action against Saddam Hussein since the end of the Gulf War. I had been summoned back to Washington, and now my career, reputation, and future were in the hands of a very angry, very powerful man. Worse, the agency I had served for nearly twenty years had let it happen without a fight. Worst of all, maybe, I wasn't really surprised. There was a reason America's human intelligence resources had dried up like the Sahara, and it began with a lack of guts right where I was sitting now—in Langley, Virginia.

After I finished with the memo, I looked back up. I knew that if the president's national security adviser didn't understand the Middle East, neither would the two FBI agents. Then again, that wasn't their job.

"None of this is true," I said.

It was obvious to both FBI agents that they weren't getting anywhere. They looked at each other and nodded. Mike turned back to me and asked, "Would you be willing to take a polygraph?"

"No problem," I said. I'd gone too far to turn back now.

Mike accompanied me to the door.

"Frankly, Justice had a hard time with this one," he said when we were in the hall, out of earshot of the others. "They weren't comfortable with 12333 and instead used Title 18, sections 1952 and 1958."

I looked at Mike for a translation.

"Federal murder-for-hire statutes," he said, then turned and walked back to rejoin the others.

As I later found out, the maximum penalty for a conviction under 1952 and 1958 is life imprisonment or death.

2

1962. LOS ANGELES, CALIFORNIA.

WHEN I WAS nine years old, my mother, not long after she separated from my father, picked me up from school one day and announced we were leaving the following week for Europe. Up until then I'd spent my entire uneventful life in California. I didn't see any need for a change, but I wasn't asked. My mother said we'd be away for two months. It ended up being two years.

As soon as my grandfather opened a letter of credit on a Swiss bank, we were on a plane to Zurich. We bought a Fiat convertible and spent the summer and most of the fall driving around the continent, doing the grand museum tour. It wasn't long before I could tell a Canaletto from a Guardi. I picked up some French and German, enough to get by on my own. I learned a little about politics, too. My mother, who had once taught political theory at San Diego State University, decided that impromptu lectures on Aristotle, Plato, Saint Augustine, and Clausewitz more than made up for my absence from grade school. I learned about realpolitik firsthand when we were caught in Berlin in October 1962 during the

Cuban missile crisis. But I think my mother hoped most of all I would take an interest in the classics. We spent months traveling around Greece and Italy, visiting every ruin she could find. We spent one snowy Christmas in Rome, touring the catacombs. She even considered depositing me at a monastery school in Austria that taught ancient Greek and Latin.

Training for a future nine-to-five job in suburban America this was not. But I was learning to adapt quickly to other cultures, and the classics my mother insisted I learn would come in extraordinarily handy: Several decades later, I parlayed my interest in them to visit places where Americans were not particularly welcome, from Lebanon's Biqa' Valley to the rugged mountains of Tajikistan.

I also learned about money during our European sojourn: about having it and not having it. The Swiss account had a bottom line. Weeks in first-class hotels—the best restaurants, the ballet or opera at night—would be followed by other weeks when we were pressed to put a roof over our heads. One time when we tried to cross the border from Germany to France, French customs turned us away because our car insurance was expired. We didn't have a hundred francs to buy temporary insurance. The French sent us back to the German side. The Germans wouldn't allow our reentry for the same reason, but they kindly offered to let us spend the night in their jail while we waited for a shift change on the French side. We stayed up most of the night playing cards and drinking beer with the guards. The next morning the French didn't even bother looking at our papers.

The first place we settled for any length of time was the Swiss ski resort of Klosters. Flush with a new infusion of Grandfather's money, Mother rented a chalet right on the slopes. To make up for my lack of formal education, she hired a tutor to teach me German, but I didn't like learning by rote and soon dropped the lessons. The ski slopes became my classroom.

The next summer, restless and bored with stuffy Switzerland, Mother got it into her head to take a trip to Moscow—a notion that conveniently ignored the cold war and the still smoldering aftermath of the Cuban missile crisis. I'll never forget our interview in Bern with a grim Soviet consul with pale, watery blue eyes. A chain-smoker, he put out his cigarettes between his fingers and almost threw us out of his office when my mother proposed driving all the way to Moscow, camping at night, and taking along our Siamese cat. Eventually, he decided we weren't spies and gave us visas, but only on the condition that we leave the cat in Switzerland and stay in hotels.

My grandfather eventually lost patience and recalled us. Since he was paying the bills, we caught the next plane home. The first place we put down was Salt Lake City, Utah, so we could ski Alta for a season. The following year, 1964, we moved to Aspen, Colorado. The town we drove into in my mother's MGB convertible wasn't the glam sandbox it is today. With a permanent population of about three hundred, Aspen was pretty much a ghost town between ski seasons. Aside from the main highway, only a few streets were paved. Three restaurants stayed open year-round: Pinocchio's pizza parlor, the Red Onion, and the soda fountain at Walgreen's drugstore. The *Aspen Times* was the only newspaper, and it came out once a week. The sole TV channel went off the air at ten P.M.

Our first winter there I joined the ski team, which in those days was one of the best in the United States. (Among my teammates was Andy Mill, later the husband of tennis great Chris Evert.) From September until April we trained without a break. In the evenings, after school, we ran slalom courses under lights, no matter how cold or icy it was. We sidestepped up, made a run, and started up again. I would come home after eight, dead tired. On the weekends we trained on downhill and giant slalom courses at the top of Aspen Mountain. A few summers we trained on the glaciers outside Red Lodge, Montana. No one cared that there wasn't any time for studying. Ski racing was everything. It became the passion of my life.

My first ski coach was Crystal Herbert, a strapping Austrian girl who had recently set the women's Alpine speed record. Following her down a slope at thirty or forty miles an hour, day after day, taught me about taking life to the edge. I remember preparing for a race at Aspen Highlands, on the fastest downhill run in North America. Halfway down there was a Z-turn that began with an abrupt ninety-degree left, a nearly vertical drop, and then an abrupt right. If you crashed, you would end up wrapped around a thick pine tree. The turn was nicknamed the "Moment of Truth."

During an inspection of the course, Crystal gave us a little advice as we stood above the Moment of Truth. In her broken English, she said that if we had any hope of winning in life, we'd have to take risks—sometimes grave ones. And if we wanted to win the race the next day we'd have to let our skis run through the Moment of Truth, not slow down as we had all been doing in the practice runs. Risk it all and you might just win, she said. Hedge your bet and you never will. In the race I let my skis run. I didn't win, but I placed higher than I ever had in a race, and I never forgot the lesson.

SKIING WASN'T ALL that was going on in Aspen. While I was learning to risk it all on the slopes, the 1960s were taking the place by storm. Hippies set up camp in the mountains around Aspen. Bishop Pike, a rogue Episcopal cleric who had replaced the cross above the altar in his San Francisco church with a fish, showed up in town and led a peaceful antiwar protest in front of Secretary of Defense Robert McNamara's house. The mayor, Bugsy Barnard, and his drinking buddies went out one night and chain-sawed every billboard from Aspen to Grand Junction—about 150 miles of them—to do their part for the environment.

Never one to miss a political movement, my mother ran for a Pitkin County commissioner's seat, in the same election that Hunter Thompson, the godfather of gonzo journalism, ran for sheriff. Happily for the proponents of condo sprawl and a drug-free jail-house, neither won.

In the middle of all this turmoil, I decided that I would ski-race for a living. My plan was simple: Quietly drop out of school and train all day. Before anyone noticed, I figured, I would be a champion. It worked fine until Aspen High School notified Mother that I had attended exactly six days of school that spring and was getting straight Fs. (Okay, there was a D in art.) Mother didn't wait for me to get home to discuss it. It took her about five minutes to find me at Pinocchio's. I was sitting in a back booth with my girlfriend, Sue, and a couple of other friends when she stormed into the restaurant.

"All Fs, you son of a bitch," she yelled across a hushed Pinocchio's. "I can't goddamn believe it. You're going to *military school*!"

I was in shock at the time, though I can now see that from my mother's standpoint, military school was about the only option she had; but, always one to put a twist on an otherwise good plan, she pulled me out of Aspen High a month early and took me back to Europe for the summer. If I was headed to military school, she would need to get my political indoctrination right beforehand.

We landed in Paris right in the middle of the May 1968 student demonstrations, the worst civil disturbance in France since the 1871 Commune. Everyone was on strike, the schools were closed, and demonstrators shut down most of the city. Unwilling to take refuge in a hotel, like a sensible tourist might, Mother dragged me into the middle of the demonstrations. One night we were charged by a phalanx of teargas-firing, baton-wielding gendarmes and came within an inch of being arrested.

Looking for a quieter place, we bought a Land Rover and set off for Moscow. To my mother's way of thinking, it was a perfectly rational refuge. The first stop was Prague, right in the middle of Prague Spring. We spent a week mingling with demonstrators there, too, and once again got out just in time. As we crossed the border into Poland, we were forced off the road by a Soviet armored column bearing down on the Czech capital and its rebellious government.

AS PROMISED, I did enroll in military school in the fall, at Culver Military Academy in Culver, Indiana. There I learned how to make a bed tight enough to bounce a quarter off the sheet, field-strip an M-1 rifle, and, to my surprise, study. I even started reading books in my spare time. My grades gradually went up to a B+ average. When the academic dean called me into his office in the fall of my senior year to discuss college, I told him I was thinking about the University of Colorado. Culver was a long way from any snow-covered slopes, and I wasn't ready to give up on my dreams yet. But the dean was a graduate of an Ivy League college, and he had other ideas for my future.

"I see you've spent a lot of time in Europe. Did you ever consider a career as a foreign service officer—the State Department?"

I hadn't, but I promised him I would, and when Georgetown University's School of Foreign Service in

Washington, D.C. accepted me, I wrote back to say I was coming. Skiing would have to wait.

I managed to make it through Georgetown, but not by much. I worked nights in a Georgetown bar, spent as much time as I could in New York City, where I had friends, and lit off for Aspen on every break, often returning to school weeks late. Sometimes merely goofing off wasn't enough. One night I rode a motorcycle with a girl I'll never forget through the basement of Healy Hall during a reunion of the class of '63. The blue blazers and khaki pants parted like the Red Sea. I rode the same motorcycle through the main reading room of the library during final-exam week. For an encore, I rappelled off the top of the Kennedy Center one evening while a performance was going on inside.

A fellow student who watched my pranks from a distance was George Tenet. I wouldn't see him for almost twenty years, and that was at a meeting in the White House. By then he was in charge of the NSC's intelligence programs—a big fish who would get even bigger when he was named head of the CIA in 1997. I hadn't forgotten Tenet, but I was hoping his memory wasn't as good as mine. Alas, it was. "This is the last place I ever thought I'd run into you," he said when he pulled me aside. I couldn't help but agree.

My mother, meanwhile, continued to drift to the left. She moved from Aspen to Venice, California, where she opened up a used bookstore near the pier and turned muse to a couple of lefty writers and poets who would sit around her bookstore debating Marx late into the night. One of them, Ron Kovick, had a measure of success. Paralyzed from a wound in Vietnam, he wrote a memoir entitled *Born on the Fourth of July*. Active in antiwar protests, Kovick and his friends periodically took over Senator Alan Cranston's office in Washington. Kovick invariably would call my mother, just to check in. We'd laugh about the FBI wiretappers puzzling over the eccentric old lady with the used bookstore in Venice.

After Georgetown, I went to Europe to "refresh" my French, which is to say I went to ski, hoping I could pick up all the French I needed after the lifts stopped. Around Christmas, though, the money ran out, and I had to come home and find a job. I considered going back to Aspen to take up acrobatic skiing, which was just coming into its own, but instead I went to San Francisco to look for a job. After all that education, I figured I should at least give it a try.

I picked San Francisco because an old friend from Culver, Mike Kokesh, agreed to let me camp out on his couch until I could find my own place. One Saturday morning Mike started reading out loud from the employment section of the classified ads. Since he already had a job he liked, I suspected that he wanted his couch back. When the classifieds proved fruitless, Mike patiently counted off all the professions he could think of that paid a salary you could live on.

"How about the federal government?" he finally offered.

I'd taken the State Department's foreign service exam in my junior year at Georgetown. I hadn't done too badly, either, falling short by only a few points.

"Take it again," he said.

It wouldn't be given for another year.

"Apply to the CIA," Mike said, laughing.

Mike never dreamed I'd take him seriously. This was San Francisco in 1976, one of those bastions of the counterculture where it was a toss-up whether the CIA or Richard Nixon was worse. But what I didn't admit to Mike was that I was curious about the CIA. In my senior year at Georgetown, the CIA had been on the front pages of the newspapers daily. Frank Church in the Senate and Otis Pike in the House headed up committees of inquiry that seemed to unearth a new CIA scandal every other day or so. I didn't follow the hearings closely, but I was left with the impression that behind the dirt there must be some deep, dark, impenetrable mystery—a forbidden knowledge. Joining the CIA would be sort of like signing up with the Knights Templar. I had never read a James Bond novel, never had a single cloak-and-dagger fantasy, wasn't in the least the sort of type-A personality who wanted to go out and charm the world. But traveling with my mother had given me a romantic view of the world, and for all the taint on it, the CIA seemed for a moment like romance itself.

Without saying a word to Mike, I called the federal center in San Francisco on Monday and asked for the CIA's telephone number. The operator gave me a number in Lawndale, California. The woman who answered the phone took down my name and address and promised to send me a personal history statement—an application—and an admission ticket for a written exam.

The personal history statement was the longest, most detailed form I'd ever seen in my life. Besides every conceivable question about my current circumstances, there were several pages asking about my extended family, friends, clubs, associations, and political affiliations. It took me two weeks and a lot of telephone calls to fill it out. A psychological questionnaire had arrived along with it. I remember one question about bed-wetting.

The written exam, which was given at the Federal Building in San Francisco, was a cross between the SAT and the Foreign Service exam. The other people taking the exam looked older than me but normal enough. I wondered if they, too, were taking the test mostly out of curiosity.

In truth, I figured I'd never hear from the CIA again. Sure, anyone could take the entrance exam, but even if I aced the test, my personal history statement was sure to weed me out. Even apart from my lefty mother, I had absolutely no experience. The last regular job I had held down was washing dishes in Georgetown.

I was wrong. One morning, about a month after the test, I received a long-distance call from a woman asking if I would be available for an interview. She gave me the time, the address of a downtown hotel, and the name of a man I was supposed to meet—Jim Scott. It wasn't until after I hung up that I realized she hadn't said she was calling from the CIA, but since I hadn't applied for any other job, it stood to reason.

The night before, I was nervous, not because I was serious about going to work for the CIA but because this was my first interview for a real job. I wanted to do well. I dug my only suit out of a trunk, hung it up in the bathroom, and ran the shower on hot to steam out the wrinkles. I paced the apartment, trying to imagine what Jim Scott would ask me and how I would respond. I didn't even have a number for him. What if I'd gotten the name of the hotel wrong? I had no way to call the CIA, except the office in Lawndale.

The next morning I called Scott's room from the hotel lobby right on time. He told me to call back in thirty minutes. *That's strange*, I thought. It was only nine, and he couldn't possibly be in another interview. I waited in the lobby imagining all sorts of things. Maybe someone was watching me to see if I was alone. When I called back a half-hour later, Scott told me to come on up.

With his slicked-back hair, tweed coat, and club tie, Jim Scott looked more like a college-football recruiter than how I pictured a CIA agent. I noticed that the bed in his junior suite was made up and there wasn't a suitcase in sight. He must have spent the night somewhere else. There was no way anyone could see in the window, but he still closed the curtains so that the only light came from a bedside lamp.

We sat down on either end of the couch. A wafer-thin manila folder sat on the coffee table. It must have been my file.

"You probably already know a lot about the CIA, but I think it would be helpful to give you a quick overview," Scott started.

I wasn't about to admit that I knew next to nothing about the CIA.

Scott must have given the same spiel a dozen times a week. Essentially, the CIA is divided into two houses: the Directorate of Operations and the Directorate of Intelligence. There are other directorates, he said, but they play mostly supporting roles. The Directorate of Intelligence—or the DI, as it's called inside—is made up of analysts: regional experts, psychiatrists, physicists, sociologists, and so on. As the name suggests, the DI analysts evaluate information and put their conclusions on paper. Information collectors, on the other hand, run the Directorate of Operations, or the DO. They are called case officers. Working mostly overseas, they gather information from their sources—agents, as the DO calls them—and pass it to the DI, where it becomes grist for the analysts.

Scott opened up the manila folder. "I see you've applied to Berkeley's graduate school in East Asian studies. It seems like you might be a possible match for the DI."

In fact, I had applied to the University of California at Berkeley after making a cursory survey of San Francisco's job market and deciding the best thing to do was punt and go back to school. I'd even started a Mandarin Chinese course and found a part-time job as a night teller at the Bank of America in San Francisco's Tenderloin district. It didn't pay much, but the hours would be perfect if Berkeley accepted me.

"You'd love the DI," Scott went on in his even, soothing, friendly voice. He was a good recruiter. I didn't realize it at the time, but our meeting was my first lesson in how it was done. "It runs very much like a university. An analyst reads the same books as a graduate student or a university professor. He keeps current in his speciality by reading periodicals and newspapers. And being in Washington, D.C. is a special advantage. He can walk in and take out books from the best library in the world, the Library of Congress." What's more, he told me, DI analysts get to travel a lot, learn new languages, and go to conferences. They go on sabbaticals, too.

"If you were to go to work for the DI, you could even continue to study Chinese," Scott said. "But the DI is a lot better than a university. Do you know why?"

I had a feeling Scott was setting the hook, but I didn't care. The DI was starting to sound better and better, maybe even a place I might really want to work. It was like getting paid to go to school.

"DI analysts not only have access to libraries, magazines, and newspapers, but also to a lot of information not available to universities—like reports from embassies, from CIA offices overseas, and from other agencies that have access to 'indispensable' information unavailable to a university. DI analysts have access to the Truth, and not just part of it. You can't claim to be an expert on a subject unless you have *all* available information."

Scott paused a second to let it all sink in. "But that's not all. There's something else unique about the DI. The DI has a very special reader. Do you know who that is?"

Scott didn't bother waiting for an answer.

"The president of the United States."

He paused again to make sure I completely understood what he'd just told me.

"The president," Scott went on, "more than anyone else, needs to know the truth about the world. But it isn't possible for him to be an expert on every country in the world or every subject. And that's where the analysts come in. They are his fact book, reference, and adviser. How can you do better than the president sitting at your elbow listening to you explain a complicated problem?"

It was, as I would find out one day, the purest sort of baloney. Pigs will fly before the president sits down for a cozy one-on-one with a DI analyst. Intelligence passes from Langley to the White House through a tight political screen. But, as I said, Jim Scott was a good pitchman, and at the tender age of twenty-two, I was a perfect mark. As he talked, I pictured myself walking the president through some knotty international crisis. I would do my best not to sound too pedantic, maybe even introduce a bit of humor. Who knows, maybe the president would take a liking to me and bring me over to the White House permanently.

Scott interrupted my thoughts: "Would an analyst's job interest you?"

"Absolutely," I shot back.

Scott picked up my application again and silently leafed through it. He looked back at me and cleared his throat.

"Frankly, it's a long shot. Without a Ph.D. or even a master's degree, I'm pretty certain the DI can't use you right now. After Berkeley, maybe. But in any case I'll pass on your application."

Oooof. The wind came out of my sails in a rush.

"But let's go back to the DO," he went on, almost without missing a beat. "It's a different kettle of fish entirely." I detected a change in his voice, an enthusiasm that hadn't been there before.

"Case officers run the DO," Scott said. "They're CIA staff employees who run agents. Agents are almost always foreigners. Being foreigners, they go places where Americans, our case officers, can't go, like inside their governments or their countries' secret scientific establishments. At the case officer's direction, the agents steal secrets, plans, documents, computer tapes, or whatever. In other words—let me be blunt—agents are traitors."

Scott had dropped his voice so that I had to strain to hear him—as if he were afraid someone was eavesdropping on us.

"And what do I mean, exactly, by spying and secrets? Let's take a hypothetical: Pearl Harbor. It's 1941. Assume there was a CIA back then, and you were in it. You're assigned to Tokyo. One night in late November you're working late. You're about ready to go home, dead tired from a long day at work. The telephone rings. The caller apologizes for dialing the wrong number. But you know it's not a wrong number. You recognize the voice. It's one of your agents, an ensign in the Japanese navy who works in naval headquarters. He's just signaled that he wants a meeting.

"At first you have a hard time following the agent as he rambles on in Japanese. He's excited. Then, all of a sudden, you realize what he's telling you: Japan is preparing to attack Pearl Harbor. He hands you a top-secret document. It's the plan for the attack, he says.

"You rush back to the office, wondering if your agent has lost his mind. You get down to translating the document. It's all there, just as he described it. You fire off an encoded message to Washington. The U.S. Navy disperses the fleet, and you've just altered the course of history.

"Knowing about the Japanese attack is information that cannot be obtained anywhere other than from a human being, an agent. There's no way we could have known with this precision about the emperor's plans to attack Pearl Harbor as early as November 1941, except from the ensign or another agent like him. Satellites and intercepts can't see inside someone's head. You need a person to do that. Agents and the secrets they steal are the crown jewel of American intelligence. It is what the intelligence business is really about."

Scott got up and went to the minibar and got us two Cokes.

"You've got to admit, that's a goddamn exciting job," he said when he sat down. "But I'm not going to tell you it doesn't have its downsides. In fact, there are very few jobs in the world tougher than a case officer's. First of all, almost every case officer has two jobs. There's his daytime job, his cover job, what he does between eight and five. More than likely it'll be a boring, routine, meaningless job. You might very well be sent overseas as a shipping clerk working for an import-export company, let's say in Penang,

Malaysia. You'll have some dreary office in the port. All day long you'll fill in import applications. Occasionally, you call the home office, let's say in Passaic, New Jersey. The person who answers the phone will have only the vaguest idea where Penang is, or even care. Everyone will take you for a ne'er-do-well. You can never tell anyone what you really do for a living. It's a thankless, anonymous job.

"And there's another downside, a lot worse than the hardship of living your cover—getting caught committing espionage. Espionage is illegal in every country in the world and, in all but a few, a capital crime. Let's go back to Tokyo in 1941. If you'd been caught meeting your agent, you'd be lucky to go to jail. And, incidentally, your agent would have been put up against a wall and shot. Sure, the CIA would have done its best to try to get you out. But it wouldn't have been able to do anything until the end of the war. Four years rotting in a Japanese jail. The same would go for Penang. A mistake in this business is unthinkable."

For a moment, I considered the possibility that Scott was trying to talk me out of the job.

Giving me some time to think, he stood up, walked over to the window, and opened the curtain, letting in the bright midday light as if it would somehow help me make a decision.

"So, what do you think about the DO as a career?"

I didn't answer.

"Well?"

"Sure," I finally said, faking all the enthusiasm I could muster. "I'd be real interested." I might have been able to see myself at the president's elbow, but I was way too immature for the job Scott had just been describing. I also couldn't stop picturing myself in leg irons, chained to the wall of some dank, foul-smelling Malaysian prison. Then again, the longer I could keep the application process going, the more I could dine out on the story for years to come; and surely the nation's supersleuths would come to their senses sooner or later.

WRONG AGAIN. In March 1976 I was invited to Washington for more interviews and to take the dreaded polygraph.

Ironically, or maybe intentionally, I was put up at the Holiday Inn across from the Watergate, the same Holiday Inn the ex-CIA Watergate burglars had used as a listening post when they bugged the Democratic National Committee headquarters. In quick succession, I went through a half-dozen interviews and exams; a couple of DO case officers, a shrink, and a security officer; and a French and German test. All the meetings took place in my hotel room. I was never brought into a CIA building.

The most impressive person I met was Don Gregg. Don would go on to be security adviser to then vice president George Bush, and ambassador to South Korea when Bush became president. Back then, though, Gregg had just been reassigned to Washington from Seoul, where he'd been ████████████ chief. For most of the two hours we talked, he described what it was like to live overseas for most of one's adult life: the isolation, the alienation from family and country, the physical hardship. Gregg was curious about my background and asked a lot of questions about the time I had spent in Europe. He wanted to know how I adjusted and whether I made friends. For the first time I had a sense that the DO might be interested in me for my overseas experience, an interesting legacy from my mother.

The polygraph was held on the next-to-last day in an apartment complex several blocks from the Holiday Inn. I found the name Scott had given me on the lobby directory—Dr. Jarmen, third floor. A balding man, about thirty-five, greeted me when I knocked on the door. With his solid white shirt, lime-green tie, and pocket protector, he looked like an accountant. He showed me into a room that was meant to be a bedroom. In the middle was an oversize plastic-upholstered easy chair, a Formica table, and a straight-back chair positioned across the table from the easy chair. Dr. Jarmen, or whatever his real name was, seated me in the easy chair and hooked me up to three pairs of wires and sensors leading to the polygraph. My right index finger was attached to a metal electrode, my chest to a respirator tube, and my upper right arm to a cuff monitor.

"Tell the truth and your perspiration, heartbeat, and breathing will remain pretty close to normal," the good doctor advised.

I was too tense at first to get a good reading, but after a pause to let my heartbeat go down, we restarted with better results. The questions came in a steady rhythm, and my answers followed in even

yeses and nos. He asked me about drugs, whether I'd
tried anything aside from marijuana, whether I'd had
homosexual relations, whether I'd stolen anything or
had any relationship with a foreign government, and
so on.

The exam lasted a little under four hours. After
running through the same questions three times,
Jarmen gathered up his charts and went out of the
room. He came back ten minutes later, unhooked me,
and said he wasn't sure whether I'd passed or not. He
would have to show the charts to his supervisor. It
could take up to a week for a decision.

When I told Scott how long the polygraph lasted,
he gave me the thumbs-up. "You passed."

I WAS FEELING PRETTY GOOD about my trip until I got
back to San Francisco and saw the boa constrictor
sleeping on the landing outside my apartment door.

The boa constrictor was my roommates' pet, not
mine. When it came time to move out of Mike's
apartment, I had gone to the Berkeley student union
to check the bulletin boards. Two students, a couple,
had a vacant room in an apartment close to campus
that would have been perfect if I had ended up at
Berkeley in the fall. I noticed the boa in its aquarium
when I inspected the place—there was no way to miss
it—but I didn't mind snakes, and the couple seemed
pleasant enough. It was only after I moved in that I
learned they were dyed-in-the-wool anarchists and
that from time to time the boa would escape the
aquarium.

Then, it had all seemed part of the local color. Now that I was job-shopping at the heart of the American establishment, it mattered deeply. I figured it would take some CIA gumshoe about five minutes of talking to the neighbors to find out about the anarchists and the boa—evidence enough of a serious character flaw on my part. I'd be lucky if the CIA didn't turn my application over to the FBI. I hadn't even been hired, and already I was developing a streak of paranoia.

One morning about six weeks after I came back from my Washington interviews, the doorbell rang. I was alone in the apartment. A gray-haired man in his early sixties, wearing a suit and tie, was standing on the stoop. He had a briefcase in one hand and a map in the other. I thought he was one of those evangelical Christian missionaries who would sometimes try their luck in Berkeley.

He apologized for disturbing me so early and asked if I was so-and-so. *Geez,* I thought, *what a coincidence, he's looking for one of my Berkeley friends.* I was about to give him the proper address when it occurred to me who my visitor was—a CIA background investigator who had mixed up my address with that of a friend I'd listed as a reference. He was in midsentence, apologizing for the mistake, when I began to push him out the door. I didn't want him to catch sight of the poster of Mao on the landing, underneath which was neatly written THE EAST WIND BLOWS RED, or the boa, which was sure to slither around the corner at any minute. Admittedly, if I had thought about it a little harder, I might have realized that an organization that couldn't even get a legman to the right address was unlikely to pick up such subtle cues as anarchist landlords.

I WAS ASLEEP on the last Monday morning of July when the telephone rang a little after eight. It took me a moment to recognize Scott's voice on the other end.

"Can you be in Washington in two weeks? Security cleared you, and the Directorate of Operations is offering you a job."

A job? I hadn't had any contact with the CIA in three months. The DO, I figured, was toast. The only thing remotely long-term on my mind was Mandarin Chinese, which I'd started during the summer session at Berkeley.

Scott was impatient. "If you can't make it in two weeks, it may be at least six months before I can get you into another class."

"Are you absolutely sure security cleared me?"

Hadn't the CIA checked with the FBI and found out about Ron Kovick or the trips to Paris and Prague? The motorcycle through the library? The anarchists and the boa? I couldn't believe they hadn't put it all together.

"Yes, at least for three years," Scott said.

I took a quick look around my shabby apartment. I thought about how far behind I was in Mandarin. I thought about another night standing at my teller's window. And then I thought about a ski run I'd made when I was fifteen. There were six of us on our last trip down when we ran into two ski patrolmen we knew, probably the wildest pair in Aspen. They invited us to come look at a new jump they'd built. We followed them off the main run to an old, abandoned mining camp. In a clearing sat three houses in a line on a steep incline. Their roofs were collapsed. Right above the highest house was a six-foot-high jump. The idea was to pick up enough speed to clear all three houses. If you took it too slowly you risked landing short—in the middle of a house. When one of the ski patrolmen pushed off, I followed without a second thought. As I sighted the jump between my ski tips, the line of houses began to look like a high-rise, but I felt a sense of inevitability. It was totally irrational. At any moment I could have turned off and avoided the jump. But I didn't. I just kept going.

I now felt the same way about the CIA. "Sure, Jim. I can be there in two weeks. I could even be there next week."

After I hung up the phone, I thought, *What the hell.* I'd finagle an assignment to Switzerland, meet from time to time with one of those shady agents Scott had talked about, gather up a few pieces of information that would save the world, and spend the rest of my time on the ski slopes. A tour in Switzerland and then out. How much trouble could I get in?

3

AUGUST 1977. SOMEWHERE IN VIRGINIA'S TIDEWATER.

CROUCHING IN THE DOOR of the C-46, I couldn't see anything. It was like looking into a bottomless well. When I leaned forward a little to look directly below the plane, the engines' backwash hit me like a fifty-pound sack of cement, almost yanking me out the door.

We'd spent more than three hours on the tarmac, waiting for God knows what, cinched up in our parachute harnesses and sizzling on the plane's hot metal floor. The swamp mosquitoes were drilling right through my Korean War-vintage fatigues. At that point I would have happily jumped onto the North Pole. Anything to get out of that damn place.

Come on, Red, tap me out.

"Red" Winstead, the jumpmaster, had his head out the door, russet hair pasted against the side of his face. He was looking intently at the ground. The rest of the stick, my team of jumpers that night, had already gone and was probably close to touching down by now. Red was spreading us out intentionally. "You don't drop everyone in a tight cluster in a combat jump," he'd drummed into our heads in ground school. "It's bad operational security." Still, it seemed like an eternity since the last jumper had gone out the door. There would be no second chance if we overshot the jump zone. I'd be going back with the plane, the only one who hadn't jumped.

A big, tough Minnesota Swede, Red was a veteran of almost every CIA covert war. No one anywhere knew more about combat jumps behind enemy lines. Legend had it that Red came up with a technique to drop Tibetans into the Himalayas. At altitudes of twenty-five to thirty thousand feet, the crosswinds made it a treacherous ride down, so Red took the Tibetans out to Camp Hale, Colorado, and taught them to wait until the very last second to pull their rip cords. Dropping like a rock into a Himalayan valley was the only way to beat the winds.

Red had started us out in jump training with parachute-landing falls into a sawdust pit. The idea was to first touch down on the balls of your feet and then roll onto your calf, thigh, hip, and back, all in smooth succession, distributing the impact as evenly as you could. Red made certain we understood.

"You goddamn well didn't hit all five points," he'd yell, leaning over me as I wiped the sawdust and sweat off my face.

Just to make sure we got the message, Red produced a former paramilitary officer who had survived a jump thanks to good technique. One night—in Laos, I think—his chute didn't open all the way and he came barreling in at twenty or thirty miles an hour. If he hadn't hit all five points, he would have died. As it was, he walked with a marked limp. Point made. At night we took to practicing five-point landings off the bar. The other trainees, who were in the operations course and wouldn't be going through the paramilitary training, would turn away, embarrassed.

After we mastered the sawdust pit, Red introduced us to the dreaded tower, which everyone agreed was much worse than jumping out of a plane. Thanks to some weird psychological quirk, jumping out from forty feet hooked up to harness and steel cable was scarier than jumping out of an airplane from a thousand feet—if you ever got to jump, that is, and on this particular night I was beginning to have serious doubts.

Red, let's go, we're gonna miss it.

Without warning, Red slapped me on the ass, and I was out the door. A sharp yank of the harness, and then the quiet. It surprised me each time. The roar of the plane's engines faded almost immediately to a monumental silence, but at less than a thousand feet, there wasn't much time to enjoy the ride.

Check the canopy.

I did, and it was fine. It was still too dark to see much, but as I pulled the right toggle hard, turning the chute in a 360-degree circle, I dimly made out the tree line in the distance. I silently thanked Red for his timing. I wouldn't be landing in the forest canopy tonight.

Never look at the ground.

Red had pounded the lesson into our heads: Look at the ground as you're about to hit and you'll unintentionally straighten and lock your legs, which is the best way to break one. I turned the chute into the wind at the last minute, slowing my speed enough so I could have landed standing up if I'd wanted. All the while I kept my eyes fixed on the horizon. I hit with my knees bent. Not quite a five-pointer, but it didn't matter; the ground was soft and wet.

I stood up and reeled in my chute, looking around for the rest of the team. I could just make out Alan. It was too dark to see the other three members of the team: Peter, Curt, and Eric.

Alan caught sight of me and pointed to a clump of trees, signaling to follow him there after I'd buried my chute. He and the rest of the team were crouching in some high sedge. We'd been warned that the bad guys had passive night-vision binoculars, and it was best to stay out of the open.

MY TEAM THAT NIGHT was fairly representative of the DO class I had come in with—about a sixty-forty split between ex-military officers and civilians. I would spend the next two decades watching the CIA evolve into an organization where garnering promotions and pleasing political masters became more important than collecting secrets, but back then the spirit of the CIA's World War II predecessor, the Office of Strategic Services (OSS), still lived. We were all adventurers—after all, we had chosen operations over the stay-at-home DI side—but a public-service ethos burned in us, too. We believed the United States needed a competent intelligence service, and we wanted to serve a higher cause.

Alan, the team leader for the night's exercise, had been a pilot in the air force. After he had pushed the envelope one time too many with the big equipment, he was switched from jets to Caribous, twin-engine planes that could take off and land on a dime and were also a lot less expensive to replace.

Alan never talked about his tour in Vietnam, but we heard about it at Fort Bragg, North Carolina, where we had gone for heavy-weapons training with the special forces. It happened one night when we were out drinking with a couple of sergeants on Fayetteville's sleazy strip.

"One of the damnedest things I saw in Nam was at an 'A' camp on the border of Laos," a crusty sergeant said as the waitress brought us our third round of beers. "We were surrounded, and Charlie was about to overrun us. We were out of everything except bullshit excuses why we couldn't be resupplied. We maybe had a day or two of ammunition left. Charlie was too close for a chopper to come in. But the captain thought a fixed-wing coming in low and fast could make it. The air force told us to stuff it because it was too dangerous.

"But then, son of a bitch if not two hours later, we heard an airplane. It was a Caribou, and it came right in at tree level, so low it clipped the tops of the trees. Branches and leaves flew everywhere. A goddamn flying lawn mower. It was the most beautiful thing I ever saw. And when it taxied up to us, we could see it was packed with ammo."

The sergeant stopped for a swig of beer, indicating the best part of the story was yet to come.

"But you know what that crazy fucking pilot did then?" the sergeant asked, looking around at us.

No one said anything.

"He jumped out of that damn Caribou, and without saying a word, he reached behind his seat and pulled out two new props to replace the ones he had chipped to pieces flying in. Then he shouted at us, 'Hurry up and unload this sucker because I'm coming back again—today.'

"As soon as the Caribou was unloaded, he took off, missing the tops of the trees by an inch. Sure enough, he came back that afternoon. New props and all. He did that for a whole week until we got regular supplies. Craziest fucker I ever met over there," the sergeant said, shaking his head.

When Alan quietly mentioned the name of the camp, the sergeant stared at him in stunned silence. The only way Alan could have known the name of the camp was if he was the crazy fucking pilot who had supplied it.

Peter was next in command. A Berkeley graduate, Peter spent a few years in the blue-water navy including a tour in Vietnam, until he was forced to resign after carelessly signing an antiwar petition while on shore leave in San Francisco. For the navy there were no second chances, but as my own case showed, the CIA was willing to forgive a few youthful indiscretions. Peter was in fantastic shape, running five to six miles a day. He was also an obsessive fisherman. Years later I would run into him again in West Africa, where he was chief in a small country. He'd managed to persuade the CIA to buy a Boston

Whaler and spent his free time fishing for barracuda.

Curt, a former marine captain who had been passed over for promotion, left the service to sell computers for IBM but soon got bored and joined the CIA to fight in the cold war. Every once in a while I'd catch him with a mad-dog grin that said he really believed he'd be dropped behind the Iron Curtain one day on some commando operation. Not surprisingly, Curt lasted only a few years in the CIA.

And then there was Eric. Like me, he'd never served in the military. Before he joined the CIA, he was an English professor at a small East Coast liberal arts college. With his thick glasses and somewhat pompous manner, he still looked and acted like he belonged in front of a classroom. At the drop of a hat he would recite some obscure passage from Milton.

One day when we were waiting in a mess line at Fort Bragg, Eric had a run-in with an 82nd Airborne Division colonel. Although Eric had a mandatory buzz cut and wore standard army camouflage like everyone else at Fort Bragg, he didn't see the point of adapting completely to military etiquette—he refused to give up his pipe. As soon as the colonel caught sight of Eric and his unlit pipe, he marched across the mess with murder in his eyes. Planting his nose about an inch from Eric's, the colonel growled: "Goddammit, soldier, get that dildo out of your mouth." We could see "Fuck you" forming on Eric's lips just as our escort, a special forces captain, stepped between Eric and the colonel, whispering in the colonel's ear, "A civilian, sir"—no doubt saving the five of us from being awarded Purple Hearts.

★

THE FIVE OF US had parachuted into Tidewater Virginia on the final exercise of a four-month paramilitary course, the last phase of the DO's yearlong training cycle and probably the most intense, grueling, expensive training offered by the U.S. government, short of something like the SEAL basic course. The next stop for many of us would be an overseas assignment.

Our exercise mission that night was to meet what was supposed to be an agent on the lam and escort him to a waiting boat. The meeting point was only a mile and a half away from the landing zone. From there to the inlet was less than a mile. What's more, we had twelve hours to do it all, and if the agent wasn't at the meeting point right on time, we weren't supposed to wait for him. A walk in the park, or so we thought.

It took Alan about five minutes to find us on the map and plot a course. We'd studied the terrain from satellite photographs and a couple of aerial reconnaissance shots. There didn't seem to be any major obstacles. Alan thought it would take less than an hour to get to the meeting point, but we decided to get as close to our destination as was prudent and wait there.

It was lucky we started early. About ten yards into the trees we ran into a wall of bramble, vines, and wild berry bushes. We had one machete between us, and the brush might as well have been made of cement. Alan started hacking through it first. After about half an hour, his hands were too bloody to continue, so Eric took over. We continued that way, taking turns, for the next two hours. So much for getting to the meeting site in an hour.

As soon as we got through, we collapsed on the ground, exhausted but heartened by what appeared in the darkness to be clear sailing ahead. Alan got everyone up after about ten minutes. Peter started off on point. As he walked along, he systematically checked for trip wires by putting the back of his hand on the ground and raising it slowly above his head.

We were making good time until we hit one of the most putrid swamps I'd ever seen. On the bottom was sucking muck; on top, thick saw grass. We quickly decided we couldn't walk around it. It was too big, and we would have been thrown badly off course. Alan checked his compass, pointed at a big tree on the other side of the swamp, and stepped into the muck. We followed in single file, sinking to our necks.

The only pleasant thought I could summon when we got to the other side was that there was no fool big enough to follow us across. If they were going to catch us, it would have to be from the front. We threw ourselves on the ground, bleeding from the saw grass, for another fifteen-minute breather.

A little after midnight, we arrived at a low hill flanked by several large boulders. Peter, Curt, Eric, and I were to wait there while Alan went ahead to pick up the agent. We couldn't be sure we had not been compromised. If an ambush was waiting, there was no point in losing the whole team.

At 0330 we got up and started to move due east and then north to intercept the route Alan would be taking with the agent. At the rallying point, Eric and Curt waited at the bottom of the ravine Alan was to follow, while Peter and I climbed the slopes to make sure we weren't being tracked in parallel ravines.

An hour later, I heard faintly one then another person moving with difficulty through the bottom of the ravine. No one had mentioned that the agent was seriously overweight and ill. We took turns holding him up by the arms and even carrying him every ten minutes. By the time we came to the gravel road, I felt like I'd just spent the last twelve hours in Everest's Death Zone.

It was now a little before six. Dawn was starting to crack, and we had yet to find the boat—if it was still there. Alan went ahead to check the inlet. We had just sat down in some bushes by the road when a car door slammed, and then a second, followed by an engine starting up less than a hundred feet away.

Eric and I each grabbed the agent by an arm, lifted him, and dragged him across the road. The car was grinding through its gears, speeding up and coming our way. We crashed through the bushes and plunged into water as the head lights lit up the foliage, and then it was complete confusion: sirens, shouts, and the burst of a machine gun. We could hear people coming through the underbrush. A grenade exploded in the water. I knew it was just a harmless flash-bang grenade, but my grip on reality was slipping.

It was then that a Boston Whaler appeared out of the darkness. Alan was standing on the bow. It was lighter now and we could be seen clearly from the shore. Automatic gunfire was everywhere, and because of the reeds, the boat could come only so close to shore. The agent was starting to go under, pulling Peter and me down with him, when Alan stuck out a gaff for us to grab on to.

"The agent in first!" he yelled. The crew and Alan hauled him up while Peter and I pulled ourselves over the side. Eric and Curt were nowhere to be seen, but the pilot turned the boat around and got the hell out of there. He'd gotten what he came for—the agent, not us.

WE HAD STARTED IN MAY at the Farm, the CIA's main training base, fieldstripping every assault rifle, machine gun, pistol, and rifle known to man. As soon as we knew our way around an M-16 or an AK-47 or a suppressed Sterling submachine gun, we took it out to the range for target practice. But that wasn't the end of it. We then fieldstripped and cleaned the same gun blindfolded. And to make sure we felt comfortable with it, we then fired it from a moving car, on a pop-up range, and at night. We even practiced on several weapons after forty minutes of physical training, to simulate the heart-thumping excitement of firing a weapon in a real combat situation.

Next came two weeks running compass courses. Everyone would line up on a numbered stick and start off across a wood, navigating only by compass. The idea was to emerge on the other side at the same numbered stick. When we'd mastered the day runs, we started walking them at night, and then through swamps, and finally through swamps at night. That was the pattern: first in the light, then in the dark.

Following three weeks of jump training, we moved south to North Carolina for two weeks of nonstop demolitions training. We spent two days crimping blasting caps to make sure we understood that if you crimped them too high, they'd explode and take your hand off. After we'd mastered that, we crimped them in the dark, by feel. Then we started blowing up things: cars, buses, diesel generators, fences, bunkers. We made a school bus disappear with about twenty pounds of U.S.-made C-4. For comparison's sake, we tried Czech Semtex and a few other foreign plastic explosives.

Not that you really need anything fancy. We blew up one bus using three sacks of fertilizer and fuel oil, a mixture called ANFO (ammonium nitrate fuel oil), that did more damage than the C-4 had. The biggest piece left was a part of the chassis, which flew in an arc, hundreds of yards away. We learned to mix up a potent cocktail called methyl nitrate. If you hit a small drop of it with a hammer; it split the hammer. Honest. We were also taught some of the really esoteric stuff like E-cell timers, improvising pressurized airplane bombs using a condom and aluminum foil, and smuggling a pistol on an airplane concealed in a mixture of epoxy and graphite. By the end of the training, we could have taught an advanced terrorism course.

In Arizona we did desert and mountain training. It was more of the same thing—compass courses, wandering around all night, improvising weapons. The only variation was that we got to catch a rattlesnake with a forked stick, cook it, and eat it. Two weeks later we were back at the Farm learning how to navigate helicopters and guide a short-takeoff-and-landing airplane onto a patch of field no larger than my backyard in Aspen. Landmarks on a map never look the same as they do on the ground, and it's a lot worse in bad weather. Afterward we spent two weeks in the Atlantic on small boats, learning some of life's useful little skills—like locating a submerged submarine off the Atlantic coast in the middle of the night.

For a little sun-and-fun time, we spent a week in Florida's Ten Thousand Islands, a miserable patch of swamp and mangrove forest. Four days sloshing around in moccasin-infested swamp and the chlorophyll in the water turned our skin lettuce green. Another four days living on mangrove roots, and our clothes started to rot. Our final exercise there was to find and dig up a weapons cache on a deserted island about a mile out in the Gulf of Mexico. By then we looked like extras from *Night of the Living Dead*. Just as we were wiping the protective grease off the cache's unloaded M-16s, we spotted a fast boat approaching the island. It wasn't until the pilot was about to run his boat up on the sand that he caught sight of us. He spun the boat around so fast it almost flipped. I would never dig up a weapons cache in a real operation, but at least I'd done my part in America's war on drugs.

EVEN AS I WAS GOING through the paramilitary

course, I knew that a case officer's job wasn't about digging up weapons caches. The course was a relic left over from the OSS, which really did fight in World War II, but the DO existed to run agents, not defend battle lines. As far as I could figure out, the only reason the DO kept the course going was to engender an esprit de corps in its new officers—a reminder that we didn't work for the pinstriped crowd down at the State Department.

The purehearts in Washington blanch at the description, but case officers are in fact second-story men, thieves who steal other countries' secrets. The DO is the only arm of the federal government dedicated to breaking the law—foreign law; but still the law. The last thing the DO wants is for its officers to run around setting off explosions and shooting it out with the bad guys in some Eastern European capital. Even back then, before political correctness had taken deep root at Langley and all around Washington, management was painfully aware that whenever the guns came out, the CIA got itself into trouble: Iran, Chile, and the Congo, countries where the CIA was accused of overthrowing governments. Better to operate in the shadows and leave the bang-bang to others. No news was good news.

Another thing I learned about the DO was that, like any other professional criminal organization, it lived according to a strict code of secrecy. Every document generated in the DO was classified, from a requisition order for toilet paper to invitations to office holiday parties. All communications were encrypted and superencrypted. Case officers used pseudonyms in place of their true names. Cryptonyms replaced the names of agents. Even geographical places were renamed. I was stunned when I found out the CIA created its own map of the Farm, with fake place names, including those of rivers and lakes—just like a real Geographical Survey map. It was as if the CIA lived in a parallel universe.

When computers were introduced, the CIA immediately understood the danger of digitized information storage. It continued to type sensitive information on manual typewriters with cloth ribbons, sometimes even recording it by hand. The DO's famous "blue-striper" intelligence reports (they were so named because of the faint blue stripe that ran diagonally across the paper) were disseminated around Washington by couriers who would stand by while the official read the report and then take it back as soon as he had finished.

My initiation into the cult of secrecy started even before I arrived in Washington to begin my training. Just as I was getting ready to leave San Francisco, Jim Scott telephoned to say that no one would be at the airport to meet me. *"It's too insecure,"* he said. "You'll be staying in a safe house for the first two weeks of orientation."

"Why not a hotel?"

"It's too insecure."

I shrugged it off. I was too excited about starting my first serious job to think about why I needed to be sequestered in a safe house in my own country.

I took a taxi from Washington's National Airport to the address in Bailey's Crossroads that Scott had given me, a new apartment building in one of those sterile complexes that were popping up like mushrooms all over northern Virginia. Another recruit, a lanky blond guy who was about thirty-five, had already moved in. He introduced himself only as Hank. I asked him for his last name. "Sorry. Can't tell you. Scott asked me not to."

The next morning, right at eight A.M., a pleasant man and a grandmotherly woman showed up from Central Cover, the DO component that fakes IDs, arranges bogus telephone lines, and works with other government agencies and businesses to hide the true affiliation of CIA officers around the world.

The woman asked Hank and me for our IDs. Everything: driver's licenses, credit cards, club memberships, and anything else with a name on it.

"You won't be needing these," she said as she dropped them into individual envelopes, wrote our first names on the outside, and sealed them.

Just as I started to consider life without any proof of identity, the man handed Hank and me laminated cards with our pictures already affixed. They identified us as civilian military employees. I took a closer look at mine. It was definitely my picture—it was the one I'd submitted with my application—but the name on it was Robert Endacott.

"Someone made a mistake," I said, handing the man back the ID.

The man looked at me, surprised. "Didn't they tell you you'd be in alias?"

No. No one had.

He then explained that from that day on, Hank and

I would live under new identities, at least until we went overseas. Only a handful of people in the CIA would know our true names.

"What do I tell my family?" I asked.

He smiled and handed me a Washington, D.C. post-office-box number typed on a yellow three-by-five card. "We'll service it once a week. You can write all the letters you want, but you can't call them, from either the safe house or any other CIA facility. And, of course, they can't call you."

I had already figured out the no-call rule. I'd checked the phone in the safe-house apartment. The line was dead.

The pair from Central Cover made it all seem cut-and-dried, but a CIA cover wasn't always airtight. During the Gulf War, one case officer was back in Washington minding a group of Arab trainees who had been put up at the West Park Hotel in Rosslyn. About midnight on their first night in town, one of the Arabs decided he was lonely. Never having been to the U.S. before and not knowing much English, he opened up the telephone book to emergencies, dialed 911, and told the dispatcher in his broken English that he needed a woman. The quick-thinking dispatcher instructed him to wait in front of the hotel until his date showed up. As promised, when he stepped out of the hotel lobby there was a woman in the park—as well as five surly Arlington policemen hiding in the bushes.

The Arab, now handcuffed, convinced the police-men to take him back to the hotel to talk to his case officer, who would confirm he was in Washington on a U.S. government training program. The case officer backed up the Arab's story. It was a language misunderstanding, he explained, and he hoped the police would be able to overlook the incident. They asked to see the case officer's own identification, a Central Cover-issued government ID that apparently looked suspicious enough for one of the policemen to check it out. True to the agency's code of silence, the CIA night operator at the agency denied ever having heard of the case officer.

As the policeman pulled out another set of handcuffs, the case officer decided if there was any time to break cover, this was it. The policeman allowed him one call to the CIA.

"We cannot confirm the employment of CIA officers," the CIA security duty officer dutifully told the policeman. At that point the case officer, an ex-marine, took back the phone and screamed into it, "You S.O.B., if you don't look up my name on your goddamned computer and confirm I work there, I'm going to break your neck as soon as I get out of jail."

A few more phone calls cleared up the problem, but most case officers spent their careers in perpetual fear that their cover wouldn't hold up at a crucial moment. In the U.S., a blown cover might mean a night in jail. Overseas, it could be a lot worse.

After the Central Cover people left Hank and me, two men in black showed up from the Office of Security, a component of the CIA that I would come to know very well over the next twenty-one years. Security took care of everything from the polygraph and security clearances to monitoring internal telephones and making sure safes were closed at night at Langley. Security even had a specialist whose only duty was to fire people: the hatchet man. While he delivered the bad news, a couple of security goons would rifle through the safe of the fallen employee, examine his computer's hard drive, and check any belongings he had in or on his desk, even such seemingly innocuous items as family photos. After that, a security team would escort him to the door.

The security officers pulled a foot-high stack of forms from their briefcases for Hank and me to read and sign. The first was a secrecy agreement stipulating that in return for a paycheck every two weeks, we agreed not to write a book, magazine article, movie script, or to go on television without clearance from the CIA. True, it covered only subjects related to the CIA and intelligence, but if you spent your life in the agency that pretty much included anything you might consider writing or saying.

Another agreement we signed was never to admit to anyone we worked for the CIA, including mothers, spouses, and even the cop who might stop you for running a red light out of CIA headquarters. It didn't matter if he had seen you with his own eyes passing through the gates, you still had to deny any connection to the CIA. When DO officers threw around the cliché "Admit nothing, deny everything, and make counteraccusations", they meant it. Although some case officers actually attempted to hide from their spouses where they worked, I found out later that most didn't. It was too hard to cover for all those late nights meeting other agents.

We also signed an agreement not to disclose anything related to "code-word" intelligence—like intercepts, satellite photography or nuclear bombs. Access to code-word intelligence requires a top-secret security clearance, which has its own stringent criteria.

I was reading some of the fine print about top-secret clearances when I came across the word "satyriasis." It was one of the things you couldn't engage in and at the same time keep a top-secret security clearance. I had no idea what it meant.

"Satyriasis?" I asked.

One of the security officers dropped his voice conspiratorially. 'A satyrist is someone who likes to have a lot of women. And regulations say if we catch you screwing a lot of women, we gotta lift your TS clearance."

It all seems comical now, but sex was one of management's biggest headaches. It boiled down to the fact that the CIA did not want its employees indiscriminately cavorting with the enemy. Because all foreigners were considered enemies of the state until proven otherwise, security strictly enforced a rule that employees must report any "close and continuing contact" with a foreign national. The problem was, no one was sure what "close and continuing" meant. A one-night stand? Writing sonnets to a platonic lover? Security wouldn't say. Eight years later, my boss in Khartoum, Milt Bearden, came up with the most sensible definition: If you keep a pair of slippers under your friend's bed, it's close and continuing.

Every six months CIA employees assigned overseas

would send in what was known as an █████████—a cable enumerating your close and continuing contacts or a certification that you had none. It was always a tense time. You knew that if some security puke was having a bad day and decided your close and continuing contact was a threat to national security he could yank you back to Washington, lash you up to a polygraph, and consign you to years in security limbo. On the other hand, if you didn't report a contact and security stumbled onto it, things would be a lot worse.

One of the odder cases I ever heard about involved a Hindu employee who was sleeping with his mother and sister. It was discovered during a routine polygraph. The hatchet man was about to fire him when the employee invoked his First Amendment rights. He argued that it was a caste thing: He couldn't find a wife from his caste in the Washington area. That threw the case into the general counsel's office, which eventually decided to fire him anyway. An extreme case, but those are the kinds of issues the CIA had to delve into to preserve its cult of secrecy.

AFTER TWO WEEKS imprisoned in the safe house, signing forms and listening to headquarters officers drone on about what they did for a living, I was overjoyed to head down to the Farm for the operations course. I knew I would be exchanging one prison for another, but this one was more in the nature of a country club, and at least I would be getting some exercise again.

Although the Farm has been described in numerous books and shown from the air in television documentaries, the CIA has asked me not to reveal its location or cover name. All I can tell you is that it is situated in Virginia's Tidewater, on a ███████████ ████████████. It's supposed to be a restricted military base, which is just what the guards will tell you if you should ever stumble upon the front gates with their flashing yellow lights and draw barriers.

Inside the gates, the Farm did resemble a country club, at least in part. There were tennis courts, an indoor swimming pool, fishing boats you could take out on the river, and several bars. There were even recreational skeet and trap ranges. The students were assigned individual rooms in dormitories. It wasn't the Ritz, but it wasn't uncomfortable, either. The instructors lived on base in white clapboard houses.

The Farm liked to project the image of a small, rural college, but it was a very peculiar college indeed. As soon as we had checked in, it was announced there would be a ███████████████████ that evening, hosted by an imaginary foreign government. I can't remember the name of the country they used, but the capital was called Wilton. The instructors played the roles of local officials, and the students American visitors. Our job was to devise a cover for our presence in the country. The purpose was to teach us how to work a social event and elicit information from people—the CIA's version of cotillion.

I picked out a short, bald, sagging, and myopic instructor who looked as if he should have retired a few decades back. Add in the martini he was sipping, and I figured he was an easy touch.

I stuck my hand out. "How's it going?"

He kept his hand in his pocket and just looked at me.

"I'm an American, and I've just arrived in town," I said, still grinning like a monkey.

"That's curious," he said in a not particularly friendly voice. "We don't see many Americans here. What do you do?"

"I work for an American gas company. We're hoping to drill some fields in your country."

"Are you a geologist?"

"No."

"Well, perhaps that explains why you don't know we have no gas reserves in our country," he said as he turned and walked away.

As soon as I got back to my room, I looked through the briefing book for the mock country. It stated very clearly that it had no hydrocarbon reserves. The next morning when students assembled in the auditorium, I could tell I wasn't the only one who had failed to do his homework.

At exactly eight-thirty a six-foot-three-inch man built like a rock entered the auditorium and walked deliberately to the podium. With his weather-beaten, ruddy face, he looked like he'd spent a lot of time in the desert.

"My name is Joe Lynch. I'm the course co-ordinator. Who got a follow-on meeting last night?"

You could have heard a pin drop. No one raised a hand.

Lynch walked up the middle aisle and stopped next to my desk. The blackboards, Formica-top desks, and bare walls made me feel like I was back at Georgetown University, but this man didn't look or sound like any professor I had ever had.

"Does anyone have any idea why we are here?" His voice boomed through the auditorium.

I knew I didn't. I was relieved when an older woman raised her hand. She looked like she could have been in the CIA for a while and was now being recycled into a case officer.

"We're here to learn how to become intelligence collectors," she said.

Lynch didn't even acknowledge her. He looked around the room and then took his place back behind the podium.

"Apparently no one got a second meeting. Did one of you at least get a telephone number?"

About half the students raised their hands.

Lynch turned to a student in the front row with his hand up. "Was it an office number?"

The student nodded.

"So what are you going to say when his secretary answers the telephone and asks who you are? If you'd read your briefing book, you'd know Wilton is hostile to the United States. Unreported contact between Americans and government officials is forbidden. By calling your friend at his office, you've just screwed him."

Lynch swept the room with his gaze.

"To go back to my question about what you're doing here. The U.S. government is spending millions of dollars to turn you into wolves, predators. Last night you were supposed to separate one of the lambs from the flock, the one who knows secrets, and lead him down the path to betrayal—of his country and everything else dear to him—and at the same time not let on what you're doing.

"If you joined the CIA as a shortcut to becoming a Foreign Service officer, drinking free booze at cocktail parties, or taking an extended vacation in Europe, I recommend you go back to headquarters and look for a desk job."

I think it was only at that moment that I finally understood the CIA was deadly serious about sending me out into the world to spy. So much for skiing in Switzerland on the agency's nickel.

FOR THE NEXT FIVE MONTHS the instructors did their best to turn us into predators. Working pretty much day and night, we learned the esoteric skills of spying—spotting, assessing, recruiting, and running agents, all in the framework of the mock country ruled from Wilton. On the surface, it seemed like some weird Kabuki play, but the stakes were high. A thumbs-down at the Farm meant you weren't certified as a case officer. Uncertified, you couldn't go overseas. You'd be permanently assigned to headquarters, and back then it was preferable to resign.

Not surprisingly, the hardest part was the actual recruitment, or the "pitch," as it was called. After you'd determined that your target knew secrets the CIA wanted to know (spotting), you then had to dope out whether he had any weaknesses that made him vulnerable to a recruitment pitch (assessing). The general rule was, you went after the weakest person— someone with money problems, a deep grievance against his country, an alcohol problem—but some of the best agents recruited by the CIA did it simply because they loved America. The point, and it was hammered into our heads, was that you had to be absolutely sure you knew your target's vulnerabilities before pitching him. Waving a hundred-dollar bill in front of someone who didn't care about money just got you into trouble.

A couple of classes after mine, the students at the Farm learned firsthand about the tragic consequences of a pitch gone bad. The story began in Kabul, Afghanistan, with a Soviet diplomat whom a case officer wanted to recruit. When it came time for the case officer to leave at the end of his tour, he still hadn't pinpointed a vulnerability to hang his pitch on. Instead, he lobbed the diplomat a softball about the need for the Soviet Union and the U.S. to get to know each other better. When the diplomat agreed, the case officer proposed introducing him to his replacement so they could "exchange views."

Too bad that wasn't the way the case officer described it in his report. He claimed he had recruited the Soviet, and his replacement, Bob ███████████, took him at his word. At his first solo meeting with the Soviet in a restaurant, Bob asked him for classified documents. The Soviet turned red, slammed his fist on the table, and started shouting. No one in the restaurant misunderstood what was going on. The incident turned into such a cause célèbre in Kabul that Bob was sent home to the Farm to teach. Deciding his career was over, and no doubt suffering from other problems, Bob shot himself on Christmas morning on the front porch of his house with his wife and children inside.

ANOTHER THING the DO pounded into our heads from day one: There's nothing more important than your agent's life. Just as a Secret Service officer is expected to take a bullet for the president, so case officers were to do anything to protect an agent's life—lie, cheat, steal, or worse. Very few people outside the business understand the nature of the bonds between a case officer and an agent, but to look at the scenario in cold institutional terms, if the word got out that the DO didn't protect its agents, no one would ever spy for the CIA again.

Sometimes a mole would betray agents and blow entire networks, but more often, agents were lost when they were spotted meeting their case officers. Accordingly, the DO spent millions of dollars training its officers to spot and beat surveillance. During our stay at the Farm, we spent almost a third of our time running foot and vehicular surveillance runs, mostly in Richmond, Virginia. Sometimes we'd follow the instructors; sometimes they'd follow us; sometimes the students would follow one another. It was all an elaborate cat-and-mouse game, and it was only a warm-up for the main event—the internal operations course, held in Washington, D.C.

The course was designed for case officers going to places like Moscow and Peking. The idea was to fire them in the crucible, replicating as nearly as possible what it was like to work against a hostile, determined, two-to-three-hundred-man surveillance team. I'll call the instructor Martha. She was a pert blonde, about thirty years old, who had just been thrown out of the Soviet Union after she was caught meeting an agent in Moscow as part of a KGB setup. Martha had been picked to instruct the internal ops course because she'd proven herself on the streets and held up to a nasty KGB interrogation. Beating surveillance wasn't something you learned in a lecture or by reading a book.

On the first day she dismissed us early. "Go home, pay your bills, and do anything else you need to clear up whatever it is you do in your life," she said, "because the next six weeks, you're mine." Since I wasn't married or otherwise attached it didn't take me long.

Martha meant it. During those six weeks, for sixteen hours a day, we were never off the streets of Washington. We put down dead drops (packages for agents), chalk marks on the walls (these were signals to agents), and took long countersurveillance routes —they turned into a blur. The teams covering us were good. Sometimes they used what's called "dolphin surveillance"—now you see us, now you don't. For two or three days they'd be all over us; we couldn't miss them. And then the next day we wouldn't see anyone. After a while, we would start to see ghosts.

Other times they employed what's called "waterfall

surveillance," in which the team walks directly at you rather than following from behind. A good waterfall surveillance requires hundreds of people and cars. As soon as a surveillant passes his target (called the "rabbit"), he turns down the first cross street, walks to a parallel street, and catches a van that drives him ahead of the rabbit so he can rejoin the flow, often wearing a change of clothes.

This went on for day after day without letup. Teams and techniques were switched at random. The objective was to wear us out and force mistakes. Just when we thought we couldn't take any more, they would turn up the heat. One night when I'd pushed it to the limit, a team picked the lock on my car and stole my notes. Sure enough, a surveillance team was waiting for me at the next drop site. It was a mistake I would never make again.

The course did more than teach us to detect surveillance, though—it also taught us to beat it. Anytime you're in motion, whether walking around a city or driving in the country, there comes a point where you're out of sight. And it is during that moment, whether it's a dip in a country road or a blind spot between buildings, that you do whatever you need to do. Chances are, you'll have only a split second. Preparation is everything.

TOWARD THE END of the course at the Farm, it was pretty clear who would pass and who wouldn't. Lynch loosened up and joined us one night at the student bar.

"I know it's been five months of hell. Do you think any of you are ready for the field?"

No one said anything.

"I'm happy you've figured at least that much out down here," Lynch said. "You've just scratched the surface when it comes to this profession.

"If there is one thing you should have learned, it's that the opposition is out to get you. It has the resources and patience, too. I don't care if it's in Moscow or Paris. Wherever you end up, there will be a million pairs of eyes watching and waiting for you to make a mistake.

"You know what I do first thing every morning when I wake up overseas? I go through my pockets. I fan the pages of the book I was reading the night before. I check my briefcase. I look under the bed. I'm a man obsessed, looking for that telltale scrap of paper with the agent's name on it, his telephone number or address—anything that could possibly compromise him. I just have to assume that the moment I leave my house or hotel the opposition will show up to rifle through my things."

Lynch ordered another pitcher of beer. A couple more students pulled up chairs to listen.

"But let me tell you something else. It's not just discipline. If you slavishly follow the rule book, you'll fail. Let's say it's one-thirty in the morning and you're finishing up with your agent. You're dead tired, and the only thing you can think about is climbing into bed. You're about ready to stop and drop off the agent when you see a pair of lights in the rearview mirror. Until then there's been almost no cars on the road. A coincidence? You can't know for sure. Another ten minutes and the lights are still there. What would you do?"

"Keep driving around until you're clean," one of the students offered.

"Maybe. But driving around aimlessly late at night is likely to tell surveillance you're operational. Red meat to the jackals. They'd flood the streets with surveillance. Now is the time for our case officer to think out of the box—break the rules."

"I know what I'd do," I interrupted. "I'd put the agent on the floor of the car, drive home, let him out in the garage, and make a place for him to sleep for a couple of hours. The next morning I'd take him out the same way. It would look like a normal day. No surveillance, and I'd drop him off in some out-of-the-way place."

Lynch reached across the table and shook my hand. "Good for you.

"Or how about this," he went on. "What if you'd prepared yourself for this eventuality—like putting a suitcase in the trunk of your car the morning of the meeting. The million pairs of eyes would have jumped to the conclusion that you were going out of town on a trip. So rather than driving around in circles, you head out of town with the agent. Surveillance thinks you're finally leaving on your trip and drops off. You leave the agent at the first town with a bus stop. The agent's not happy, but at least he's not in jail."

Lynch was mentoring, talking from years of experience in the field, and he was dead right. As I'd find out in my career, spying wasn't something you learned from a book, a training film, or a lecture. You learned it by doing it, with someone looking over your shoulder.

4

MY PAN AM TICKET pretty well told the story: seven hours to Frankfurt; another five to Tehran, where I overnighted; two more hours to New Delhi and another stayover; then a final two hours to Madras. I'd come to the other side of the world, but I didn't realize how remote a place the CIA had sent me until I stepped out of the plane and slammed into the sweet stench of rotting vegetation and open sewers. In the pitch black, it took me a while to figure out that the tin shed on the other side of the runway was the Madras airport terminal.

Inside the terminal, the wobbly ceiling fans only managed to stir up the hot air. Sweat was dripping off my nose. Thanks to a broken luggage belt, bags from who knew how many flights formed a mountain in the middle of the concrete floor. Two porters fought each other climbing to the top to retrieve the same bag. Three other porters followed me around, pestering to carry mine. They wouldn't listen when I told them I intended to carry my backpack myself. All the while a beggar with a withered arm and an amputated leg scooted behind me, pulling and pushing himself along the filthy floor with his good arm and leg. Every once in awhile he'd reach up and grab at my pant leg. It didn't seem to matter how many rupees I dropped into the pouch around his neck or how fast I hopped from one side of the terminal to the other. He just kept following. I was the only white person in the place.

I finally surrendered and gave one of the porters a fistful of rupees to go find my backpack. It took him about two minutes to come back with it.

"Madras isn't Paris," the branch chief for India had told me before I left for Dulles. "Do your two years there, keep your nose clean, and you'll be in line for a good assignment the next time around."

In other words, I was on probation. Although I had graduated from the Farm, the Near East Division, which recruited me for Madras, had decided I needed a tour in one of its true shit holes to see if I could make it as a case officer. The practice back then was to send Arabic-speaking rookies to Sana, North Yemen, and the rest to the CIA's small outposts in South Asia, which we called the night-soil circuit. (If you've ever seen South Asians walking into the fields as if picking their way through a minefield, you'll understand where the term comes from.) In fact, it wasn't such a bad system. The Madrases of the world really did determine who was cut out for the work and who wasn't. Some got sick, hated living overseas or couldn't hack the work. Some were caught meeting an agent, and sent home in disgrace. One or two went crazy. And some of us just soldiered on, hoping to make a difference.

India was better than most places to get your feet wet in operations. For a start, you learned how to operate against real, live surveillance. India's Intelligence Bureau, whose job it was to keep an eye on the CIA and India's other enemies, had been created by the British, which meant it was focused, disciplined, and tough. The IB could field thousands and thousands of surveillants. The ones on foot were nearly impossible to spot because they wore the same white dhotis or loincloths as every other male loitering on the street. They could flood any Indian city and disappear in the knot of humanity. Four-wheeled surveillance wasn't any easier: There were only two models of cars in India back then, and in the rearview mirror, one car looked like another. Short of Moscow or Peking, India was one of the toughest operating environments in the world.

Several years before I got to India, the IB caught a Delhi officer dropping off an agent after a meeting. The case officer had kept a pretty steady eye on the rearview mirror, looking for the giveaway of car lights hanging back. When he was ready to let off the agent, the case officer cut down a small street, stopped, and took off as soon as the agent was out. Problem was, an IB surveillance car had been hiding behind some foliage at an intersection the case officer had just passed. The IB team caught up with the case officer's car just in time to see the passenger door open and the agent climb out. Disaster followed: The agent and a dozen subsources were arrested. The case officer and Delhi's chief were sent home. Indian operations were shut down for almost two years.

On the bright side, India was the perfect place to collect first-rate intelligence. The CIA's interests there narrowed down to SOVMAT and India's nuclear program, both subjects of intense study in Washington. SOVMAT was CIA-speak for Soviet military manuals. By the 1970s India had become one of the world's biggest buyers of Soviet weapons, from tanks to airplanes and submarines. Since the Soviets typically would sell India their most advanced weapons, it had also become the most important country in the world for vacuuming up information on the Soviet military. Thanks largely to its offices in India, the CIA was in a position to tell the Pentagon what was going to come through the Fulda Gap if World War III were to break out. On the potential global-cataclysm front, India had tested a nuclear bomb in 1974. The White House wanted a heads-up on when the next one might go off—especially if it were in Pakistan.

India also was the perfect preserve for a young officer to bag his first agent. As one of the founders of the Non-Aligned Movement, it hosted missions from just about every country in the world. You could go to a cocktail party and meet a Mongolian diplomat or the ambassador to the African National Congress. But the real attraction was the thousands of Soviet diplomats, military officers, and technicians. About all you had to do to find one was step out your front door. If you were ever lucky enough to actually recruit one, you were a made man.

Finally, India was a place you could polish up on your social skills—cope with servants, make a dry martini, properly clip a cigar, keep up with the mindless chatter at the cricket club. You could hire a tennis pro for pennies. Some case officers even learned to play polo. Even in Madras, the living conditions weren't too shabby.

After the squalor of the airport, my mood definitely brightened as the driver drove through the gates of the estate that would be mine for the next two years. It was a white, two-story stone and stucco house with a huge banyan tree and a pergola of jasmine that arched over the entire length of the driveway. Lined up under the veranda were my servants—all seven of them. A cook, a bearer, a maid, an inside sweeper, an outside sweeper, and two gardeners. Although they were barefoot, the men were dressed in white starched uniforms and the women in brightly colored saris. They bowed as I got out of the car. When the bearer brought me a glass of cool, fresh mango juice on a silver tray, I decided India wasn't going to be half bad after all.

MADRAS TURNED OUT to be the ideal place for me to start out as a spy. I inherited only two agents, and they weren't stars, either. I had plenty of time to prepare for meetings, take long countersurveillance routes, and polish my cables back to headquarters. A rookie case officer thousands of miles from Washington either rose or fell on his cable prose.

Madras also was a great place to make the inevitable first mistakes. One night after a particularly hard monsoon rain, I took a wrong turn and ended up on a beach road with one of my agents in the car. I stalled in about two feet of water. Afraid the police might come along at any moment, I shooed the agent out of the car and watched as he disappeared into the darkness, shoes in his hand and pant legs rolled up above his knees. Another time my second agent didn't show up for a meeting. He didn't come to the alternate meetings, either. My choices were to sit on my hands and hope he'd turn up one day or to go look for him. Breaking the rules for the first time, I went to his house and knocked on the front door. If the IB teams in Madras had been as good as the ones in New Delhi, both of us would have been cooked, but Madras was a backwater posting for both sides.

The chief there, Chris ▮▮▮▮▮▮▮▮, was old-school CIA. The son of an ambassador, Chris had joined the agency right after graduating from Harvard and had worked in Africa before landing in India. Prior to each agent meeting, Chris and I would sit down to talk about it. He wanted to know what counter-surveillance route I planned, what papers I would carry with me, when the alternate meeting was scheduled if the agent didn't show up, what questions I intended to ask, and so on. After the agent meeting, Chris and I discussed every detail of what had happened and what was said. Then he would go through my cable drafts with a thick red pencil.

Happily, Madras wasn't all work. I rented a beach house south of the city. Built on stilts and surrounded by palm trees, it wasn't more than fifty feet from the water. I spent most weekends there, reading and swimming, sweet relief from the boredom of South

Asia. Madras also had good clay tennis courts, and I took up tennis seriously. It wasn't skiing, but I was learning to make do.

I'd just settled into a comfortable routine when Chris was seen meeting an agent. Rather than wait for the Indian government to lodge a complaint, the office in New Delhi sent him home. I wasn't happy to lose his company or mentoring, but now that I was on my own, I intended to show headquarters and New Delhi just how good I was. The rule was never to leave a rookie untended, because he'll eventually screw up. I intended to prove myself the exception.

Shortly after Chris left, a recently recruited spotter —or "access agent," as the DO called them—introduced me to an Arab military officer on assignment to the Indian military. Sami, as I will call him, was assigned to a base about a ten-hour drive from Madras. He was an attractive target because relations between his country and the U.S. were going from cold to frigid. Diplomatic channels were about to close down, which meant that very soon only the CIA would have eyes and ears on the ground in Sami's country. Also, his government bought a lot of Soviet weapons, and the manuals that came with them were never far from our minds.

Ever since my first unhappy reception at the Farm when I tried to pass myself off as an oil man, I knew the first contact was tricky. As soon as I shook Sami's hand, I plunged into an aw-shucks routine, rambling on about how dull India was, how difficult it was to make friends, how awful the weather was. It was a relentless torrent. Sami didn't have a chance to say anything or walk away. Just around the time I needed to take a breath, I set the hook. I mentioned the beach house, how refreshing the breeze was, how nice it was to spend a day away from the bustle.

"When you get to Madras, give me a call. You'll love it," I said.

Sami looked at me for a second or two before deciding the invitation was innocent. "Sure," he answered, "I'd be happy to."

When Sami accepted my card and gave me his in return, I had to bite my lip to hold back a smile. It worked! And this guy was a bona fide hard target definitely worth recruiting, my first developmental. I was as excited as I was the first time I asked a girl out on a date.

When I called Sami at his base two weeks later, he sounded genuinely happy to hear from me. He apologized for not calling. We were about to hang up when he let it slip that he would be passing through Madras the following week. I again mentioned the beach house. He hesitated for a beat and then accepted, adding he would bring his wife. *Bingo.* Now it was just a question of reeling him in.

I spent a week preparing the beach house for Sami and his wife. I stocked it with a couple of bottles of Johnny Walker Black Label Scotch, a case of good California white wine, and American food you couldn't find in India. I brought over my stereo so there would be music, and I dispatched the cook the day before to have everything ready.

On the big day there wasn't a cloud in the sky. A steady breeze blew off the Bay of Bengal. You could barely feel the humidity. In the morning we swam and spent an hour sitting on the beach talking. We moved back to the house for lunch, and afterward we sat on the balcony drinking wine. Sami and his wife were completely relaxed. They talked about Islam, about Sami's childhood growing up as a Bedouin, about his blind father.

The day was going fine until about four o'clock, when the ayah, my maid, went into labor. With her loosely wrapped sari, I had no idea she was even pregnant. I don't think her husband knew, either. We quickly closed up the house and packed everything into the car. Sami and his wife insisted on going to the hospital with the ayah and me.

While Sami's wife stayed with the ayah, he and I sat on a bench under a tree outside the hospital and talked. He slipped easily into telling me about his country's military. He was on duty during the 1967 Israeli-Arab war, he said, assigned to a listening site monitoring Israeli communications when Israel attacked the U.S.S. *Liberty*, killing thirty-four American sailors. Until that day he believed the Arab propaganda that Israel was America's pawn, but listening to the Israeli pilots talk to one another as they strafed the ship, he understood how far he had been misled. The East and the West needed to keep open their channels of communication, he added. Otherwise there never would be peace in the Middle East.

All I could think of as he talked was how he was playing my song. Not only had I corralled a hard target, I had pinpointed an actual vulnerability:

Sami's concern about the need for a dialogue between Arabs and Americans. He had opened a door that I intended to walk right through.

Two weeks later Sami was back in Madras and called me. I had already received from headquarters what is called a provisional operational approval, or POA. A POA meant headquarters had done a background check on Sami and nothing derogatory had come up. He wasn't a known fabricator or a double sent by his country to stir up problems with the CIA. Headquarters didn't decide whether Sami was recruitable or not—that was up to me. But now I had the nod to take down my prey.

Sami offered to take me out to lunch. I agreed but suggested that he first pass by my office to pick me up. The Farm had been explicit: I needed to control the venue of the pitch.

As Sami walked around my office, drinking coffee and looking at my meager brag wall, he seemed less talkative than he had been at the hospital. I didn't pay attention, though. I was silently rehearsing the pitch I'd prepared the night before, including the part where he said yes.

"Sami," I finally started, alarmed by the tremor in my own voice. I could feel myself starting to sweat even though the air-conditioning was blasting out a stream of arctic air. "I need to ask you something."

Sami looked at me quizzically and sat down in a chair on the other side of the office. I was sitting behind my desk.

"A couple weeks ago, we talked about the need for a dialogue between our two countries. Well, I was thinking that maybe you could help with something."

Sami listened without saying a word as I fumbled through what was undoubtedly one of the most awkward pitches ever delivered by a CIA case officer. When I got to the part about having to keep this arrangement secret from his government, Sami shot out of his chair. He was trembling with anger.

"Are you asking me to spy?" he asked in a low, raspy voice.

When he hurled his cup on the floor, I knew "yes" wasn't going to put this toothpaste back in the tube.

I mumbled something about the understanding between countries being his idea. Sami cooled down a couple of degrees, but we didn't go to lunch. I would see him again a few more times, but he always made sure someone else was present.

5

197█. NEW DELHI, INDIA.

A DAY AFTER I sent New Delhi a cable about the botched pitch, its chief, Bill ███████████, asked me to fly up to see him.

Wild Bill, as he was affectionately known, was a tough little fireplug of an Irishman and one of the best street officers, maybe ever. He'd recruited the first North Korean as well as dozens of other hard targets. He was also a wizard with gadgets and disguises. One story held that when he was assigned the task of bugging a conference room, Wild Bill fashioned an ice arrow to shoot a miniature microphone into the conference room's acoustic tile ceiling—at night through an open window from the street. The arrow, in theory, would melt away, leaving the microphone embedded in the ceiling. I never learned whether it worked or not, but the story was Bill ███████████ to a T. Another story went around that when he was in Tokyo, he tailored his own reversible jacket and hat. When the Japanese had him under surveillance, he'd follow a walking route until he was momentarily out of sight, then reverse his jacket and hat and move back through the surveillance team undetected.

The first time I walked into Bill's office I was surprised to find the American ambassador to India, Robert Goheen, leaning over his shoulder, looking at something I couldn't see at first. Bill was wearing jeweler's goggles and had a pair of tweezers in one hand and a razor blade in the other. When I got closer, I could tell he was cutting under a period in a typed letter, making a pocket for a microdot—a photographic negative tiny enough to be hidden in such a minute space.

"This new generation doesn't even know what a microdot is," Bill mumbled to the ambassador, nodding in my direction.

When he finished, Bill changed places with Goheen and walked him through the procedure. Goheen's résumé included a tenure as president of Princeton University, as well as a stint as a classics instructor. I doubt he had had the slightest interest in spying before meeting Bill, but he clearly loved these microdots. Bill was that type of person; his enthusiasm was contagious.

Another thing about Wild Bill: He never flinched from risks. When the Pentagon needed to know the composition of the T-72 tank's frontal armor, Bill found a sergeant at an Indian tank-repair depot who would give us access to a T-72 overnight. A tech team with a high-speed precision drill was brought in to take a core sample of the armor. Another time he had one of Delhi's case officers recruit a T-72 driver to steer one of the tanks across the border into Pakistan. Both operations came up short—the CIA wouldn't let me write about them here if they had succeeded—but the point is that Bill was prepared to do whatever was needed to get the job done.

I went directly to Bill's office as soon as I got off the plane from Madras. When I walked in, he got up and closed the door.

Uh-oh, I thought, *here it comes—he's sending me home.*

"Well?" Bill asked.

I was stammering something about having hustled Sami too fast when Bill cut me off. "Kiddo, I didn't call you up here to flog you for pitching that joker. My only gripe is that you didn't go up to his base and pitch him again."

Before I could recover, he asked, "How much does Uncle Sam pay you a year?"

"About $26,000."

"And how much did your training cost?"

I didn't know for sure, but I'd heard a figure of $250,000 batted around.

"Okay. Now let me add up the rest. There's your car, your rent, your electricity, your airplane tickets, and all the money it costs to send your stuff to India. And then there are the salaries of all the people who support you back at headquarters. That brings us to a ballpark figure of 500K. Do you think you've earned it back so far?"

I'd never thought about spying in those terms, but $500,000 definitely sounded like a lot of money. By the time we finished talking, we had agreed that I'd come up to New Delhi to start paying down my debt. Bill liked my initiative with Sami. Maybe with a little mentoring, he could turn me into a decent case officer.

★

Two months later I moved to New Delhi and was assigned an apartment in one of the newer suburbs— a big four-bedroom place, but definitely not my Madras mansion. I had only two servants now and no beach house, but none of that mattered. I was in the big leagues now.

The first week Wild Bill handed me an agent file. "Here," he said, "go cut your teeth on this one."

The agent was among Delhi's best counter-intelligence sources. He was supposed to be working for the KGB but had volunteered to be doubled back against it. Over the years he'd provided spectacular information on the KGB in India—names of its case officers, its American targets, even the names of some Indian agents. But we still weren't absolutely sure he was doubled. There was always the possibility that the KGB ran him in to collect information on us. Or maybe the double himself didn't know whom he really worked for—one day for us, one day for the KGB. Counterintelligence was like playing chess blindfolded.

In fact, the KGB aggressively targeted the CIA. India was a training ground for them just as it was for us. The Soviets fielded a lot of hungry young officers who would do just about anything to recruit one of us. They bugged our houses, put surveillance on us, and from time to time pitched us.

The KGB had its successes, too, as I found out, including one of our communicators, the people who handled our cables between the boonies and Washington. Arresting the communicator would have compromised our source of information—a Soviet "mole," or double agent—so the CIA left him in place and monitored him day and night, no easy task. The officer running the case communicated with headquarters using a onetime encryption pad. He had to encrypt and decrypt each and every message manually—hideously time-consuming but the only way to keep the surveillance secret from the communicator. In a separate case, a surveillance team had caught a KGB officer dropping off a State Department communicator a little after four in the morning. The only possible explanation was another KGB recruitment.

Paul ███████████, the double's current case officer, was a Soviet targets officer and Delhi's walking reference on the KGB. He could rattle off such things as the name of the deputy chief of the KGB's First Chief Directorate in 1958 and a lot of other spy arcana without missing a beat.

When I asked Paul to introduce the double to me, he pulled out of his safe a half-dozen thick volumes, nearly two feet of background on the double.

"Go read these and come back in two weeks," Paul said.

It was some of the most tedious prose I would ever have to suffer through—hundreds of long contact reports mixed with near-verbatim accounts of meetings with the double. Each report started with a review of the previous meeting, then went on in excruciating detail about whom the double had met since then, what his KGB case officer had told him, how he'd responded, and so on. By going over and over the same ground, the hope was to either catch the double in a lie or establish his bona fides, but the density of detail was overwhelming. I started skimming.

Paul eyed me warily when I came back a week later carrying the files in my arms. "Did you notice how the double only mentioned Oleg Ivanovich's name once?" he asked before I could sit down. "We know Oleg is a prodigy, the rezident's wonder boy. But why doesn't our double know that?"

I didn't even remember reading Oleg's name. Paul pointed at the door, and I left the same way I came in—with the files stacked in my arms.

This time I devoured them. A month later I knew the first name, patronymic, and family name of every damn Russian in the KGB rezidentura. I'd even memorized their dates and places of birth and their wives' names. I knew everything about their careers. I studied their pictures. I could have picked them out in a lineup. Paul gave me another quiz. I passed and now was ready to take over the double. As for Paul, he enjoyed looking over my shoulder, offering help when I needed it.

I met him twice a month, usually after midnight in old Delhi. At that time of night, when the streets were deserted, you could spot an IB watcher, whether he was wearing a dhoti or a three-piece suit. Nor was there any place for IB surveillance cars to hide. I'd drive around for a couple of hours debriefing the double. Every once in a while I would stop to take notes. After the meeting I'd go home to catch a few hours of sleep. The next morning I'd be at my typewriter, banging out a contact report as detailed and tedious as the rest. I probably added two volumes to the double's file.

But writing the contact report didn't mean the job was over. Just as important, I had to cross-check the double's information. Once, I asked him to look into Oleg Ivanovich, and he came back with Oleg's home address and license-plate number. The following morning, very early, I drove by the address. A car with the right license plate was parked in the driveway. I drove by four or five more times to make sure it wasn't a coincidence. Another time, when the double told me Oleg had left on a trip to Moscow, I had an agent at the airport check Aeroflot's passenger manifest for that day. Oleg's name wasn't on it. I had the agent go back and check Air India's Moscow flight for that day. His name wasn't on that one, either. At that point it was one of two possibilities: Either Oleg had traveled on an alias passport or the double had lied to me. Running a double agent is a very long walk in the wilderness of mirrors. In the end, we finally found out he was really working for the KGB, which ran him into us to collect information on our officers.

The technical term for what I was doing was "building matrices"—a fancy name for basic detective work. The idea was to sift out suppositions, assumptions, hearsay, poorly sourced information, and wishful thinking, leaving the facts to stand on their own. No matter how thin they might be, they were the only conclusions you could trust. It was indispensable training for anything you wanted to do in the CIA.

★

I HAD THE KGB double and a handful of other agents, but I still wanted to recruit an agent of my own—to start paying down my 500K debt.

I decided to go after an Indian military officer. It had been just eight years since the last Indo-Pak war, and there was always the possibility that another would break out at any time. The next might go nuclear. An Indian military officer in our pocket could give us forewarning.

The problem was getting close enough to the flock to separate a lamb. Indian military officers were a segregated class, forbidden to go to cocktail parties that foreigners attended or to join the same clubs foreigners did. When they did meet a foreigner, they were supposed to report it immediately. While most things in India were inefficient, the government's effort to isolate its military officers from foreign contact wasn't.

I soon discovered that a back window had been accidentally left open. Indian military officers loved to hunt. On weekends and on vacation, they would go up to the Punjab to shoot partridge and sometimes a large Indian deer called a Blue Bull. I figured by simply reinventing myself into an avid hunter, I could run into some of them.

On my first vacation back to the U.S., I bought a Browning double-barrel twelve-gauge shotgun and a crate of shells. To be as unobtrusive as possible, I picked up a surplus Indian-made military jeep on my return, one modeled on the original 1942 World War II Willy's. It was in fantastic condition, including its original camouflage paint. The owner told me it had been decommissioned after the 1971 Pakistan war, but it looked newer than that to me. Sorting out the registration took forever, but I went ahead and slapped some civilian plates on it, thinking no one would notice, and then I finagled a weekend invitation to a partridge hunt.

We started about nine in the morning, when the sun was up and the grass dry. To flush the partridge from the high corn where they fed, we mustered field hands to walk through and beat the stalks with sticks, yelling, *"Titah, titah,"* Punjabi for "partridge." By midafternoon we had bagged a good hundred of them. At night, while we sat around a bonfire in the courtyard, the cook roasted a dozen for dinner.

On my fourth trip to the Punjab, I met a Sikh who looked to be about thirty-five. He introduced himself as Major Singh and said he was the cousin of the landlord who owned the farm we were hunting on. I kept away from any sensitive subjects—hunting would do. Nor did I try to set up a follow-on meeting. I knew if I came back to his cousin's farm, I would run into him again.

The next Saturday I hunted with Major Singh. Like most Indian military officers, he was a magnificent shot. I never saw him miss a bird. At the end of the day when we were low on ammunition, he'd shoot only if he had a chance of taking down two partridges as they crisscrossed. Even then he rarely wasted a shot. That night around the bonfire we talked for several hours about India and the U.S. He loved America. He thought it was a mistake for India to ally with the Soviet Union, both for ideological reasons and because Soviet military equipment was vastly inferior to America's. His secret desire, he told me, was to attend staff college in the U.S. We turned in about midnight.

That fall Singh and I spent almost every weekend together. We became friends. I eventually offered to buy an Italian shotgun for him, a magnificent weapon not for sale in India. When I presented it to him several weeks later, he hugged me. At our next meeting Singh brought some money to pay me back. I refused, telling him it was a gift and it would be an insult to accept money for it. He hemmed and hawed before accepting. The hook was set.

Worried that people would notice how much time we were spending together, I started taking Singh out to hunt during the week. There wasn't time to go deep into the Punjab, but good partridge could be found closer to Delhi.

We were driving back into town one evening along a side road, to avoid the traffic on the Grand Trunk Road, the main highway that links Calcutta in the east to Kabul, Afghanistan in the west (it runs 1,600 miles diagonally across India) when Singh suddenly shouted, *"Stop!"* At first I thought there was something in the road, but as soon as I stopped the car, Singh jumped out, clutching his new shotgun, ran across the road, and hopped over a low stone wall. About two minutes later I heard a shot. The next thing I saw was Singh throwing a dead peacock over the wall. He was about to follow it when a half-dozen men wearing side arms and carrying automatic weapons came running up from all directions.

I stayed in the car as Singh talked with the men. Every now and again they'd look over at the jeep, and I'd get terrified that they were going to ask for the paperwork. I was starting to suspect the jeep was hot, liberated from the Indian army. If that was the case, both Singh and I would be hauled off to jail. Happily, it was too dark for them to see that I wasn't an Indian or that the jeep had civilian plates on it. Singh was wearing his uniform, and no doubt they thought we were both army.

Singh finally handed the peacock to one of the men and walked back to the jeep, grinning sheepishly.

"That was Mrs. Gandhi's estate," he said as we pulled away.

Not only had Singh trespassed on Indira Gandhi's estate, he'd killed an Indian national bird, which was also illegal. Close calls like that weren't part of the course at the Farm.

The more I saw of Singh, the more it looked like he was ready to be separated from the flock. One weekend I brought Wild Bill on a hunting trip. It never hurt to have a second opinion. Bill and Singh hit it off. Afterward Bill agreed with me that it was time to pop the question. In fact, I invited Bill to be there for the show.

Singh knew something was up as soon as he walked in the room and saw Bill. He kept smiling, though. We were all friends. I brought Singh a beer.

I started about as steadily as when I had pitched Sami, rambling about our long friendship.

"Major," Bill cut me off. "Let's don't horse around. Bob and I work for the CIA."

Now that that grenade was thrown, I took back over. I asked Singh if he wanted to work for the CIA as an agent. He went pale. It looked for a moment as if he was going to get up and leave. He thought better of it, though, probably remembering he'd broken the rules by not reporting his contact with me and accepting the shotgun. He'd already compromised himself. When I finished, he hesitated and then said he would think about it.

Major Singh eventually turned down the pitch, but making it did wonders for my confidence. We remained friends for years. Soon recruiting agents became as natural as ordering a pizza over the telephone. It's all a matter of listening to what people are really saying. Money problems, an awful boss, secret desires or allegiances can all be windows into small compromises that grow into larger and larger ones. It took me a while, but I finally learned how to read the dark forest of other people's minds and then walk them into espionage small step by small step. Toward the end of my career, I never had a pitch rejected.

FOR MOST OF MY TOUR in New Delhi, I was extremely lucky to fall under the IB's radar. It put only sporadic surveillance on me. The lax coverage mattered, too, because in addition to the double I had been handed and my efforts to recruit Singh, I'd picked up five other agents. I was meeting an agent every two or three nights—a lot in a hostile environment like India.

My luck almost changed for the worse one night in August. A week of monsoon had left half of Delhi's roads flooded and impassable, bad conditions for meeting agents, but since Madras, I had learned to avoid the low areas. Besides, I expected the meeting to be brief. Pass the agent some cash, I figured, and kick him out the door in the first dark alley.

As soon as I turned the corner, I could see he was carrying a bulky duffel bag. He was also breathing heavily as if he had run to the meeting.

"T-72 manuals," he said, pointing at the bag as he climbed in the car.

"What?" I asked, almost certain I'd heard him wrong.

Grinning from ear to ear, he repeated himself.

The T-72 tank manuals were the Holy Grail we'd been after for years, the keys to the kingdom of knowledge. My heart started racing, especially when the agent said he had to have them back in two hours. The sergeant who had borrowed the manuals needed to return them to the safe before he went off duty. There wasn't enough time to go to the office, copy them, and run a good countersurveillance route. Worse, at that hour New Delhi would be crawling with IB, but I could take them that night or maybe never.

The choice seemed obvious. I slammed on the brakes, pushed the agent out of the car, and yelled at him to meet me in two hours behind guest house number three at Delhi's Gymkhana Club. The agent looked at me, confused. I reiterated, "You're either in the goddamn bushes behind number three or you don't get your manuals back." I sprayed him with gravel as I spun the car around.

As soon as I got into the office, I called the officer who did our technical operations, or the tech as we called him, to come help. He worked the document copier, and I the lone Xerox. Inevitably, the paper jammed not long before the machine ran out of toner. The toner was locked in a closet, which neither of us had the key to. The tech had to drill the lock. By the time we finished, I had exactly seventeen minutes to get to the Gymkhana Club.

As I passed through the first circular intersection, I saw a parked car turn on its lights and pull out after me. A second fell in behind it. I checked my watch. I now had six minutes to get to the handoff with the agent. Ordinarily I would have driven around until I'd flushed out the two cars, but there was no time.

I continued along the main road, which was bumper-to-bumper with cars. With all the swimming lights in my rearview mirror, I couldn't tell whether the two cars were still behind me or not.

About half a mile away from the Gymkhana, I cut down a back street, a shortcut I'd taken hundreds of times and one I knew would be empty of traffic at that time of night. As soon as I turned the corner, I slammed down on the gas pedal. I must have been doing fifty by the time I was halfway down the block. No one drove that fast on Delhi's side streets, and anyone trying to keep up with me would have to show himself. I kept my eyes fixed on the rearview mirror.

I don't know if it was because of a premonition or not, but when I looked back at the road, an enormous cow was spanning it. I knew in that split second that if I hit the brake, I would skid and hit the cow, dead center. That left me the option of going around it. The problem was that India's sacred cows are completely unpredictable. When they panic, they're as likely to bolt forward as to turn and bolt the other way. Flipping a mental coin, I headed for the cow's rear end and cleared it by a good two inches. The right side of the car had dipped into a mud-filled sinkhole on the side of the road—I could hear the axle scraping along the edge—but my momentum carried me through. It was a miracle I didn't flip. As soon as the car stopped fishtailing, I looked in my rearview mirror. The cow was gone, but in its place there were now at least three pairs of lights. They had to be IB. Worse, they were gaining on me.

I knew I had broken all the rules. The last thing you want to do when you're under surveillance is to tweak the adversary's interest. It only makes him more determined. But I had no choice. I could either hand back the manuals—I had three minutes now—or abort, and the agent had made it clear that if the sergeant didn't return them that night, he would be caught and arrested, bringing the whole house of cards tumbling down.

By the time I pulled through the Gymkhana's gates, the three pairs of lights had grown to five. In my rearview mirror I watched them file through the gates one by one. The closest car was maybe ten feet from my rear bumper. There wasn't any more road, but I kept going—right down a gravel walking path between two tennis courts. I figured they wouldn't follow me. I was right. All five cars stopped in front of the club's main building and started deploying on foot. I hit the brakes, stuffed the duffel bag with the manuals in it into a tennis bag, and ducked between two tamarind trees. Footsteps echoed behind me as I followed a path bordered by tall myrtle until I came to a protected section of the hedge that fronted guest house number three. I could see the agent's shadow through the foliage, right where I had told him to be. Without stopping, I pulled the duffel bag out of the tennis bag and tossed it through the hedge in one quick motion. Out of the corner of my eye, I saw the agent pick it up and walk away.

I continued along the path and entered the Gymkhana's bar through the back door. The place was empty except for a distinguished Indian gentleman in a three-piece suit, sitting alone and reading a newspaper. I walked over and sat next to him. Without saying a word, I summoned a waiter and ordered two double Scotches, straight up and no ice, for both of us. It wasn't until I struck up a conversation as if we were old friends that he looked like he might run for it.

I glanced at the back door and saw two of my surveillants. They were looking alternately at my tennis bag, the Indian gentleman, and me. I could tell that their interest was quickly narrowing down to the Indian gentleman, trying to figure out why I'd been in such a hurry to come see him. By the time they got around to questioning him, the agent would have long cleared the area and returned the manuals to the sergeant.

Nothing like beating the odds. I ordered another round for my new friend and me.

AFTER THREE YEARS IN INDIA, I was like a carpenter finishing up an apprenticeship. I had all the tools and skills to go out on my own. The only thing I needed now was a speciality. I asked to study Chinese, but before the East Asian Division could answer, the Near East Division came in with an offer to put me through its two-year Arabic course. I knew next to nothing about the Middle East, but I accepted without a second thought. I'd been hanging around in the frying pan. It was time to jump into the fire.

PART II
INTO THE FIRE

6

APRIL 18, 1983. BEIRUT, LEBANON.

A DENTED, LATE-MODEL GMC pickup truck pulled off to the side of the road, just beyond the burned-out husk of the St. George's Hotel. The driver left the engine running and calmly watched the traffic along Beirut's seafront corniche.

No one paid any attention to the pickup or noticed that it was sitting low on its springs. The civil war was over, as far as most Lebanese were concerned. The Israeli army, which invaded Lebanon in June 1982 to crush Palestinian guerilla groups operating there, had already withdrawn well south of Beirut and was about to pull back even farther. And the Palestinian guerrillas, who had owned Beirut's streets since the start of the Lebanese civil war in April 1975, had withdrawn too, to Tripoli in the north and the Biqa' Valley. The American, British, French, and Italian troops that made up the Multi-National Force now patrolled in their place. Even the Lebanese who detested foreigners and blamed them for the country's problems took grudging comfort in the French LeClerc armored personnel carriers driving up and down Hamra, Beirut's central business district. Although they would never admit it, they were also pleased that American marines, with their M-16s and flak vests, guarded the airport. Lebanon wasn't exactly at peace, but it was closer than it had been in a long time.

You could smell the optimism in the air. The Lebanese who had left during the civil war were coming back, and they had money in their pockets to rebuild what had once been one of the most European and modernized of Arab cities. Only six months after the Israeli invasion, Beirut was one vast, sprawling construction site. Hardly a building wasn't being painted, patched up, or torn down to put up another one. Cranes, scaffolding, backhoes, and street crews clogged the streets day and night. A beat-up truck sitting low on its springs, idling by the side of the road, wasn't about to attract anyone's attention.

At 12:43 P.M. the pickup's driver spotted the old green Mercedes as it came flying around the corner in front of the 'Ayn Muraysah mosque, darting in and out of traffic and trying to make headway against the usual crush of traffic. As the Mercedes got closer, the pickup driver recognized the two men in the front seat. He had been with them only a few hours before, when they had met for final preparations. The driver waited until the Mercedes flashed its lights three times. That was the prearranged signal that the approach to the target was clear. The driver then slammed his pickup into first gear and pulled into traffic, barely missing a dump truck. He headed along the corniche toward 'Ayn Muraysah, in the direction the Mercedes had just come from. On his right, strollers walked along the esplanade, beside the teal blue, silver-speckled sea. On his left, the upscale apartments of 'Ayn Muraysah seemed to tumble down the hill toward him. The driver, though, stared only at the car in front of him. That was the one thing they hadn't taken into account: lunchtime traffic.

As he neared the seven-story American embassy the driver searched for a chance to cut across the oncoming lane. He slowed, nearly to a stop, as the drivers behind him pounded furiously on their horns. When a gap opened between two cars, he abruptly swerved the truck into it, almost colliding with a woman who was driving her two children home from school.

Now the driver pushed the gas pedal against the floor and pointed the truck toward the exit of the embassy's semicircular covered driveway. By the time it entered the driveway the truck was moving too fast for the guards to draw their weapons. The guard understood what was about to happen. They'd seen it so many times before in Beirut. All they could do was throw themselves on the ground and pray.

The pickup truck hit an outbuilding but continued forward, ascending the short flight of steps leading to the lobby. Just as it crashed through the lobby's door—at exactly 1:03 P.M. local time, according to the State Department's official announcement—it exploded. Even by Beirut standards, it was an enormous blast, shattering windows for miles around. The U.S.S. *Guadalcanal*, anchored five miles off the coast, shuddered from the tremors. At ground zero, the center of the seven-story embassy lifted up hundreds of feet into the air; remained suspended for what seemed an eternity and then collapsed in a cloud of dust, people, splintered furniture, and paper. The lobby itself was blasted into powder. The thick Plexiglas window protecting Guard Post 1 imploded at about 27,600 feet per second, disintegrating the young marine on duty. The only part of him found was the melted brass buttons of his tunic.

Sixty-three people, including seventeen Americans, were killed in what was then the deadliest terrorist attack against the U.S. ever, but the CIA was hardest hit. Six officers died, including the chief, his deputy, and the deputy's wife. The deputy's wife had started working at the embassy only that morning. Bob Ames, the CIA's national intelligence officer for the Near East, was killed, too. Bob had stopped by the embassy on a visit to Beirut. His hand was found floating a mile offshore, the wedding ring still on his finger. Never before had the CIA lost so many officers in a single attack. It was a tragedy from which the agency would never recover.

IN THE NEXT twenty-four hours, swarms of CIA and FBI investigators descended on Beirut. The problem was, there wasn't much left to investigate. The explosion completely consumed the driver. There was no trace of the detonator, either, leading to the hypothesis that the bomb maker had placed a small amount of explosives inside the device to make sure it was destroyed in the explosion. Detonators are signatures—something an expert would not want to leave behind.

The mystery only deepened when the FBI forensic experts were unable to take a swipe from the rubble to determine the composition of the explosive. Semtex? RDX? C-4? They had no idea. Eventually they found a trace of PETN, but most military explosives contain some PETN. It added little to solving the bombing. One explanation was that half-filled acetylene tanks wrapped around the explosives not only served to enhance the brisance of the charge—the destructive fragmentation effect—but also to ensure the obliteration of the explosives along with the driver and detonator. As for the truck, the FBI finally found a piece of the chassis with a VIN number and traced it to its original buyer in Texas. Someone had bought it used and shipped it to the Gulf, but the trail went cold there. The FBI couldn't figure out how it got to Beirut, let alone who owned it.

Lebanese intelligence and the CIA fared no better. The Lebanese investigators assumed the driver was a Shi'a Muslim, but only because the Shi'a were more inclined to commit suicide in a terrorist operation than other Muslims. The Lebanese agents fanned out across Beirut's southern suburbs and the Biqa' Valley where most of the radicalized Shi'a lived, but they couldn't come up with a credible rumor or any leads. The CIA's sources also came up empty.

Three groups would call in to claim responsibility, but the CIA wasn't even sure whether they existed. All three calls could have been hoaxes. The Lebanese arrested a half-dozen people, but it looked like a case of rounding up the usual suspects to make it look like they were on top of the investigation.

The bombers left no return address. Whoever they were, they were very, very good.

I WAS IN TUNIS studying Arabic when the news of the bombing hit like a sonic boom. All of us, the students and the instructors, knew someone working in the embassy in Beirut. I'll never forget Khaldiyah, an older woman who had worked in the Beirut embassy for many years, putting her head on the table and sobbing uncontrollably.

I figured some radical Palestinian group was behind the explosion, and it would be only a matter of weeks before someone was caught and the plot exposed. I turned out to be wrong. I had no idea the bombing would never be officially solved or that it would become for me a lifelong obsession, but the seeds of the latter were already sown. I'd visited Beirut a few months before the bombing and talked to some of our people there, including the chief and his deputy who had died. Even today I can close my eyes and see them and their offices and imagine them crumbling into dust. Between the mystery of who did it and the memory of who died there, I would never be able to leave it alone. (The account of the bombing just given, I should point out, has been assembled from fact, contemporary rumor, bits and pieces of information I've gathered over the years, and speculation based on nearly two decades of research.)

Four months after the bombing, I finished up my two-year Arabic course and was assigned to ███████ ███████, then a small but important outpost in the

Middle East. Its reporting was avidly read in Washington. I had an outstanding agent who produced a stream of documents and firsthand intelligence. There were plenty of hard targets, too, and after New Delhi, the local surveillance was a breeze. It felt great to be back on the streets, running agents, and putting my Arabic to use. And, frankly, I needed all the practice I could get. Even after two solid years of training, I was still a long way from any sort of fluency. It would take years before I was comfortable in the language.

Things started off well enough with my new chief, John ██████████, but it wasn't long before I realized he wasn't Wild Bill. A slight man with a nervous tic, John wore a meticulously pressed suit and a pair of brilliantly shined wing tips to the office every day, including weekends. I could have lived with the fact that he dressed like a Foreign Service officer, but not that he had an account-book mentality about spying to match. John refused to take risks. He thought the worst thing that could befall a case officer was to be caught trying to recruit an agent.

Instead of worrying about intelligence, John fretted over meeting headquarters' paper deadlines. When a request came through from Langley for some inconsequential progress report, John would stop everything to have it in a week early, before any other office in the Middle East. It infuriated him when I handed in my accountings late, even though the office invariably owed me money. It was clear we were headed for a blowup. It came when I tried to bug a terrorist safe house.

During the first year of my Arabic course in Washington, D.C., I'd made friends with a young Palestinian student. He had no idea I worked for the CIA. He helped me with Arabic; I helped him with English. We hit the Georgetown bars together, and he introduced me to Arabic cooking. But what cemented our friendship was when I helped him polish up an essay that won him a grant for graduate school. When it came time for me to leave, he pulled me aside and told me he had a brother living in the city I was headed to. I'll call the brother Khalid. He gave me Khalid's address and telephone number, adding cryptically that Khalid could help me with any security problems I might have.

I called Khalid shortly after I arrived, and he immediately agreed to meet. It turned out Khalid was a member of a Palestinian terrorist group. We both knew he would lose his scalp if he was caught with a CIA officer, but Khalid took the risk because his brother had told him to. That was one of my first lessons in how the Middle East works: You don't recruit an individual; you recruit families, clans, and tribes.

Late one night when we were driving around—by then we'd put our meetings on a clandestine footing—Khalid was oddly quiet, though grinning from ear to ear. At last, unable to contain himself any longer, he dropped the news. He'd just found out about a secret Abu Nidal office, and he thought terrorist operations were planned there.

Khalid was right to be excited. Abu Nidal was at the top of the CIA's hit parade. A cold-blooded murderer, he had attempted to assassinate the Israeli ambassador to London, provoking Israel to invade Lebanon on June 6, 1982, and very nearly drawing the whole Middle East into war. We knew he would try again, given the opportunity.

As I let Khalid out of the car, he handed me the address of the Abu Nidal office. Without saying a word to John, I checked the address out the next day, walking around the neighborhood. Although it was a three-story apartment building, common in that part of town, a guard with a machine gun stood in the building's unlit vestibule, barely visible from the street. Since nothing identified the building as a government office, which would have explained the guard, I figured the odds weren't bad that it was just what Khalid had said.

Two adjoining buildings shared walls with the Abu Nidal office. If you could get access to one of those apartments, it would be only a matter of drilling a hole in the wall with a silenced drill and putting in a microphone. Providing you didn't drill all the way through to the other side, the operation would be a piece of cake. In a pinch, we probably could have listened straight through the wall with an accelerometer, or contact microphone—a little like putting a glass up to the wall to hear through.

Back in the office, John looked at me wide-eyed as I explained my plan. "There's absolutely no way State's going to approve it," he interrupted.

"What does State have to do with it?" I asked, thinking he might have misunderstood me. "We find an agent to rent an apartment in one of the adjoining buildings, bring in a tech team, drill, stick a mike in the hole, and then keep our fingers crossed that we get some take from it."

"Bob, you don't have the slightest idea what political sensitivities are involved. This country is important to the United States. No one wants to risk alienating it by undertaking a risky operation. We can't afford a misstep that would give it an excuse to drop out of the peace process."

Clearly, John thought I should be able to grasp the political nuances on my own. I was about to let the matter go when he made the mistake of trying to appease me.

"You know we can do quite well with the softer targets here," he said. "TheAustralian national day is coming up. Why don't you try to finagle an invitation?"

"You've got to be kidding me," I said. "Who in God's name do you expect me to meet at an Australian embassy reception?"

John pulled out a rag he kept in his top desk drawer and started buffing his wing tips. When the buffing rag came out, I knew the conversation was over.

IF I HAD REALIZED then that John was a kind of see-no-evil, hear-no-evil, do-no-evil model for the new CIA that was quietly building back in Washington and around the globe, would I have walked away then? I don't think so. For one thing, the bombing of our embassy in Beirut was starting to really intrigue me.

Officially, the embassy investigation continued.

Unofficially, it was dead in the water. After the initial bogus arrests made by the Lebanese, no leads surfaced. The FBI forensic teams sealed and labeled their plastic bags of evidence, boxed what they could find of the pickup truck, and headed home to write their reports. It was left up to State and the CIA to continue the investigation on the ground, but that soon hit a snag when the Lebanese investigators beat a suspect to death during questioning. The rumor started that a CIA officer observed the whole thing and did nothing to stop it. Whether the story was true or not, Washington abruptly cut off all cooperation with the Lebanese.

The Lebanese carried on alone, but like the FBI, they were unable to identify the driver, the owner of the truck, or the type of explosives used. Six months after the bombing, they produced a final report that was a dog's breakfast of unsupported and politically motivated accusations against enemies of the Lebanese president, Amin Jumayyil: Syria, Iran, Yasir Arafat's Fatah, and three other Palestinian groups. It even tried to tie in one of Jumayyil's Christian rivals, all without offering a shred of evidence. No one paid any attention to it.

Besides, the White House and State Department had other things to think about. Neither the withdrawal of Israeli troops from Beirut in August 1982 nor the arrival of the American-led Multi-National Force a few months later—not even the Washington-brokered May 17, 1983 truce between Lebanon and Israel—could get around the funda-mental fact that Lebanon had no functioning government. Once the Israelis left and Syria let loose its supporters, the last vestiges of central authority melted away like a snowman in the desert. Disaster was around the corner.

The Multi-National Force troops came under increasing attack. At first it was only ambushes and sniping, but then on October 23, 1983—six months and five days after the American embassy bombing— the United States suffered its worst peacetime military loss ever. A suicide driver drove a truck filled with explosives through the front door of a building the marines had converted into a barracks. Two hundred and forty-one troops were killed. A French barracks was also destroyed by a truck bomb, killing fifty-eight. The Reagan administration was forced to move the marines to ships off Lebanon's coast and eventually home. By December 1983, the U.S. didn't even pretend to support the May 17 agreement. The denouement came on February 6, 1984, when the Lebanon's central government finally collapsed completely and a ragtag coalition of Muslim militias took West Beirut. West Beirut was now Indian country and all of Beirut—indeed, all of Lebanon— was about to become a very dangerous place.

Back in Washington, the Reagan people quietly conceded that there was no point in asking the Lebanese to reopen the investigation. Nearly a year after the explosion, we still didn't know any more about who had done it. The bombers had disappeared like a diamond in an inkwell.

★

FOUR DAYS AFTER THE EXPLOSION at the marines' barracks, I sat looking out my office window in my new post. At the official level, I knew no more about this bombing than I did about the embassy's, but the tom-toms beat hard and fast in the intelligence business, and rumors had been flying.

It was a little after one in the afternoon, and the streets were deserted. Everyone was at home, eating or napping, and taking refuge from the unseasonable heat. They wouldn't come out again until early evening, when it cooled off. The only sign of life was in front of the small mosque up the hill from our offices, where a group of old men in long robes had assembled in front of the arched entrance to the courtyard. A call to prayer came over the mosque's loudspeaker. I checked my watch. It was too early for a regular prayer. A funeral? A memorial service? There was no way to tell. In the Middle East, life goes on behind high walls, out of view of strangers, especially foreigners.

And it wasn't just walls made out of mortar and stone. The Middle East is a place wired to obscure the truth. Television and newspapers don't report news; they report whatever propaganda the government want them to report. Investigative reporters don't exist. Books on politics and society aren't worth reading. The only time a scandal spills into the public is when the government decides it should. At the personal level, things are no different. Middle Easterners believe that the less they give up about themselves, the better. They'll talk about politics only in the most general terms, and they wouldn't even consider discussing terrorism. In their eyes, terrorism is a state activity; expressing your opinion on it just gets you thrown in jail.

You didn't have to be stationed in Beirut to know that there was one place in the Middle East more walled off than all the rest—Balabakk, Lebanon. Balabakk had become the Sodom and Gomorrah of terrorism. Every terrorist, radical, and lunatic who thought he could drive the Israelis out of Lebanon had set up shop there. But the real turning point for Balabakk had arrived on November 21, 1982, when Husayn Al-Musawi, the head of a radical Islamic group known as Islamic Amal, and what amounted to his extended family seized the Shaykh Abdallah barracks from the Lebanese gendarmerie. Clearly acting on Tehran's orders, Musawi immediately turned the barracks over to Iran's Islamic Revolutionary Guard Corps, or the Pasdaran, as the Iranians themselves call it. The Syrian troops, who had occupied the area since 1976, watched and did nothing. The Lebanese central government couldn't do anything, or at least wouldn't. Iran now had a sovereign piece of Lebanese soil. It would decide who could set foot in Balabakk and who couldn't, and every source we had indicated that the Pasdaran was about to go to war against the West.

In fact, the first act of the war had already occurred. On July 19, 1982, David Dodge, the acting president of the American University of Beirut, was grabbed in Beirut, boxed up and trucked across the Lebanese-Syrian border, and delivered to a waiting Iran Air flight at the Damascus airport. The Iranian

Pasdaran ran the whole operation out of Balabakk. Dodge would end up spending six months in Tehran before Syria—Iran's closest ally in the Arab world—pressured Iran to release him.

In June 1983, almost two months before Dodge was released, we picked up a onetime report that Iran intended to kidnap more hostages. The Pasdaran intelligence chief for Lebanon, now comfortably situated in the Shaykh Abdallah barracks, had urgently summoned a Lebanese contact to a meeting. Once he arrived, the Iranian took him outside, out of range of any bugs, and told him that the Pasdaran had screwed up with Dodge. Moving him out of Lebanon allowed the Americans to pinpoint Dodge's whereabouts. Worse, in holding him in Tehran, Iran directly implicated itself in the kidnapping. Although Tehran had no choice but to release Dodge, it still intended to kidnap foreigners in Lebanon—only now more carefully. It needed plausible denial and wanted Lebanese agents to run the campaign. When the Lebanese agreed to help, the Pasdaran officer instructed him to start setting up a kidnapping apparatus: surveillance teams, secret prisons, non-attributable cars. Iran would foot the bill, identify the victims to be kidnapped, and provide other assistance that could not be directly tied to the abductions.

Even though we leaned hard on all our sources in the area, the CIA was not able to pick up additional information on Iran's new kidnapping campaign. The closest we came to knowing what was going on in Balabakk was by way of the glossy black-and-white satellite photos that headquarters sent us from time to

time. To be sure, they offered a pretty good view of
the Shaykh Abdallah barracks. You could pick out
trucks and cars parked inside the compound,
shadows of people walking around, from time to time
even a military formation. Apart from that, they were
a waste of quality paper. From ninety miles up, you
couldn't distinguish one uniform from another. In
fact, if it weren't for the local press, we never would
have known the Iranian Pasdaran had taken over the
barracks.

Neither then nor now, nor ever in the future, can
photos tell you what is happening inside buildings or
in the heads of the men who occupy them. To do that,
you need a human source, and the way I saw it, the
only way to find one was to quit speculating about
what went on behind all those walls put up to hide the
truth. I needed to go to Lebanon, to the Biqa' Valley.
If you want to run with the big dogs, you have to get
off the porch.

I STARTLED JOHN when I knocked on his door. Since
our flare-up over the Abu Nidal office, relations had
gone from bad to worse. It was rare when I talked
with him at all, and then only when I'd stepped in
something.

"How about my taking a trip to Lebanon, to the
Biqa'?" I asked.

Out came the buffing rag. After he had worked up
a high gloss on his shoes, John finally said: "It's not
our turf, you know. Beirut won't like it."

Maybe, but John and I both knew that the Beirut

CIA office didn't have any turf. It still hadn't recovered from the bombing. Officers rotated in and out every couple of months and rarely ventured more than a block or two from the new embassy. No one was there long enough to care about whether I was poaching or not.

The more John thought about the idea, the more he grudgingly approved. If I were caught doing something in Lebanon, I'd be expelled, which wouldn't be his problem. (If I were expelled far enough, it might even solve his problem.) And even he had to admit my nosing around the Biqa' couldn't possibly screw up U.S. relations with the Lebanese government—there weren't any. John finally agreed to a short trip, but only to Shtawrah, a small Biqa' town on the Beirut-Damascus highway. Although Shtawrah is forty kilometers from Balabakk, I would open the door at least a crack. Who knows, I might even get lucky.

Shtawrah's commercial center had made it through the years of civil war largely untouched. The Syrian elite shopped there, as did the UN, aid organizations, and diplomats from Beirut and Damascus. Almost everything was available, from American detergent to Swiss chocolate. Cuban cigars went at a fraction of what London Heathrow's duty-free shops sold them for. You could exchange any currency in the world at Shtawrah's banks, at rates better than Zurich's. You also could buy arms, from pistols to rocket launchers, or just about any other contraband you might need. If your tastes ran more toward a kilo of pure coke or heroin, you had only to ask the concierge at the Park Hotel.

Beyond the shops, though, Shtawrah was no different from the rest of the Biqa'. The day I arrived there, I passed by the smoldering ruins of a training camp for the Popular Front for the Liberation of Palestine/General Command (PFLP/GC) on the edge of town. A squad of Israeli F-16s had flattened it the day before. I was curious about the raid and asked Ghazali, whose supermarket was Shtawrah's main grocery store, if the raid worried him. He shrugged. "We're in business. What can we do?"

Actually, Ghazali's answer made perfect sense. There was nothing any of the Lebanese in the Biqa' could do about a roster of neighbors that included Hizballah, the Japanese Red Army, Baader-Meinhof, Sendero Luminoso, the PFLP, Abu Nidal, ASALA, and half a dozen other suicidal and/or genocidal terrorist groups. As long as the Israeli air force continued to shoot straight, the Lebanese could get on with life and make a little money, especially if they took care of their own safety. Ghazali's clerks carried 9mm semiautomatics in shoulder holsters; and his assistant, whose office was behind a bulletproof window, kept an AK-47 with a drum magazine on his desk and a clear field of fire down all the aisles.

On that first visit, I walked around Shtawrah for a while, then drove up into the mountains above the town on the Beirut highway and stopped at a restaurant with a sweeping view of the Biqa', although it was too hazy to see Balabakk. Just as the waiter brought a tray of mezzah, the restaurant shook, rattling the windows and the crockery. The waiter looked away, pretending he hadn't heard anything. I caught his eye.

"Your *New Jersey*," he whispered.

The U.S.S. *New Jersey*, a refurbished World War II American battleship parked off Lebanon's coast, would periodically hurl shells the size of Volkswagens into the mountains around Beirut. Washington's thinking was that if the *New Jersey* had scared the Japanese in World War II, it might do the same for the Lebanese who still rejected the May 17 agreement with Israel.

After lunch, I decided it was time to start meeting the locals. I drove to Barilyas, a village a few miles beyond Shtawrah, and pulled up beside two police-men standing on the corner. When I announced that I was an American classicist interested in making a tour of the Biqa's Roman ruins, they looked at me as if I'd just stepped off a spaceship. They directed me to Masna', the last town before the Syrian border, where the Lebanese Surete Generale kept an office.

The Masna' Surete building had taken several direct hits in 1982. Its red tile roof had been blown off and all the windows broken. Burned-out car hulks still decorated the parking lot. Sergeant Ali was standing out front, sunning himself and smoking a cigarette. With his two-day beard, open tunic, and AK slung over his shoulder, he matched the scenery. When I approached him he was friendly enough.

I walked up to Ali and started as innocently as I could, asking about 'Anjar, a nearby village that had been the site of an ancient Roman trading post. A few ruins remained, I knew, which made the question not too odd for a Westerner, but 'Anjar was also one of the few villages in the Biqa' not occupied by terrorist groups hostile to the United States. ASALA, the Armenian terrorist group that had attacked the Turkish Air counter at Paris's Orly airport in July 1983, kept a camp there, but ASALA had no beef with America. Some of its leaders were even American citizens. This was the Middle East: Balabakk, my real interest, needed to be approached in crablike fashion.

Ali led me into his office and served me a thimble-size glass of tea, which tasted like it was mostly sugar. He wanted to talk about the U.S. He had several cousins living in Michigan and New Jersey, he said. He himself would move there if he could, but he didn't think he'd be given a visa. I dropped 'Anjar and let Ali take the conversation where he wanted. When I could see he was starting to get antsy I got up to leave. As we said good-bye, I promised to look him up the next time I was in Masna'. Ali told me the days he was on duty.

When I returned, I brought Ali an application for a U.S. visa and a couple of tourist brochures. I didn't promise him help with a visa, but the offer was implicit. This time we spent more than an hour talking, about America but also about the Middle East. Ali didn't say a word about Balabakk or Iran, and neither did I. As I walked out the door Ali handed me a piece of paper. He'd written his full name and home telephone number. Only then did I realize he was related to Husayn Al-Musawi, the Iranian Pasdaran agent who had seized the Shaykh Abdallah barracks.

I continued to see Ali every few weeks. He liked having an American friend, and he was seriously starting to think about making a trip to the U.S. to visit his cousins. He fished around to see if I could help him. I offered to see what I could do.

It wasn't until January that our conversations produced anything interesting. Just as I sat down and Ali put a glass of tea in front of me, I told him I'd been invited to visit Balabakk the following week to see its famous Roman ruin, theTemple of the Sun. I hadn't, of course, but it was time to get around to talking about my intended destination. I asked him if it would be safe. Without saying a word, he took me by the elbow and led me out a back door to a lot behind his office. We talked between two mounds of rubble.

"Mr. Bob, you can't go," he said gravely.

"Why not?"

"Forget your Roman ruins for now."

"Why, Ali?"

It was obvious he was having a hard time bringing himself to say more.

"They're going to kidnap an American in Lebanon," he finally whispered. "An official."

I knew there was no point in pressing for details like who, when, and where. Ali's body language said he had told me all he was going to tell me, but what a mouthful! Or so I thought.

"That's bullshit," John said.

"John, he's a Musawi. He's from Balabakk. He might have picked up something. We can't dismiss the information out of hand. We have to write it up in an intelligence report."

"Look, this dirtbag doesn't have a POA. He's not a recruited source. You don't even know his date of birth. You can't expect me to send this rubbish in as intel. Go back, get his bio, do the paperwork you hate so much, and then we'll see."

There was no point in saying anything. The POA was meaningless here. Ali wasn't interested in becoming an agent. He might give me a tip from time to time, but he was completely loyal to his clan, the Musawis. None of that meant his information was wrong. I gave Ali's warning to a friend at the embassy who sent it to Washington via State Department channels. Consular Affairs picked it up and included it in a classified consular brief. Years later I would come across the brief. It was the very first piece of paper in what would grow to become the CIA's huge hostage file.

AT 10:38 A.M. on March 16, 1984, I was still at home drinking my third cup of coffee and reading a week-old *Herald Tribune* when my push-to-talk Motorola radio crackled alive. It was John. "Get into the office as fast as you can." John always sounded nervous, but now I detected pure panic.

By the time I got to the office, John was a sickly pale yellow. "Buckley's been kidnapped," he said as he handed me a cable. That morning Bill Buckley, the CIA chief in Beirut, had been hit over the head on his way out of his apartment building, pushed into a car, and driven away. No one got a plate number or a description of the kidnappers. The Islamic Jihad Organization (IJO), one of the groups to claim responsibility for the embassy bombing, would eventually take credit for Buckley as well, but that didn't tell us anything. We still didn't know anything about the IJO.

Buckley wasn't the first American kidnapped in Lebanon since the 1982 Israeli invasion. In addition to David Dodge, Frank Regier, an American professor of electrical engineering at the American University in Beirut, had been snatched in February 1984. CNN bureau chief Jeremy Levin had been grabbed a month later. But they were civilians. This was a family member loaded with secrets.

"I've got to go back to the Biqa' and see Ali, John."

John looked at me as if I'd finally lost my mind.

"We can't just sit on our hands," I went on before he could interrupt. "I've seen with my own eyes how Syria administers the Biqa'. It won't let anything happen to a foreigner under its authority. Buckley and the rest were kidnapped in Beirut, where Syria doesn't have any troops. John, you've got to let me—"

"Forget it," John said, cutting me off. "Washington would bring me home in a straitjacket if I even asked."

I turned around and walked out. There was no point in reminding John about Ali's warning. And besides, John was right. Headquarters would never allow it. It was closing down operations in Lebanon as fast as it could.

During the next seven months, not a single lead surfaced on Buckley. Not only did we not find out who kidnapped him, we weren't even sure he was still in Lebanon. The CIA went to every government and private source it had, but no one could tell us anything, not even a plausible rumor. As for myself, I was convinced Balabakk was as good a place as any to start looking, and the more I brooded on the kidnapping, the more certain I became that I could get in and out safely. Eventually, curiosity got the better of me.

The first thing I did was to arrange to meet ██████, an adviser to ████████ ████████. A branch of his family who had settled in the Biqa' lived peacefully with the Shi'a neighbors, including the Musawis. I felt confident that under ██████'s aegis, even the Pasdaran wouldn't dare touch me. When I told him what I wanted to do, ██████ called another relative, a Lebanese army captain, and the two of us agreed to meet up in Shtawrah and take the captain's car to Balabakk. The captain, I should note, didn't have the slightest idea who I was or why I wanted to visit Balabakk.

The drive to Balabakk was like descending into hell. Just outside of town, lurid, menacing murals were painted on the sides of bombed-out buildings. One was of Jerusalem's Dome of the Rock mosque, the third holiest site of Islam, bursting through an American flag. Another was Ayatollah Khomeini leading a demonstration against the American embassy in Tehran; a third, an American flag spattered with blood. In Balabakk itself, banners in

Farsi and Arabic proclaimed DEATH TO AMERICA.

The captain suggested lunch at a friend's house. I agreed. We were already through the front door when he mentioned that it was the house of one of Husayn Al-Musawi's cousins.

The dozen guests sitting on the floor in the salon eyed me warily when we walked in. I was probably the first Westerner they'd seen in months. After a cup of tea, we were brought a plate of leeks, fava beans, and bread.

Things were going fine until one of the guests took a particular interest in me. With his long, ungroomed beard and armband that read *We Crave Martyrdom*, he made me nervous. After staring at me a few seconds, he asked, "What brings you to Balabakk?"

Rather than drag out the classicist spiel, I went for the big lie.

"I'm a Belgian. I work for an aid organization," I said.

I kept my fingers crossed that no one spoke French or, worse, Flemish. I didn't speak a word of Flemish, and my French was definitely rusty.

"Sir, may I ask your name?" the ungroomed beard persisted.

"Er, Rémy."

"That's your family name?"

"No, it's Martin," I said before I could stop myself. It wasn't like Rémy Martin cognac wasn't sold in Lebanon. Fortunately he went back to eating.

Afterward the captain took me to the Temple of the Sun. When we knocked on the closed gate to the old Roman section of Balabakk, the gate swung open and there were our two guides—khaki-uniformed Iranian Pasdaran soldiers. They couldn't have been happier to show us around the site.

We were driving out of town when I casually asked the captain about the compound on the hill, which I knew was the Shaykh Abdallah barracks. He stopped the car by the outside perimeter wall, and I had a chance to take in all of the buildings. It was remarkable how different they looked from the ground than they did from satellite photography.

One building in particular caught my attention. Two Pasdaran soldiers were guarding the front door, and either cardboard or blankets covered the inside of the windows. A wooden sign on the wall identified it as the married officers' quarters.

It wasn't until years later that I would learn Bill Buckley was inside, blindfolded and chained to a radiator, along with five other Western hostages. Nor would I know for years that this same building was a key link in my search for the embassy bombers. But, in truth, I wasn't really surprised by either revelation. Everything in the Middle East is interconnected. Pull on one thread and a dozen more will come out. Sniff up one trail and you'll come to twenty forks in the road, each of which could be profitably followed.

But you've got to have human intelligence to do it—people on the ground, agents, access agents, a network of traitors, and a case officer willing and able to work it. No aerial reconnaissance photo could have put together the covered windows and guarded door at the Shaykh Abdallah barracks. No electronic intercept could have placed a set of human eyes on the ground that day in Balabakk. In the end, intelligence boils down to people. I think the CIA knew that back then—the spirit of our founding fathers still lived in the agency—but it wouldn't be long before we were running pell-mell in the opposite direction, with disastrous consequences from the Middle East to finally America's own soil.

I'LL BE FRANK. My visit to Balabakk was a gross fracturing of all the rules. It may have given me a feel for the terrain, a knowledge you couldn't get from satellite photos or from a book, but it was risky and did nothing to help Buckley or anyone else.

Shortly afterward, I was transferred to Khartoum, Sudan. Even without knowing about my trip to Balabakk—and he never found out—John had had enough of me and my late accountings.

7

JANUARY 1986. LANGLEY, VIRGINIA.

THE G CORRIDOR on the sixth floor looked like a construction site. Boxes, furniture, coils of telephone wire, and trash were piled up everywhere. The offices on either side of the hall were swarming with electricians and painters. Construction crews were ripping up floors, tearing down partitions, and putting up new ones. No one had any idea where the new counterterrorism chief's office was. I had to go from room to room to find it. When I did, though, there was no mistaking its singularity.

For starters, cigar smoke hung in the air like a low-lying cloud, thick enough to close down most airports. Unlike most everyone else in the CIA, Duane "Dewey" Clarridge didn't believe in desks. Instead, he had a round table with half a dozen chairs in the middle of his small office. He figured an informal atmosphere encouraged younger officers to wander in and talk. The best ideas percolated up rather than down.

Dewey perhaps didn't need to worry about the trappings of office; unlike most CIA officers, he was plugged into the White House. As head of the Latin

American Division, he had cut every corner necessary to help Ronald Reagan's beloved Contras. For good measure, in November 1985 he had also expedited the first shipment of arms to Iran. Dewey was the White House's kind of spy. It didn't surprise anyone that after Abu Nidal's Christmas 1985 attacks on the Vienna and Rome airports, the White House tapped Dewey to head a new CIA counterterrorism unit, one with teeth.

As soon as he saw me standing in his door, Dewey motioned me to come over and sit down next to him at the round table. I'd heard enough about him to know there was no point in beating around the bush.

"I want to work in terrorism, Mr. Clarridge. I'd be happy to take any job."

The truth was that I was not only interested in terrorism, I was bored. After the Libyans started targeting me for assassination after they found out I was meeting with the Libyan opposition, headquarters pulled me out of Khartoum after only four months and gave me a deadly dull desk job in Africa Division. I also told Dewey about my unsuccessful search for Bill Buckley and how I'd ended up pissing John off.

"That asshole's still on the streets?" was Dewey's only comment. Before I could answer, he asked, "How good's your Arabic?"

After nearly three years in the Middle East, it was a lot better than when I got out of Arabic school.

"You'll travel anywhere, anytime?"

"I'd get on a plane today if you want me to."

That's all Dewey needed to know. He didn't even

ask to see my file. I asked him if I should tell anyone, like the Near Eastern Division, to which I still technically belonged.

"Don't do anything," he said as he motioned me out of the office with his cigar. "Go back to your desk and sit by the telephone."

Two weeks later I was drafted into Dewey's new organization: the Counterterrorism Center, or CTC.

THE FIRST FEW MONTHS serving as a foot soldier in Dewey's war against terrorism were about as exhilarating as the spy business gets. I'd seen the face of evil in the Biqa' Valley and was both fascinated and appalled by it. I also wanted to get back to my private quest to find out who was behind the embassy bombing. CTC looked like the ideal place for both. Also, Dewey had a new presidential finding— authority to do pretty much anything he wanted against the terrorists. He had all the money he wanted. The CIA director, Bill Casey, promised him carte blanche; he could cannibalize the DO and the DI to stock CTC. He even recruited a handful of Los Angeles cops. He was planning to deploy them around the world and start hauling in terrorists in handcuffs.

By the time I started, CTC's new offices were miraculously up and running. It was pure frenetic energy. Everyone worked in one huge, open bay. With the telephones ringing nonstop, printers clattering, files stacked all over the place, CNN playing on TV monitors bolted to the ceiling, hundreds of people in motion and at their computers, it gave the impression of a war room. I kept thinking of those World War II propaganda films of Churchill's underground bunker during the Battle of Britain.

Expectations were high. Everyone had heard about Dewey's successful counterterrorist operation as head of the European Division. One of his offices helped run an agent in a lethal Palestinian terrorist group known as the May 15 Organization, which specialized in airplane bombs. The agent was a gold mine, providing information that stopped a couple of terrorist attacks, and Dewey had no intention of losing him. When the agent's May 15 boss ordered him to attack an American target, Dewey crafted an operation in which the CIA exploded a car inside an American embassy compound in such a way that the agent could take credit. No one was killed, but the agent's boss was convinced the agent had tried, and he continued as a fantastic reporter for us.

All of us new recruits expected operations like that to be the norm in CTC, but it wasn't long before the politics of intelligence undermined everything Dewey tried to do. Although CTC looked like a high-tech command center, the truth was that Dewey had no one to command in the field. In spite of Bill Casey's promises, the CIA's offices abroad still answered to their geographic division chiefs back at headquarters, and as the chiefs made absolutely clear, not one of them was interested in fighting Dewey's war. It was too risky. A botched—or even successful—operation would piss off a friendly foreign government. Some-one might be thrown out of his cushy post, and sent home. Someone might even get killed. No matter how much Dewey waved around his finding with President Reagan's signature on the bottom, the division chiefs weren't going to have some ex-L.A. coppers runnin' 'n' gunnin' in their backyards.

We'd ask the Paris office to put together a surveillance team to watch the apartment of a suspected terrorist, and Paris would come back and tell us it couldn't because the local intelligence service would find out. We'd ask Bonn to recruit a few Arabs and Iranians to track the Middle East émigré community in West Germany and it would respond it didn't have enough officers. Once we asked Beirut to meet a certain agent traveling to Lebanon, and it refused because of some security problem. Security was never *not* a problem in Beirut, for God's sake. Instead of fighting terrorists, we were fighting bureaucratic inertia, an implacable enemy.

Dewey couldn't even recruit the staff that he had been promised. After six months, he could put his hands on only two Arabic speakers, one of whom was me. But since the other officer managed a branch, that left just me to travel and meet agents. That wasn't a lot, since about 80 percent of CTC's targets spoke Arabic. There were no Persian, Pashtun, or Turkish speakers at all.

I was assigned to a branch tasked with finding the hostages in Lebanon, but I was the only one there with any experience in the Middle East. The branch chief had never set foot in the Middle East, let alone Lebanon. At one point he was conned into an operation to buy maps of the sewers of Beirut's southern suburbs: He had no idea the southern suburbs were illegally constructed and didn't have sewers. Other branches were worse off. Analysts were in charge, which was insane. People who'd never met an agent in their lives, didn't know what a dead drop was, and rarely traveled out of the Washington metropolitan area were directing field offices abroad on how to run their cases. It was like assigning a hospital administrator to head the surgical team.

MY FIRST SHOT of reality came early, about a month after I joined CTC.

Bonn cabled that a leader of Syria's Muslim Brotherhood who was living in Germany wanted a meeting with the CIA. Bonn, of course, refused to meet him for fear of irritating the Germans, but it grudgingly agreed to let someone from CTC fly out to see what he wanted.

I took the cable to Dewey. "What's in it for us?" he asked.

Good question. The Muslim Brotherhood was an amorphous, dangerous, unpredictable movement that shook every government in the Middle East to its bones. Founded by an Egyptian, Hasan Al-Banna, in 1929, it was dedicated to bringing the Kingdom of God to earth. The Egyptian Muslim Brothers had unsuccessfully tried to kill Egyptian President Abdul Nasser. The Syrian branch had tried to kill Syrian President Hafiz Al-Asad a couple of times. In 1982 its followers seized Hama, a historic city in central Syria, provoking Asad into shelling them and Hama into the next life.

The Muslim Brothers are also distant cousins of the Wahabis of Saudi Arabia, the most puritanical sect of Islam. Underwritten by the Saudi royal family, the Wahabis spawned Osama bin Laden. They also served as the inspiration for the Taliban in Afghanistan and other radical Sunni movements. Many Muslims consider the Wahabis dangerous because they adopted the beliefs of Ibn Taymiyah, a fourteenth-century Islamic scholar who condoned political assassination. Al-Jihad, the Egyptian fundamentalists who murdered Egyptian President Anwar Sadat relied on Ibn Taymiyah as justification for what they did.

I'd had some experience with the Muslim Brothers during my abbreviated tour in Khartoum. One of my jobs there was to ███████████ ███████████ against Mu'ammar Qaddafi's. One evening soon after I got to Khartoum, I invited two of the Libyan dissidents, a political boss and a military commander, over to my apartment for tea. As usual, there was a sandstorm and the electricity was off. We sat in the dark, sweating and talking about the normal things you use to warm up a conversation with Arabs—marriage, children, the price of bread. My apartment was near the airport, and every so often we heard the roar of a plane taking off.

The military commander finally came around to talking politics. He mentioned in passing that he'd been able to quickly rebuild the group's military cadres in Libya after its failed May 1984 attack on Qaddafi's residence, even though most of the attackers had been killed.

I asked the military commander why he thought he could take Qaddafi in a place so well defended.

"God told us to do it."

"God?"

"Yes." He then added without the slightest hint of irony. "He told us the day and hour."

That set off bells, at least in my head. These Libyan dissidents hadn't been billed in Washington as Muslim Brothers, but when people told you God was calling the shots, there was a good chance the Brothers were nearby.

I was curious now and I had a way to check on my suspicions. When I was studying Arabic in Washington, I had met a Sudanese graduate student who worked nights at the front desk of my apartment building. Just as I had with the Palestinian student earlier, I would sit with my Sudanese friend for hours, practicing Arabic. In return, I helped him with his English. One night in a heart-to-heart talk, he confessed he was a Muslim Brother. He explained to me the group's ideology—its commitment to changing any Muslim leader who had fallen away from Islam. He agreed the Egyptian Jihad, an offshoot of the Muslim Brothers, was legally justified in murdering Anwar Sadat. Sadat was an apostate, he said, and the Koran, Islam's Holy Book, mandates that apostates must die. My friend returned to Sudan about the same time I arrived there, and we renewed our friendship. When I asked him about the Libyan dissidents, he confirmed they were Muslim Brothers, noting that his own organization backed them to the hilt.

I brought my preliminary findings to Milt Bearden, Khartoum's burly chief ███████. This was the same Bearden who defined a close and continuing relationship as keeping a pair of slippers under your friend's bed. Bearden was a popular boss. His case officers called him Uncle Milty.

As soon as I finished telling him about my suspicions about the Libyans, he said, "So?"

I fell back on the standard line that while Qaddafi might be as crazy as a tree full of owls, the Muslim Brothers in power in Tripoli would be a lot worse. With Libya sharing borders with Algeria and Egypt, they could destabilize those two countries.

"Do you know how they refer to Qaddafi in the White House?" Bearden asked.

I didn't.

"They call him the Mad Dog of the Middle East. Look, Baer, if Genghis Khan were to crawl out of his grave and declare his intention to get rid of Qaddafi, this administration would support him. So forget about it."

Bearden had a good nose for politics, so I accepted his word for it. Besides, the Sudan was imploding. The country was nearly bankrupt, and President Jafaar Numeiri was mentally unstable and incapable of dealing with the crisis. Demonstrators of uncertain ideology had shut down the government. As the office's only Arabic speaker, I volunteered to go out in the crowds to find out whether they were anti-American or not. I passed myself off as a Lebanese journalist. When demonstrators moved close to the embassy or the American residences, I would call in a warning with a concealed radio.

The two Libyans dropped out of sight during the upheaval, but a couple of nights after the Numeiri regime collapsed, they unexpectedly reappeared. Apparently they had heard that Qaddafi's henchmen had shown up in Khartoum, looking for revenge, and they were hoping I'd smuggle them out of the country. Too bad I wasn't home when they came calling. In their excitement, the Libyan dissidents mistook my neighbor's door for mine. An elderly administrative officer at the embassy, my neighbor was on her first tour overseas. Already nervous about the coup, she panicked when she looked through the peephole to see two bearded, wild-eyed fanatics with AK-47s. When they started banging on her door with the butts of their rifles, she lost whatever remained of her sangfroid and ran out her back door, down the fire escape, and across Khartoum to her boss's house. She was still in her nightgown. The next day the embassy sent her to Germany for a rest.

I knew, in short, that dealing with the Muslim Brotherhood was playing with fire. These guys were programmed for trouble. But if the Reagan administration really was determined to fight it out with our enemies in Syria and Lebanon, we couldn't have found better surrogates. The only question was what they were prepared to do for us, and to find that out, we had to talk to them.

Dewey agreed that I should meet with them, and I was on an airplane to Frankfurt the next day.

Not bothering to check in with Bonn, I took the train directly to Dortmund. The plan was for me to wait by a designated kiosk in the Dortmund railway station until I was signaled by a Brotherhood cutout— not the best of arrangements, but since I knew Bonn wasn't going to help, I didn't have a choice.

At the stroke of two, a dark bearded man with a paunch, about forty-five years old, walked up to me and, without saying a word, motioned me to follow him. We were heading toward a side exit when he pulled me by the arm into the baggage claim room. The baggage handler, who also looked like an Arab, nodded at my escort as we set off between a long row of baggage racks and out a back door to a rear loading dock. Waiting there were two identical charcoal-gray Mercedeses with smoked windows. We got in the backseat of the first one.

After a short warm-up through Dortmund, the two Mercedeses turned onto the autobahn and opened up their throttles. We never got out of the fast lane, which in Germany is reserved for drivers who think 120 miles an hour is a prudent speed. Every time a car got in our way our driver madly flashed his lights until it moved. The second Mercedes drafted right behind us.

About twenty miles later, just as I was getting used to the German version of NASCAR, the driver swerved abruptly right, cutting diagonally across the two slow lanes without ever easing up on the gas pedal and dropping down an off-ramp I hadn't even seen. The second Mercedes followed, but I noticed it starting to hold back, blocking anyone who might try to follow us. *These guys are serious,* I thought.

The Mercedes took what looked to be an aimless

route through a new, modest, scrubbed German suburb. By now it was early afternoon. Almost no one was on the street when the driver turned into the driveway of a house identical to all the rest and pulled into a bottom-floor garage. As soon as we were inside, the door closed behind us. I never would have been able to find the place again.

Waiting in a small office adjoining the garage was a frail, elegant man with a neatly trimmed beard. He was in his late fifties, I guessed, wearing a soft gray flannel suit and a starched white shirt with a straight collar. He struck me as particularly calm and collected. The concept doesn't exist in Islam, but the word that came to mind was "beatific." He motioned for the others to leave us alone and closed the door.

For the next hour the Muslim Brotherhood leader vilified the regime in Damascus. He described Hafiz Al-Asad as a heathen, the incarnation of evil, and in other terms you didn't hear even in Washington, where Asad was never particularly popular. He pulled out a loose-leaf notebook full of pictures of Hama after the bombardment—people burned, crushed, and buried under the rubble. Whole families had been put up against the wall and shot.

Finally, I interrupted to ask what could be done.

The man smiled. "We are ready to go hand in hand with the United States and remove this cancerous sore from God's sight."

"How?" I asked, suspecting the worst.

"We have buried in Ghuta, near the Damascus airport, an SA-7 missile," he said matter-of-factly, as if telling me he'd planted a bed of petunias in his garden back home. "What we need is for you to inform us when Asad's airplane is ready to take off and he is on it."

My first thought, as a case officer, was *Damn, this is hot information.* The sourcing couldn't be better—this man was a boss in the Syrian Muslim Brotherhood, and he was talking about capping Hafiz Al-Asad, the biggest hurdle to a Middle East peace. Since our new friend was proposing an assassination, in violation of Executive Order 12333, I'd have to report it to Dewey but I still hoped that we could keep meeting this man and maybe redirect his energies to a common goal. Even if we couldn't, I didn't see any harm in keeping our lines of communication open. Who could tell when we might need the Muslim Brotherhood?

Back in Washington, Dewey listened carefully as I told him about the meeting, from the moment I was picked up at the Dortmund rail station until I had told the Muslim Brotherhood leader I'd have to consult with my bosses.

"Go write it up," Dewey said.

"Wait," he added as I was heading out the door. "Nothing on a computer. Use a typewriter instead. Destroy the ribbon afterward. And don't make a copy. I want to keep this between Ollie, you, and me."

Ollie was Oliver North, the NSC staffer who would take the fall in the complicated interplay of missiles, hostages, and funding for Nicaraguan rebels that became known as the Iran-contra affair. Although the Muslim Brothers had nothing to do with Iran-contra, dealing with them was right up North's alley.

As instructed, I gave Dewey the only copy of my contact report—the last I was ever to hear about it.

Bonn was unimpressed with the cable I sent about the meeting (minus the part about the SA-7). Bonn was sticking to its original position: It did not want to meet anyone from the Muslim Brotherhood. I didn't have the time to go back, and the CIA wouldn't meet the Syrian Muslim Brothers again. But the Muslim Brother I met in that innocuous suburban house in Dortmund would pop into my life again, in the days after September 11, 2001, when the FBI came calling to tell me that one of the Syrian's associates was a suspect in the global network that had supported the attacks on the World Trade Center and the Pentagon.

The really bad guys—the ones capable of doing great harm for or against our side, depending on which way God is talking to them that day—don't just go away. It was better, I always figured, to have a line into them, even if it meant keeping our hands a little dirty in the process. There is, of course, no guarantee even if we had kept communications open that the Syrian I met in 1986 would have led us to Muhammad Atta or any of the German cells of Osama bin Laden's Al Qaeda network that may have played a role in the September 11 attacks. But closing down the channel assured that the Syrian wouldn't lead us to anyone. For Bonn and the CIA, it remains an unforgivable error.

THE WHITE HOUSE was still on Dewey's back to do something about the hostages, and as was his style, he was still looking for an answer to bubble up through the ranks of his counterterrorism troops.

I'd been back from Germany for about a week when Dewey hailed me into his office one morning. "You have good instincts," he began. "What's the craziest idea you can come up with to free the hostages?"

For a lot of reasons, there was no obvious answer to that question. As late as 1986, the intelligence community was divided over who even controlled the hostages. The CIA's corporate position was that the IJO—it still knew next to nothing about it—held them and that it operated largely independent of any state control. Although the CIA conceded that the group had lines to Iran and Syria, it didn't think either country had any real influence. Other analysts around Washington, especially in the Pentagon, disagreed. They were convinced the IJO was no more than a puppet of the Iranian Pasdaran.

The CIA's position wasn't based on rock-hard evidence, but the hypothesis had become so ingrained it was getting hard to ignore. For a year after Buckley's kidnapping, the CIA had absolutely no idea who had taken either him or the other IJO hostages. A break wouldn't come until Algeria stepped forward to inform us that a young Shi'a Muslim from southern Lebanon named 'Imad Fa'iz Mughniyah had kidnapped Buckley as well as CNN's Jeremy Levin and the clerics Benjamin Weir and Laurence Martin Jenco. Before 1982 Mughniyah worked for PLO chairman Yasir Arafat, the Algerians told us; now he operated on his own. According to this source,

Mughniyah was looking to trade his foreigners for seventeen prisoners being held in a Kuwaiti jail on charges of bombing the French and American embassies there on December 12, 1983. One of the seventeen was Mughniyah's brother-in-law Mustafa Badr-al-Din.

Mughniyah had dropped mostly out of sight until June 14, 1985, when TWA Flight 847 was hijacked out of Athens and flown to Beirut. Three days later the hijackers shot a young navy diver and threw his body out onto the runway. The hostages were eventually handed over to Amal, a Lebanese Shi'a militia, and they were scattered around Beirut's southern suburbs, but four remained with the IJO. A well-placed agent identified Mughniyah as the mastermind of the hijacking, which fit nicely with the Algerian portrait of Mughniyah as a lone operator. The agent's information was good enough for the Department of Justice to indict Mughniyah and three accomplices for the hijacking.

All of that was on my mind as I stood in Dewey's door.

"No limits?" I finally asked.

"Yeah, anything," Dewey said.

"We hit Mughniyah where it hurts—his family," I said.

Dewey didn't see what I was getting at.

"Look, Dewey," I said. "Let's assume three things are true: Mughniyah really controls the hostages, Mughniyah is devoted to his family—as most people in the Middle East are—and finally this administration would consider anything to get the hostages back. If all of these are in fact true, then we might consider grabbing some of Mughniyah's family to trade for the hostages."

The idea, of course, was over the top, but back then the CIA was expected to operate on the edge, do things no other government agency would consider. One of the instructors at the Farm had told us a story of how, after the 1967 Arab-Israeli war, the agency's skunk works had come up with the idea of filling a captured Soviet transport plane—Soviet markings and all—with live pigs and dropping them over Mecca, Islam's most holy city. The idea was to light the Middle East's fuse and direct the blast toward the Soviet Union, whose influence had been growing in the area. Compared to that, what I was suggesting to Dewey sounded almost sane.

"Fine, go find me 'Imad's family," he told me.

I knew better than to actually get started; Dewey would still have to run it by Ollie North or someone else at the NSC. When I never heard anything back, I forgot about it. Only when the Iran-contra story broke did I learn that North had circulated my idea around the White House via one of his infamous messages on PROF, an internal White House e-mail system.

DEWEY WAS TO COME to me one final time about the hostages, and the next time I had a bit more confidence in the outcome.

During my trip to Balabakk in October 1984, I had seen with my own eyes that Syria was not entirely comfortable with having the Iranian Pasdaran camped in its backyard. It bothered Syria that the Pasdaran supported just about every Islamic terrorist group in the Middle East except the Syrian Muslim Brotherhood. Hafiz Al-Asad, a committed secularist, couldn't be sure when Iranian-backed fundamentalism would slosh back over the Syrian border. My idea was to make Asad believe Iran had decided to destabilize his regime. If it worked, Syria, I hoped, would act without thinking and crack down on the Pasdaran and its agent, Hizballah. Even if it turned out the IJO was an independent organization, eliminating its ideological allies couldn't hurt.

The plan I came up with was unconventional but certain to attract Asad's attention. The objective was to scare Syrian diplomats in Europe and make them believe they were the targets of Hizballah terrorist attacks. It was supposed to work like this: One night a half-dozen clandestine CIA tech teams would hook up low-order explosives to the ignitions of the Syrian diplomats' cars. The next morning, when the diplomats started their cars, there would be a pop and a fizz. (Low-order explosives burn rather than explode, but the chemical composition is nearly identical to a real explosive. The police, I figured, would assume the terrorists had simply been sold a bad batch of plastique.) Afterward we'd put out a fake communiqué claiming the attacks in the name of Hizballah, and an angry Asad would come down on Hizballah as he had on the Muslim Brothers during the Hama insurrection. Or at least that was my plan. I wrote it up in a cable to all our offices in Europe.

"Ollie is going to go nuts," Dewey said as soon as

he finished reading it. He ran out the door to show it to Clair George, the director of operations.

It wasn't five minutes before Dewey was back, standing beside my carrel with the cable in his hand.

"Clair said forget it. No, I'll tell you the truth—Clair screamed at the top of his lungs to forget it. He said it would be over his dead body that the CIA would set off bombs in Western Europe. Think of something else—minus the plastique."

Eventually we did get an operation through the bureaucracy. The CIA has asked me not to describe it. I can say, though, that while it managed to irritate Hafiz Al-Asad—sort of like a twenty-four-hour diaper rash—it wasn't enough for him to shut down Hizballah.

I DON'T KNOW if Dewey ever told the White House about this last operation, but if he had, I doubt it would have been impressed. The White House wasn't interested in palliatives. It wanted the hostages free. But again not until Iran-contra broke would I understand how desperate the administration had been or how close I came to being sucked into its scheme.

One morning in April 1986 I turned around to find Dewey standing behind me in the office. The weather had turned warm, and Dewey was wearing a double-breasted linen suit with an enormous carnation in his lapel. He had an unlit half-smoked stogie in one hand and an agent's file in the other.

"Read this," he said as he dropped the file on my desk. "You and Cave are going on vacation."

George Cave was the CIAs legendary Iran expert. Fluent in Persian and good in Arabic, Cave was probably the most experienced Middle East hand in the CIA—so valuable that he had been brought back from retirement because the ranks of Middle East experts in the CIA were thinning out so fast and there was no program to train new ones.

When Dewey went away I noticed the cryptonym, or the agent's code name, on the file jacket: ██████████/1. The first two letters indicated the agent was either an Iranian or reported on Iran. I looked at the first document with the agent's true name—Manucher Ghorbanifar. It meant nothing to me, but on the left side of the file I noticed what we in the DO called a "burn notice," or a directive to stay away from an agent. These things were sent to every CIA office around the world after the DO had a wrenching experience with any agent, like fabricating information that badly embarrassed the CIA in the press or with the White House. Ghorbanifar had reported on March 17, 1984 that an Iranian radical, Mehdi Karrubbi, was plotting to assassinate President Reagan. The following day Ghorbanifar was polygraphed and confessed he'd invented the whole story to make some money, but not before the Secret Service had been put on red alert.

I didn't bother reading past the burn notice. Once you've established a fabricator, you never deal with him again. I put Ghorbanifar's file on top of a stack of other files I would never read.

Dewey was back a couple of weeks later. "Well, did you read it?"

When I admitted I hadn't, he took back the file, and not long afterward, I was plucked off the counterterrorism team and sent to Beirut. There was nothing Dewey could do about it. The Near East Division couldn't find anyone else to go. Not only was it dangerous, it was considered a bad career move. I didn't care, though I knew the only place to learn about terrorism was on the ground.

George Cave did take up Dewey's offer of a "vacation" to Tehran and came close to being indicted once the Iran-contra scandal broke. Dewey didn't escape quite so cleanly: He was indicted but eventually pardoned. If I had read Ghorbanifar's file as instructed, chances are I would have wound up being sent to Tehran and almost certainly indicted as an Iran-contra coconspirator. This was one time I could pat myself on the back for not following orders.

I'VE OFTEN THOUGHT about how the Reagan people got sucked into Iran-contra. It's clear now that the Iranians were playing the White House for suckers. As soon as Iran received its first planeload of arms in exchange for a hostage, it went into the hostage business full-time, kidnapping dozens more. But it was more than that. When the White House employed Ghorbanifar, a known swindler, to handle one of the most sensitive diplomatic channels in American history, it ensured the channel would fail. It was sort of like using the local paperboy to do your investing in the stock market. No, it was a lot worse.

I think there were two things at play. First of all,

after the 1983 bombing of the marine barracks in Beirut, the option of a military rescue operation was off the table. There was no way the Pentagon was going to commit troops short of a full-scale invasion. It wouldn't even agree to send a Delta Force team, the army's elite counterterrorism unit, unless a Delta member had "eyes on" the hostages at least twenty-four hours in advance—a condition that could never be met.

That left diplomacy. The only problem was that no one in the national security establishment had a good back channel to Iran. The State Department worked through Switzerland, but the hostages were too sensitive a subject for the Swiss and the Iranian Ministry of Foreign Affairs to deal with. The CIA itself didn't have a channel to Tehran. During the Shah's rule, the White House had been formal in its instructions to the CIA: Stay away from the Iranian opposition lest the Shah be offended. Even when Ayatollah Khomeini was in exile outside of Paris, the CIA avoided him and his entourage. So when the Iranian revolution went down in 1979, the CIA was blind and deaf in Iran—all thanks to Washington politics.

With diplomatic and military solutions taken off the table, the White House was bound to accept Ghorbanifar as a channel when Israel dished him up. For me the surprising thing was when the White House figured they'd been had by this swindler, they turned to the American-Iranian middleman Albert Hakim, who set up the second "channel" to Iran. Like Ghorbanifar, Hakim was in it for the money. Unlike

Ghorbanifar, Hakim could cut out all the other
middlemen and go directly to the hostage outlet—the
Iranian Pasdaran. The main point of contact was Ali
Hashemi Bahramani, an officer in the Pasdaran and
the nephew of Ali Akbar Hashemi Rafsanjani, the
Iranian Speaker of Parliament.

8

APRIL 1986. WASHINGTON, D.C.

BEFORE I WAS SENT to Beirut, I had time to give myself a crash course in terrorism. There wasn't a better place to do that than in the CTC. I had complete access to all of the CIA's files and databases on terrorism. I was like a kid in a candy store.

The first thing I turned to, inevitably I suppose, was the embassy bombing. By now the mystery had grown roots in me. One look at the thin, tattered, apple-green file, and I could tell the case was stone cold. The most recent piece of information was nearly two years old. There were a couple of reasons: The embassy bombing decimated the CIA ranks in Lebanon, and then later, when the embassy moved to East Beirut, the CIA lost most of its best Muslim agents. Few of them could travel across the Green Line that separated the Christian and Muslim halves of the city. The Green Line got its name from the grass that grew up in the abandoned streets that formed the demarcation line.

Not that reopening the case would be easy or maybe even possible. Lebanese president Amin Jumayyil had quietly released all of the suspects in the bombing. We suspected he'd been bribed, but whatever the cause, with the only suspects in the bombing scattered across the Middle East, we were back at ground zero. All we had to go by were the three claims called in to the press on the day of the bombing. The only difference was that one of those groups, the IJO, now had a name to go along with it— 'Imad Mughniyah. He was as good a place as any to start.

'Imad Mughniyah was an enigma. According to his passport application, he had been born in 1962 in Tayr Dibba, a dirt-poor village in southern Lebanon, but even that was uncertain. Often poor Shi'a Lebanese recorded the family village as a birthplace to conceal an illegal residence, more often than not in Beirut's southern suburbs. Mughniyah, we knew, had grown up in a makeshift cinder-block house with no running water, in 'Ayn Al-Dilbah, one of the poorest parts of the southern suburbs. Located at the edge of Beirut's airport—planes passed only a few hundred feet overhead—the house was the best that Mughniyah's vegetable-seller father could afford. During the civil war, the suburb was a main axis on the Green Line. As a teenager, Mughniyah would have woken frequently to the sound of artillery and gunfire. From time to time stray bullets and shrapnel hit his house.

All of this we were able to piece together from agents, but no CIA officer of any complexion or ethnic origin could go into 'Ayn Al-Dilbah to verify it. 'Ayn Al-Dilbah was a fortress as secure as any in the world. Everyone there knew everyone else. If a stranger couldn't explain himself, he would be lucky to be escorted out the way he came in. Even Lebanese authorities couldn't enter 'Ayn Al-Dilbah.

Mughniyah, we had confirmed, joined Yasir Arafat's Force 17 (Arafat's elite personal security organization) at an early age, maybe fourteen or fifteen, but was always a low-level bang man, one of dozens who spent their days and nights sniping at Christians across the Green Line. He reportedly spent a year at the American University of Beirut. If he had, though, someone lifted his records. One of Mughniyah's distant relatives was an Islamic scholar, but other than that, he had no apparent grounding in Islam.

That's what we knew, but it still didn't add up. How did a poor boy from 'Ayn Al-Dilbah rise out of the ashes of the 1982 Israeli invasion and in less than a year put together the most lethal and well-funded terrorist organization in the world? Was this the man who kidnapped and held dozens of foreign hostages? Was this the man who blew up the American embassy in April 1983 and covered his tracks so well that there wasn't a single lead tying him to it? The more I got into the files, the more convinced I was that the Algerians were wrong about Mughniyah operating independently.

I spent two months searching through CTC and anyplace else I could burrow into for stray pieces of information that hadn't made it into the files. I would often show up before six A.M. on my bicycle at the CIA's front gates on Route 123. Sometimes I'd have to knock on the guard's glass booth to get him to look at my badge. Around seven or eight in the evening, I'd finally notice that most everyone in CTC had left, but I would read another hour or two more. The mountain of files and paper on my desk and surrounding floor grew into a standing joke.

Still, I didn't have enough information to come to any final conclusion about Mughniyah's role in the Beirut embassy bombing. But as I sorted through the parade of hostages who had been seized in the Middle East, I became increasingly convinced that if Mughniyah was largely responsible, he was getting a heck of a lot of help from Pasdaran and, behind it, the sovereign government of Iran.

We knew with absolute certainty, for example, that the Pasdaran had kidnapped David Dodge. We knew, too, that in June 1983 a Pasdaran officer in the Biqa' had outlined a plan to kidnap foreigners. Wasn't it as likely that the current spate of kidnappings traced back to that plan, at least as much as it could be laid at Mughniyah's feet? Finally, there were the circumstances surrounding Bill Buckley's death. He probably died in July 1985. Although we could never fix a date, we did find out with near certainty that the Pasdaran commander Ali Salch Shamkhani, who is, at this writing, the defense minister of Iran, went into a rage, screaming at his subordinates at a Tehran meeting that it was senseless to let the hostages in Lebanon die out of pure neglect. Shamkhani, we had been told, had ordered that the Pasdaran unit stationed in the Shaykh Abdallah barracks immediately arrange for a doctor to take care of any other sick hostages. Subsequent to this report, a Lebanese

Jewish pediatrician, Elie Hallak, already a Hizballah prisoner, was brought in to examine Michel Seurat, a French researcher kidnapped by the IJO. Hallak ultimately couldn't do anything for Seurat, who would die the following year, probably of cancer. Nor could Hallak do anything for himself: He was executed as soon as the IJO found a cooperative doctor to tend to its captives.

Finally there was the curious case of CNN's Jeremy Levin. The IJO had grabbed Levin in Beirut on March 7, 1984. Nothing was heard about him until nearly a year later, when on Valentine's Day, 1985, he walked up to a Syrian army checkpoint near Balabakk. Levin explained that when he awoke that morning and found his chains loose, he tied two blankets together, lowered himself from a window of the apartment building serving as his prison, and took off. It was easy—so easy, in fact, that Levin would wonder whether he'd been allowed to flee. Based on Levin's description, it seemed likely that he, too, had been at the Shaykh Abdallah barracks. If that was true, then it was the Iranian Pasdaran who had held him, even though the IJO had snatched him.

All this was sloshing around in my head early one morning when the CTC's deputy chief, Fred Turco, called me into his office. "Jenco's out," he said. Fred sounded exhausted, as if he'd been up all night. "He's on his way to Wiesbaden. Get home, pack, and go out to talk to him."

Father Lawrence Martin Jenco, the American priest, had been kidnapped in Beirut on January 8, 1985. As with Levin, there was no trace of him until his release on July 26, 1986. Another hostage, Reverend Benjamin Weir, had been released earlier, but Weir had refused to talk to either the FBI or the CIA. We hoped Jenco would be able to fill the gap between Levin's escape and now.

There wasn't time to ride my bicycle home and make it over to Andrews Air Force Base. Fred had one of CTC's war wagons—an armored Chevy Suburban 2500—take me home to get some clothes and then drop me off at Andrews, where I joined up with a debriefing team of some twenty people. We were almost ready to board the C-141 to Wiesbaden when an air force major trotted out to tell Ambassador Bob Oakley, the State Department's counterterrorism chief, that our departure would be delayed. Two storm fronts were converging over the Atlantic, and the FAA was giving strict priority to inbound flights, some of which were already backed up two hours and running low on fuel. The FAA didn't care how urgent our mission was—we would have to wait.

Undeterred, Oakley asked around for a quarter to call Ollie North at the White House. A couple minutes later he came back smiling. "Let's go," he said. Only when we were taxiing down the runway did Oakley explain. North had called the head of the FAA and, speaking in the president's name, ordered him to give us immediate clearance for takeoff. I filed that fact away: A staffer at the NSC carries a big stick in Washington—someone you wouldn't want to unnecessarily piss off.

Jenco didn't turn out to be the gold mine we'd hoped for. Although he had a remarkable memory, he had been chained to a wall and blindfolded for most of his captivity. The few conversations he'd had with his guards revealed nothing. Jenco didn't recognize pictures of Mughniyah or anyone else.

I was beginning to think it was a wasted trip until Jenco got around to talking about Jeremy Levin. When the guards learned Levin was gone, they reacted with a genuine mixture of surprise, anger, and panic, and hurriedly dispersed the hostages to private homes around the Biqa' and eventually to Beirut's southern suburbs, out of the reach of the Syrians. That told us that Levin had in fact escaped; and it also said that his captors wanted to avoid a confrontation with Syria.

When we showed Jenco the satellite photos of the Shaykh Abdallah barracks, he presented us with yet another bright, shining nugget of information. His captors apparently had made a grave error in not completely blocking the view from the bathroom Jenco used. Through a tiny crack, he had on several occasions seen khaki-uniformed Iranian Pasdaran soldiers delivering food from what appeared to be a military mess to the apartment building he and the other hostages were held in. Jenco was able to identify the building from the photos: the main mess of the Shaykh Abdallah barracks. Best of all, he was able to pick out the married officers' quarters as the building he'd been held in—the same one I had seen protected by Pasdaran guards during my October 1984 visit to the Biqa'.

★

LIKE MANY THINGS in the Middle East, the Mughniyah story was becoming more complicated under further scrutiny, but what I came across next made absolutely no sense at first.

On September 30, 1985, a group calling itself the Islamic Liberation Organization kidnapped four Soviet diplomats in Beirut, wounding one of them so severely that he would die in captivity. No one had ever heard of the group, but its demand that the Syrians stop their offensive against fundamentalists in Tripoli convinced us it was a cover name for the Syrian Muslim Brothers, who at the time were holed up in Tripoli. A little later, an unknown Palestinian by the name of Khudur Salamah was arrested, confessed to the kidnapping, and was traded for the three surviving Soviet diplomats. (Salamah's confession might not have been entirely voluntary: There was a rumor that his interrogators cut off his testicles to loosen up his tongue.)

We didn't know what to believe—the Salamah story had the earmarks of what passes for an urban legend in Beirut—but when the truth came out, it was stranger than fiction. It was 'Imad Mughniyah who had arranged the Soviets' release, flying to Tunis to negotiate with none other than Yasir Arafat, who by then was serving as the Soviets' intermediary to the hostage takers. Mughniyah, we learned, sought and received Arafat's assurance that the Soviets would not take revenge against the kidnappers. As a sweetener, Arafat had Abu Iyad, the head of security for the Palestinian Liberation Organization, transfer $200,000 to Mughniyah's account. The Soviets lived up to their part of the bargain; they never went after Mughniyah or the Islamic Liberation Organization. Whatever the ILO was, it would never kidnap anyone again.

This showed Mughniyah in a completely new light. Yes, he had apparently once been a member of Arafat's Force 17, but the Algerians also seemed to have been wrong about his having cut his ties with Arafat. At the very least, we now knew he was feeding at the Palestinian's trough.

The story became even more intriguing when we found out who Khudur Salamah was. His real name was 'Ali Dib. A Lebanese Shi'a born in 1957, he joined Arafat's Fatah at an early age and was eventually moved into intelligence. In 1975, at the beginning of the civil war, he had been appointed sector commander in 'Ayn Al-Dilbah, which meant he was Mughniyah's boss. After the Israeli invasion, Dib apparently became involved in international terrorism. His name was found in the address book of a Hizballah terrorist who was arrested in Ladispoli, Italy in 1984.

Dib led us to another Fatah operative—'Abd-Al-Latif Salah, born in Jordan in 1950. After graduating from the American University of Beirut, he married the daughter of a prominent Shi'a politician. About the same time, he joined Fatah intelligence. In 1982, after Fatah pulled out of Beirut, Salah joined a stay-behind cell to fight the Israelis. He wouldn't resurface, for us at least, until the arrest of 'Ali Dib (aka Khudur Salamah), when he served as a point of contact with Mughniyah. And then, on December 17,

1985, he and a subordinate were arrested in Cyprus in possession of a gun concealed in a bottle. (The glass was meant to defeat an airport X-ray scanner —the same technique the TWA-847 hijackers used to smuggle their weapons on board.) All through this, Salah remained on Arafat's payroll. Moreover, we learned later that Arafat regularly sent subsidies to Mughniyah and Hizballah through Salah.

THE ARAFAT ANGLE sent me back to the embassy bombing. I remembered that one of the suspects arrested after the bombing was a Fatah member named Muhammad Na'if Jada'. He was the only prisoner who had told a credible story. In fact, it would prove crucial in unraveling the embassy bombing.

Jada', a Palestinian, had been hired by the embassy as a guard a few months before it went up. Afterward he immediately confessed to his participation in the plot, telling his interrogators that he was an active lieutenant in Fatah. In the fall of 1982, his Fatah boss, Azmi Sughayr, had instructed him to wangle his way into a job with the embassy. Without asking why, Jada' set up a concession stand on the corniche directly facing the embassy, made friends with a couple of marines who worked there, and was hired to work in the marine house. From there he moved over to the embassy guard force. A few weeks before the bombing, two of Sughayr's lieutenants asked him to keep track of the movements of Ambassador John Habib, who was traveling in and out of Beirut, helping to negotiate the May 17 agreement. Again without asking any questions, he agreed; but a couple of days before the bombing, Sughayr's lieutenants called on Jada' again, this time asking his help in an operation to "scare" Habib. As soon as Habib was inside the embassy and the driveway was clear, the plan went, they asked Jada' to signal a car that would be passing back and forth in front of the embassy. On the morning of April 18, 1983, a guard mistakenly told Jada' that Habib was in the embassy. Seeing the driveway clear, Jada' walked out to the street and signaled the green Mercedes. The last thing he remembered, he told his interrogators, was a flash and a wall of flying debris coming at him. In fact, it was a miracle Jada' lived, and almost certainly not the bombers' intent. The CIA polygraphed Jada' after his arrest. He passed on all questions. But after the incident in which the Lebanese tortured a suspect to death and the CIA dropped out of the investigation, no one from the CIA would ever talk to Jada' again. By 1986 we had no idea where he was.

BY THE TIME I FINISHED rifling through headquarters files and absorbing everything I could find on the IJO and Mughniyah, it was time to leave for Beirut. I knew now with a fair degree of certainty that at least at one point the Iranian Pasdaran had controlled the hostages, that Mughniyah had hijacked TWA-847 and was still closely tied to Arafat and Fatah, and that a Fatah network was more than likely responsible for the Beirut embassy bombing. It was time to get on the ground and start connecting the dots.

9

AUGUST 1986. LARNACA, CYPRUS.

THE DRIVER WAS more than forty minutes late. If
the chopper left for Beirut without me, the next one
wouldn't be for another three days. Dead time in
Cyprus would be bad enough. Missing my agent
turnover meetings in Beirut would be a disaster. Most
couldn't be rescheduled for an entire month. I was
waiting in a nearly deserted airport cafeteria, checking my watch on the minute.

I considered calling Nicosia to find out if I'd gotten
the time wrong, but my instructions from headquarters were explicit: Don't talk about helicopter
schedules over the telephone. I'd need to take a taxi
all the way up to Nicosia—about an hour away—to
find out what had happened.

A commercial flight into the Beirut airport was out
of the question: Hizballah checked all incoming
manifests. I'd be lucky if I even made it out of the
terminal before being kidnapped. A boat sailed
nightly between Larnaca and Junieh, a fishing port on
the Christian side of Beirut, but I couldn't go over
that way either, because from time to time the Syrians
and their Lebanese allies used it for target practice.

Again I calculated the time difference between London and Larnaca. No, I'd gotten that right. I checked my ticket, too—in the top left corner I'd penciled the helicopter's departure time and the time and place I was to meet the driver. I was where I was supposed to be, when I was supposed to be. This would be hard to live down: Veteran case officer loses his way to Beirut. Dewey and Fred would have a field day when they read the cable notifying the world I'd gone missing.

Just as I was about to get up and take another look around the airport, the driver came running into the cafeteria, clipboard in hand. "Baer?" he asked, out of breath. An accident on the road from Nicosia had snarled traffic.

We hurried to the van he had left running in front of the terminal. Around the back of the airport, a gate guard recognized the van and let us through. The driver threaded his way through a couple of small airplanes, turned a corner, and pulled up between two U.S. Army Blackhawk helicopters. The crews, wearing olive drab jumpsuits, were waiting for me.

"You're it for Beirut, right?" the loadmaster asked, taking my duffel bag and handing me an inflatable life vest. "It's a one-hour trip. We're taking two birds over. If one goes down, the other will pick up the survivors. And I'm here to tell you, these things don't double as boats. After it hits the water, it'll be less than a minute before it sinks to the bottom. But don't jump into the water right away, either. If the blades are still rotating, they'll chop you into hamburger. It's all in the timing." He winked and smiled his best stewardess smile.

"Oh, one other thing. We're on the ground only twenty seconds, and not a second more. If we take fire, don't even try to get out. You won't like flying back to Larnaca hanging from a skid."

The two helicopters lifted off the tarmac in tandem, turned slowly to face the sea, dipped their noses, and headed off, going from 0 to 220 knots in about two seconds. We flew at a little under twenty-five hundred feet, side by side. It was a clear day. The Mediterranean shimmered below us.

About ten minutes from Beirut, the crew shrugged on inch-and-a-half thick Kevlar flak vests, while the loadmaster shoved open the cargo door, letting in a blast of air. The pilots then took the helicopters down to about twenty feet over the water, an altitude hard to see from land and nearly impossible to shoot at. I'd heard the helicopters were flying even lower than usual these days because they had recently been painted by radar—probably by Syrian surface-to-air missile batteries.

If Lebanon was there, I couldn't see it. A thick brown haze hugged the coast. We flew right through it, and I found myself directly over the shore and coastal highway. I expected the helicopters to turn south over the highway and fly in a straight line to the embassy. Instead they continued, one after the other now, straight into and up a ravine. We were still only about twenty feet above the ground. People came out on their balconies to look at us.

Just as the ravine tapered off, the helicopters veered right, flew perpendicular to the ground for a second, then leveled off and popped up over a ridge.

Immediately on the other side was what remained of the four-story embassy in East Beirut. A suicide car bomber had destroyed it on September 20, 1984, killing fourteen people, just seventeen months after its seven-story predecessor along the waterfront had been blown sky high. The siding that hadn't been blown off in the explosion was stripped off afterward, leaving a skeleton. A haunted building on haunted ground.

Two gunners on the roof manned belt-fed .30-caliber machine guns. They faced away from the helicopter pad, ready to shoot anyone foolish enough to pop his head up while the helicopters were on the ground. These guys took their jobs seriously. A couple of months before, they had fired on a UN helicopter that strayed too close to the embassy, wounding the pilot.

As I watched, the two Blackhawks diminished to a dot, then disappeared as they skimmed away over the Mediterranean. Even after I'd flown into Beirut more than fifty times, I always felt like I had been abandoned in the bottom circle of hell. The eerie quiet after the beating of the rotors, the shells landing around the port and tracers from a .50-caliber machine gun arcing over the city, the thick pall of black smoke from burning buildings that always seemed to sit over the downtown—anyone who stayed on in Saigon in 1975 and watched the last helicopter taking off from the embassy roof must have felt something similar.

The new Beirut embassy, a two-story villa a hundred yards from the skeleton, was among the most heavily protected properties in the world. The ten acres of land surrounding it were covered with a sea of coiled razor wire, fortified bunkers, watchtowers, machine-gun positions, and sandbagged trenches. Foot-thick steel walls protected the villa from artillery and rockets. Antirocket screens covered the roof. With more than six hundred local guards, the U.S. embassy had the fourth largest standing militia in the country. An armored division would have had a fight to capture it.

But the ring of protection extended only so far. During the previous three years, the CIA had lost two chiefs, another five officers, and plenty of agents. And, of course, Beirut and Lebanon weren't dangerous just for us. Thirty-seven foreigners had been taken hostage since January 1984. A half-dozen of them were executed.

About the time I got to Beirut, the assassinations started creeping into the Christian East, where the embassy was. The French military attaché was shot at point-blank range in the parking lot of the French embassy. The deputy in the French intelligence station was machine-gunned in front of the Lebanese intelligence headquarters, no doubt fingered by one of the Lebanese officers he was supposed to be working with. Three armed French gendarmes were shot one afternoon on their day off. Since American officials were on the same hit list as the French, we took these attacks seriously.

To cope with the violence, the State Department imposed a rule that Beirut embassy officers never set foot outside the embassy compound, except to go home. Even then, they traveled in heavily armored cars, accompanied by a dozen heavily armed guards in lead and chase cars. Embassy residences were protected around the clock by guards and roving patrols carrying automatic Uzis. Just to be extra safe, State Department officers met their contacts in the embassy screened by metal detectors and protected by marines with M-16s.

As a general rule, only the ambassador ventured out, and then in a twelve-car convoy with sirens and bodyguards shooting in the air to clear traffic. The point vehicle was an armored Suburban crowned by a shooter manning a .50-caliber machine gun, finger on the trigger. He was more serious about his job than the guy who shot up the UN helicopter. Seeing the ambassador move around Beirut was impressive, even for the Lebanese who'd seen it all.

In the CIA, we took a different approach to staying alive. Sure, we carried guns, but in a country where just about everyone from the age of twelve owned a machine gun, small arms weren't all that useful. Instead, we relied on tradecraft learned from the terrorists: Constantly move around, blend in with the environment, and stay completely unpredictable. We must have had some thirty apartments and twice as many cars. Switch residences and cars often enough and you become a moving target; move fast enough and you're impossible to hit. I might spend one night in an apartment in Ashrafiyah, an old part of Beirut on the Green Line, and the next at a beach condo twenty miles north of Beirut. Sometimes we used two or three different cars in the same day, generally old rust buckets indistinguishable from any other Lebanese car. From time to time I drove a dented broccoli-green 1964 Mercedes taxi. It fit in beautifully. Lebanese would wave me down from the side of the road for a ride, never suspecting an American was at the wheel.

MAYBE IT SOUNDS WACKY, but I loved working in Beirut. Instead of dealing with the distractions of headquarters, the meetings and paperwork that ate up time, I would move around on the streets, where I had always been more comfortable. Best of all, I was away from Washington politics, maybe the greatest hindrance we had to doing our job.

Jerry, the chief when I arrived this time, was a wiry, cigar-smoking, ex-airborne officer who had once worked as rodeo cowboy. Jerry had a healthy respect for just how dangerous the place was—we kept an outfit belonging to Bill Buckley in a storage locker on the off chance that he would reappear—but once he decided I knew what I was doing, he gave me all the rein I needed. It didn't matter that I'd be gone from the office for days, meeting agents and working out of safe houses.

Running agents in Beirut was like no other place in the world, but then again, Beirut itself was like no other place. Once we asked for a polygrapher to come to Beirut to box a Palestinian source, and they sent us Bernie, a skinny African-American who wore large-frame plastic glasses and took an instant dislike to Beirut, from the moment he boarded the helicopter in Larnaca.

As soon as we dropped off Bernie's things at one safe house, we headed across town to another to do the polygraphing. It was a beautiful day. A wind had blown off the haze. People were swimming and walking along the beach. The guns along the Green Line were oddly quiet. Squint a little bit and you could almost pretend to be driving up the Pacific Coast highway from Santa Monica to Malibu. I could see Bernie was starting to feel better about Beirut—not exactly relaxed, but at least he'd stopped threatening to shoot his boss for sending him there.

Before Ashrafiyah, we cut up into the hills to a part of Beirut called Hazmiyah. Several Lebanese army artillery positions hid in the woods, but otherwise it was a quiet residential neighborhood popular with military officers. As Bernie set up the polygraph on the dining room table, I wrote down the questions I wanted him to test the Palestinian on. Because the Palestinian spoke fluent English, Bernie didn't need me to translate during the exam. My plan was to wait in one of the back bedrooms and catch up on my sleep.

I'd just closed my eyes when a boom shook the building, rattling the windows. A second boom quickly followed.

Bernie flung the bedroom door open. "That's it," he said. "We're finished."

"It was outgoing. Nothing to worry about, Bernie," I said, trying to calm him down. It was true, too. I knew from the sound that it was the local artillery position firing into the West. "You'll be able to tell the difference if it comes back the other way," I made the mistake of adding.

"No, you don't fucking get it," Bernie yelled,
apparently convinced the artillery had made me deaf
or stupid. "*That* son of a bitch didn't react. And I
mean there wasn't a squiggle. Not after the first shot
or the second. It was like he'd died. When someone's
got ice water running through his veins, there's no
fucking way I can box him."

I suppose we all got that way after a while in Beirut,
even the foreigners. The fighting always seemed to be
going on somewhere else, and during the few times it
did get close—like the time a militia in West Beirut
hosed the hillside around one of the apartments I was
staying in with 107mm rockets—it was always over
quickly. A few minutes of a pounding heart, and then
life was back to normal. Sort of.

10

PICKING UP THE TRAIL of the embassy bombing was like putting together a Roman mosaic scattered in an earthquake and scorched by fire. You had no idea what was a lead and what wasn't.

Actually, it was worse. Sitting in Christian East Beirut meant we were working in the dark. We couldn't cross into West Beirut, where most of our best remaining agents were. On top of that, none of our agents was in a position to infiltrate Hizballah or any other radical Shi'a Islamic group, and no one could even get close to 'Imad Mughniyah or the IJO. That left us making do with what the CIA calls access agents—those who don't know secrets themselves but can access people who do.

One of my best access agents was a freelance journalist I'll call Farid. Although he was a Christian, Farid's job allowed him to travel back and forth across the Green Line. A slight, balding man with a winning smile, Farid could pass unnoticed almost anywhere in the world. He had friends and contacts all over Lebanon and could talk to pretty much whomever he liked, with the exception of Mughniyah or Hizballah. The limitation was okay with me: Sidling up to the really toxic guys would only draw attention to Farid. Moreover, Hizballah was in a particularly foul mood in those days. The year before, on March 8, 1985, a car bomb had detonated in front of the apartment building of a Shi'a spiritual leader, Muhammad Husayn Fadlallah, killing eighty people. Hizballah immediately accused the CIA of training the bombers. It was absurd—no one could teach the Lebanese anything about car bombs—but logic didn't matter, since anyone who fell under Hizballah's suspicion was summarily executed.

The first thing I asked Farid to do was to collect public records on people we suspected of being close to the IJO. To ease the burden on him, I rented a safe house in Sinn Al-Fill, a poor Christian neighborhood near the Green Line. I would always get to the meeting first so I could watch Farid maneuvering with his scuffed leather briefcase between the cars parked on the sidewalk and the vendors.

Once he was inside, I'd get him a soft drink and he would dump the contents of the briefcase onto the sofa between us—stacks of civil registration documents, political membership lists, old newspaper articles, and news photos from Hizballah demonstrations. Most of it was junk, but I never discouraged him from bringing it. It was up to me to pick through for that one gem I could use. I always paid Farid a bonus if he brought something good. Money was never a problem for the CIA in Beirut.

I had Farid collect the Lebanese civil registration documents for Muhammad Hammadah, one of the

TWA-847 hijackers whom we suspected of being an active member of Mughniyah's group. It took him about four weeks to put his hands on them, and then he couldn't contain himself when he came to the meeting. He gleefully told me how he had finally found the right civil registration office, waltzed in, plunked down the equivalent of a nickel, and watched the clerk copy the page for the Hammadah family. No one asked any questions.

I picked it up as if it were a rare manuscript. There, in front of me, was the entire family from Muhammad's father, here 'Ali Hasan Hammadah, born in 1929 in Al-Sawanah, to his mother, Fatmah 'Abd-al-Hasan Dabbuk, born in 1931 in Khirbat Silm. All of his living siblings were listed, including Muhammad's older brother 'Abd-al-Hadi Hammadah, a dangerous leader in Hizballah.

Someone who doesn't make a living in counter-terrorism might scratch his head and wonder why I'd risk an agent's life for information like this, but in fact it represented the kind of detail that could break open a case. The records gave us addresses, telephone numbers, marriage ties. It helped us check the bona fides of other agents. Eventually I or another case officer was sure to run into an agent who claimed to know Muhammad Hammadah. Now we could start vetting the agent by asking about the facts we already knew. The Hammadah civil registry, for instance, told us that Muhammad's sister Samira had been born on February 13, 1969, and was still unmarried and living at the Hammadah home in Burj Al-Barajnah. If the contact didn't know about her, something was wrong. Maybe he wasn't as close to Muhammad as he claimed. Maybe he had been sent to draw us into an ambush. Knowledge was power, and self-preservation. Muhammad Hammadah eventually would be arrested on January 13, 1987, at Frankfurt Airport trying to smuggle through customs a bottle of methyl nitrate, a highly explosive, unstable liquid. It was probably intended to be used in terrorist attacks in France.

Farid even helped solve a terrorist case. On December 25, 1986, four Lebanese hijacked an Iraqi flight from Baghdad only to have it crash over Saudi Arabia, killing the hijackers along with most of the crew and passengers. The Iraqis told us one of the hijackers was Ri'bal Khalil Jallul, a young Shi'a from the southern suburbs. To confirm the story, Farid searched for and found a Jallul family registered as Burj Al-Barajnah, registration #117. Listed among the children of Khalil Jallul was a Ri'bal Khalil Jallul, born February 10, 1967. One of Farid's sub-sources then found a Hizballah poster pasted on a mosque wall, a picture of a young martyr whom the caption identified as Ri'bal Jallul. Finally, Farid managed to dig up a copy of the passport Ri'bal had used. The name was an alias, but the passport photo matched the Hizballah poster. We'd come full circle, and one more piece of the mosaic was in place.

WHERE FARID LEFT OFF, telephone taps picked up.

In Beirut, everyone's phone was tapped. You could walk down almost any street and see jerry-rigged telephone wires draped across the street. Part of it was just practical business. If you were to move into an apartment in, say, Hamra—Beirut's old central business district—and find that there was no telephone line, you couldn't ask the telephone company to come out and install a new line. The telephone company no longer existed, along with anything else that approached everyday infrastructure. What you did was find a working line and tie into it, legally or illegally. You might steal a line from one of Hamra's mostly abandoned hotels. Since the hotel never got a bill, it wouldn't know. Or you might just go down into the basement and hook up to your neighbor's line in the telephone distribution box. With all this freelance telephone wiring going on, installing a tap was a cinch, which meant they were everywhere.

I went back through tap transcripts looking for a reference to a Ri'bal Jallul. I found a call between 'Abd-al-Hadi Hammadah, the brother of the TWA hijacker, and a Jihad Jallul. Since the Jalluls are a big family, I couldn't be sure Ri'bal was related to Jihad. But in checking the Jallul registration records, I found a Jihad Khalil Jallul, undoubtedly Ri'bal's older brother. I came across another interesting tap transcript from April 16, 1986: A Hizballah mole in the Lebanese police named Muhammad Murad had called what we suspected was an IJO office. He first asked for Mughniyah and was told he wasn't there; he then asked in succession for 'Abd-al-Hadi Hammadah, Jihad Jallul, and Zuhayr Jallul. (Zuhayr was another brother of Ri'bal, according to the civil registration documents.) I now had Mughniyah tied, circumstantially at least, to the Iraq Air hijacking. For his part, Murad later helped kidnap four American professors at Beirut University College.

I didn't stop there. I found out from another agent that the Jalluls lived in Mughniyah's neighborhood, 'Ayn Al-Dilbah. I even got a sketch of the outside of their apartment, above a candy store and only a few blocks from Mughniyah's house. We found out a lot of other things about Jihad—his car's license-plate number, his telephone number, even the make of the pistol he carried. We got into his family history as well. His father was an alcoholic. Jihad had accidentally killed his mother while cleaning a gun in the kitchen.

I had five other agents doing the same thing as Farid. Piece by piece, I put together a picture of Mughniyah's group. I would spend hours poring over the take, making connections between people, eliminating false leads, adding to my matrices. My makeshift charts started to look like the wiring diagram for a Boeing-747 cockpit. The mounting details made it easy to see how Mughniyah had been able to keep his group so secret. Everyone was either related by blood, had fought together in Fatah, or hailed from the 'Ayn Al-Dilbah neighborhood. We started calling them the 'Ayn Al-Dilbah gang, but it was those same bonds that made the IJO such a hard target to crack.

★

ONE NAME that kept popping up alongside Mughniyah's was Husayn Khalil, but it wasn't until

Khalil's involvement in the kidnapping of former ABC correspondent Charles Glass that he became worth zeroing in on.

Glass had come to Lebanon in June 1987 to do research for a book. Born to a Lebanese mother, he knew the country better than most American reporters and even earned a brief measure of celebrity by interviewing on camera the captain of TWA-847 through an open cockpit window in the middle of the hijacking. But apparently Glass didn't know Lebanon well enough to avoid the fatal error of advertising his travel itinerary. As soon as the Iranians got wind of Glass's plans to visit Sidon, a Pasdaran officer drove to Husayn Khalil's house in the southern suburbs and ordered him to kidnap Glass. Although we knew when and where the kidnapping was going down—we even had the license number of one of the cars to be used—we had no way to get in touch with Glass. We watched helplessly as he was grabbed near the airport.

Although the horse was out of the barn, I had Farid run down everything he could on Khalil. It took him less than a week to come up with the family's civil registration records. Khalil's full name was Husayn 'Ali Husayn Jawad Khalil, born to 'Ali and Samira Khalil. He was married to the sister of 'Ali 'Ammar, a senior member of Hizballah who one day would be elected to the Lebanese parliament. Another agent brought me a handful of photos of Khalil.

The background data was all well and good, but it was only when I ran Khalil's name by a former Fatah agent that his story became really interesting. Samir, as I'll call the agent here, was a Lebanese military officer, but in 1975 Fatah had recruited him to stay out of the fighting for Beirut's hotel district. After Arafat evacuated Beirut in 1982, Samir stopped working for Fatah, but he still kept in touch with some secret members left behind.

Samir and I met in his former mistress's apartment in Ashrafiyah, on the Christian East side of Beirut. He always brought along one or two soldiers—as a Muslim, he could never be certain some Christian thugs might not try to grab him. I got used to the soldiers, but it was unnervmg to see a pair with rocket-propelled grenades barring entry to the apartment.

About halfway through our first meeting after the Glass kidnapping, I handed Samir three pictures without saying a word. Two were of Palestinians who belonged to a left-wing group; I didn't care about either of them. The third was of Khalil praying in a mosque, along with a large group of other worshipers.

Samir immediately handed me back the picture of Khalil. "That one there is Husayn Khalil," he said, putting his index finger on Khalil's face. "He was with Fatah in the seventies. I think he joined in 1971. We worked together for a couple of years."

"And now?"

"In 1982 Khalil left Beirut just ahead of the Israelis. He signed up with Husayn Al-Musawi as chief of security. I heard he led the takeover of the Shaykh Abdallah barracks. I don't know what's happened to him since, but I'll check."

That afternoon I sent a cable to headquarters,

asking for a complete trace on Khalil. What came back was stunning. Tucked away in a five-page cable was a tap transcript that placed Khalil as the Lebanese in charge of the married-officers' quarters at the Shaykh Abdallah barracks in early 1985—at the same time the IJO hostages were held there. The authenticity of the information could not be challenged.

At our next meeting, Samir started droning on about the Shi'a fighting each other in the West. Finally, unable to contain myself, I interrupted: "Anything on Khalil?"

"Oh yeah, I almost forgot. I ran into one of his old colleagues from Tyre."

"Khalil was in Tyre?"

"Yes, for a couple of years. After a stint in a Fatah student cell in Beirut, Khalil was recruited by Force 17 and transferred to Tyre. He worked for a guy I'm sure you've never heard of."

"Try me."

"Azmi Sughayr."

I almost got up and kissed Samir. Sughayr was not a common name. It had to be the same Sughayr who recruited Jada' to work in the embassy. If I was right, it was like hitting a grand slam to win the World Series. I had finally tied someone other than Jada' to the bombing. Better by far, I had, for the first time, one person connected to both the hostages and the bombing. Khalil was all of a sudden a lot more important than Mughniyah.

I went back to headquarters and asked for everything on Sughayr. There was a lot. My predecessors in

Beirut had done their jobs well. According to headquarters records, Sughayr had been born in Palestine in 1944 and joined Fatah's elite security organization, which would become Force 17, in 1969. He fought for Yasir Arafat against the Jordanian army in 1970 and then in 1971 he joined Black September, a fictional organization used by Fatah to conduct terrorist operations. In 1973 Abu Iyad appointed him head of the Security Office for Foreign Operations. He was probably involved in almost every major Black September terrorist operation, including the massacre at the Munich Olympics. After putting in several years in Libya, he was appointed Fatah commander for Tyre in 1979. Shortly afterward Husayn Khalil had gone to work for him. In 1982, during the Israeli invasion, Fatah put out the false news that Sughayr had been killed. In fact, he stayed in Beirut to run resistance operations against Israel. Khalil apparently had studied at the feet of a master terrorist.

There was one piece of missing evidence that bothered me: What happened to Jada' after he was released? It was a long shot, but I asked headquarters once again. Two days later I got my answer, and it was a lot more than I had hoped for. Jada' had gone to Dubai, where he was taken in by a man named Anis 'Abdallah Hassan (Abu 'Ali), the head of a Fatah sleeper cell in the Gulf. The next day I went through our telephone tap records looking for an Abu 'Ali. I was about to give up when I found three calls from an IJO office to an Abu 'Ali in Dubai. Not only that, according to the taps, Abu 'Ali worked directly for 'Abd-Al-Latif Salah—Mughniyah's associate and Yasir Arafat's representative to the IJO.

This was all rock-solid evidence, and it was all consistent. You'll have to take my word for it: Evidence doesn't get much better in the intelligence business. Just as important, for all the twists and turns the story had taken—and I realize the reader has just been through quite a number of them—the intelligence had been gathered the way it has to be: at the ground level, through human sources, by wire taps, and by correlation with untold hours of similar research by predecessors who still cared about doing the job right.

The only conclusion a reasonable person could make was that a Fatah cell—with or without Yasir Arafat's knowledge—blew up the American embassy in Beirut on April 18, 1983. Mughniyah and Khalil were almost definitely involved. There was only one significant question: Who gave the orders?

TO GET TO THE NEXT STEP, a lot of details needed filling in, like who actually drove the truck through the front door. If we could find that out, it might well lead us to the bombers.

The break came in October 1987. I was at my desk late in the afternoon when the embassy security officer came to say that a Mr. Walker wanted to see me. Mr. Walker was the code for a walk-in who wanted to see a CIA officer. It wouldn't win any originality prizes, but I got the message.

As with any potential agent, I had to begin with the

assumption that I would run him as an agent. That required protecting him from the very beginning, and it meant isolating him from the local guards, who could be working secretly for anyone. Rather than have Mr. Walker pass through the embassy check-in system, I went to the outer perimeter to meet him.

The man waiting for me was probably about thirty-five, although he could have passed for much older, and scarred all over, including a crater in the top of his head. Slight and gaunt, he wore a faded and patched shirt. His sandals flagged him as a Muslim. (Lebanese Christians usually opted for stylish European shoes.)

After he passed through the metal detector, I led him along the embassy's metal labyrinthine sandbagged trenches, down a hill, and out a back exit, where I had prepositioned a car.

As soon as we turned onto the coastal highway I asked Mr. Walker for his national identity card. When he pulled it from his shirt pocket and showed it to me, I almost drove off the road. He had the same family name as a member of Mughniyah's group. I held my breath when I asked Mr. Walker—I'll call him Hasan—if he was related to the terrorist of the same name. "He's a first cousin," he told me.

My objective became putting our relationship on a clandestine footing as quickly as possible. As the first cousin of a notorious IJO terrorist, Hasan had a half-life in Christian East Beirut of about five seconds. I needed to find a secure place to let him off and another secure spot to pick him up for the next meeting. The less terrain he had to cross in East

Beirut to meet me, the better. I headed to Sinn Al-Fill, the same neighborhood where I met Farid.

We talked on the way. I wanted to know everything about him: where he lived, whether he was married, how many children he had. I also needed to learn whom he was close to in Hizballah and the IJO. He wasn't a member of either, he told me, but even as he spoke, I was contemplating how to insert him into one of those assemblies of worthies.

We also talked about how he could justify coming across the Green Line to the east if challenged. It wasn't as if you could pop over to Sinn Al-Fill to buy a pizza: No one crossed without a very good reason. We agreed that he would say he was buying Islamic books for a German scholar of Islam who lived in the east. Since the fictional German couldn't go into the west, Hasan, if challenged, would explain that he did his buying for him. It wasn't the most ingenious cover, but it was all I could come up with on short notice. I gave Hasan a sterile telephone number—one not associated with the office.

Finally, as I was about to drop Hasan off, I asked him why he had decided to meet with the CIA.

"I can't stand the murder of innocent people. What Hizballah does is wrong."

"But it's risky," I said. "You have children. If you're caught, you'll be tortured to death."

"I know. But God protects me."

I waited for Hasan to explain. I thought I knew where the conversation was going. I was wrong.

"I play Russian roulette," Hasan said sheepishly.

I'd heard the rumor that fanatic Muslims had taken

up the sport to test divine determination. A round in the chamber was God's way of letting you know your time was up. But I never took the rumor seriously, at least until now. Before I let Hasan out, I made him promise to stop playing Russian roulette. Just meeting me, I told him, was all the fate he wanted to tempt.

HASAN JOINED HIZBALLAH, found a job in one of its offices, and turned into a fantastic agent, the CIA's first in the group.

The analysts back home sent me reams of questions about what shaykh so-and-so thought about shaykh so-and-so, how much Hizballah was spending on its social welfare programs, or when it was going to enter mainstream Lebanese politics. But what interested me were 'Imad Mughniyah and the IJO.

Since you had to be recruited to the IJO, I asked Hasan to work the problem on the edges. Not surprisingly, my first order of business was the April 18, 1983 bombing. Hasan and I talked it over at length. I knew he was politically savvy so I simply confessed that the U.S. government had no idea who blew up the embassy. The canned Middle East response was that it was inconceivable the CIA didn't have a clue about a terrorist attack that killed seventeen Americans. Hasan didn't go for it. "For lack of a better lead," he said, "why not let's start with 'Imad?" At that moment, I knew Hasan had as good a chance as any agent to come up with some of the answers I was after.

Hasan started praying at a mosque whose imam

was close to Mughniyah. Hasan went every Friday
and soon joined a religious study group. A good
writer, he started crafting tracts for the imam.
Because the imam knew Hasan was related to an IJO
terrorist, he accepted him as one of the faithful.

One day when Hasan was alone with the imam, he
decided the time was right to bring up the bombing.
As we'd agreed, Hasan started with a ploy. Instead of
charging ahead and asking who the suicide bomber
was, he mentioned the name of a young man who had
been in the imam's congregation for many years but
had disappeared. Lowering his voice conspiratorially,
Hasan said he'd heard the young man was the suicide
driver who blew up the U.S. embassy in April 1983.

"Where did you hear that?" the imam asked.

Hasan responded vaguely that he'd heard it from
his IJO cousin. He knew the imam would never check
back with his cousin.

"No" the imam answered. "No, he was not the
blessed martyr who destroyed the American spy
nest."

Hasan insisted he was right.

"No, you're wrong." The imam didn't appreciate
having his authority challenged. "It was Brother
Hassuna. I know very well."

"Who?"

"Muhammad Hassuna."

THIS WAS THE FIRST TIME we'd ever had a name for
the suicide bomber, but the story still needed to be
nailed down. I invited Bernie back to Beirut to

polygraph Hasan. Two days later he was scrambling out of the door of a Blackhawk.

It was another flawless day. Bernie was calmer than on his first visit; the fighting along the Green Line had died down. If everything went smoothly, Hasan would be in and out of the polygraph before lunch.

Things were going fine until we turned down the main street into Sinn Al-Fill. We were about three blocks from the pickup site when a blast from a .50-caliber machine gun hit a neon sign hanging over the road, spraying glass over the car. Just above our roof, wires sparked and sizzled. I looked at Bernie. The expression on his face seemed to say, "Do I shoot him for putting my life in danger, then run? Or do I just run?"

A second burst from the .50 thudded into the wall of a building farther down the street.

Bernie pointed at my foot. "That's your foot. And right under it is the gas pedal. Now apply one to the other—*and let's get the fuck out of here!*"

We found a quiet street out of the line of fire, and Bernie waited in the car, glumly resigned to spending the rest of the day with a lunatic, while I went looking for Hasan.

Eventually, he came walking down the main street of Sinn Al-Fill, looking like he was taking a stroll along the corniche. Although the shooting had stopped, the street was completely deserted. Maybe the Russian roulette paid off after all.

Hasan passed the polygraph with flying colors, including whether the imam had told him Hassuna was the suicide bomber.

The polygraph was a start, but I couldn't rely on it.

Perhaps the imam had lied to Hasan, or maybe he didn't really know the identity of the suicide bomber and was simply covering up his ignorance. Since I couldn't polygraph the imam, it was time to go back to the matrices.

Hassuna was not a common name in Lebanon. That helped. I had all of my agents look into the Hassuna family. Samir knew a Major Hassuna, and promised to check with him to see if any members of the family were missing. A week later he dropped the bombshell on me—one of Major Hassuna's brothers, Muhammad, had died on the Iraq front in Iran.

"Iran?" I asked incredulously. "How's that possible? Lebanese don't simply pull up stakes and go fight for Iran."

Samir shrugged. "I'll find out."

At the next meeting, Samir said that Major Hassuna had told him his family was nonpracticing Muslims. They rarely went to the mosque or read the Koran, but Muhammad was different. Their father was alcoholic and abusive, and Muhammad took it particularly badly. In his search for a deeper faith, he had embraced Shi'a Islam, and in early 1983 he had unexpectedly informed his family that he was going to Iran to fight in the war with Iraq. That was the last they heard of him until they received a letter from the Iranian embassy that Muhammad had died in a battle on the front. There were few remains, the letter said, and he was buried in a military cemetery in Iran. Included in the letter was a Polaroid of Muhammad's gravestone. The major didn't know anything more about his brother's death.

I had Farid dig up the official records on Muhammad Hassuna. Although Hassuna had a passport, there was no record that he had ever traveled out of the country. According to the family civil registration records in Sidon, the Hassuna family's residence was Awza'i, a neighborhood near the airport controlled by Hizballah.

ALTHOUGH I was a long way from producing evidence that would hold up in court, I was getting closer every day. I wrote up what I knew about Hassuna in a long, detailed intelligence report—the first in a series I would do on the bombing.

A few days later, headquarters advised that the report would not be disseminated. "While the information is compelling," they wrote, "it is only of historical interest." In plain English, the national security community no longer gave a damn who had bombed our embassy in Beirut.

IN A WAY, I could almost understand Washington's not caring. The CIA was falling into the hands of people who had never put their lives on the line to learn about terrorism in places like Beirut. The embassy bombing for them wasn't just ancient history; it was a distraction from their career ambitions. Why mess up a spotless record by bearing news of one of the agency's darkest hours? I saw my job differently. If we didn't know who we were up against, we wouldn't know what they were capable of, and might not learn until they showed up on our shores, armed to the teeth.

Besides, there was still an outstanding arrest warrant for Mughniyah. All I needed was someone with the balls to exercise it.

I'll call the man I found Jean. Jean was about thirty-two and, like Mughniyah, had spent his life fighting on the Green Line. The only difference was, he killed and kidnapped Muslims rather than the other way around. Jean had made a name for himself when he flattened a foreign embassy to improve his field of fire.

Jean was waiting for me at a nightclub called Dominos.

"I always knew one day the CIA would come knocking at my door when it had some work too dirty to do itself," Jean said, shaking my hand.

I kept quiet while I looked around. Although it was already past eleven at night, Dominos was only now starting to fill up. Arms dealers, Colombian narcotics traffickers, Christian Gucci warlords—an entire demimonde did its business there. Aside from the inset lighting over the bar, Dominos was pitch black, and the music was just loud enough to mask a conversation but not drown it out.

I turned back to Jean. "I need a network in the west, people who are not going to waste my time."

"I don't do intelligence. Go talk to the Lebanese Forces if you want information."

The Lebanese Forces were the main Christian militia. We both knew its intelligence wasn't very good.

"It's not information I'm after. I need to do an operation."

Jean grinned. "So Syria has finally crossed the line."

"No, I want to get someone in the southern suburbs."

"A hit?"

"No. I need the guy alive."

"Who is it?"

"You find me the people and we'll talk."

Jean wrote down the name of a video store in Zuq, an out-of-the-way neighborhood in East Beirut. "Tomorrow morning at ten."

He was sitting in his Range Rover in front of the video store when I arrived. He got out and motioned me to follow him, and we walked through the store, out the back door, and into an apartment building through its alley entrance. The electricity was off. We climbed five flights of stairs.

A Lebanese army captain opened the door. A second officer was sitting behind him on the sofa. On the dining room table sat a cutoff M-16 with a suppressor and a laser sight: not exactly your standard-issue weapon for the Lebanese army.

The captain's left hand looked like a webbed duck foot. My guess was that it had been mangled by an explosive charge. When he went into a corner of the room to talk with Jean, I noticed that one of his legs was shorter than the other as well.

"The captain is ready to hear you out," Jean said when he turned back to me.

As soon as I started talking about needing a

network in the west, the captain grinned just as Jean had.

"The target's not Syrian," I said. "It's Hizballah. I want to grab a member of the Islamic Jihad."

"Forget it," the captain said, without any hesitation. He spoke English with an American accent, although he never volunteered his name. "You want to whack him, fine. But you'll never find anyone to do a kidnapping in the southern suburbs."

Jean and the captain again spoke to each other privately. I picked up the cutoff M-16. The action was Teflon-coated to reduce noise.

"There's one person just maybe crazy enough to try something like this," the captain said, "but we haven't worked with him in years. He's too crazy."

"Does it make any difference?" I asked. "He either brings the guy across the Green Line or he doesn't. I'll only pay a success fee."

The captain agreed to see if he could recontact him.

When we got outside, I asked Jean who the two officers were. Both, he said, had gone AWOL from the Lebanese army and were now members of an anti-Syrian guerrilla group working in the Biqa' Valley. They'd carried out several successful attacks on the Syrians, but they had lost people each time. "In another six months there won't be any of them left," Jean said.

A week later at dusk he picked me up in Babda, a Christian neighborhood that bordered the southern suburbs. We waited in Jean's Range Rover until dark, then drove slowly down the hill. The closer we got to the Green Line, the more the buildings started to look like sand castles washed over by a wave. The last buildings before the fields that separated Babda from the southern suburbs had been reduced to piles of rubble.

We passed through three checkpoints manned by the Lebanese Forces. Everyone knew Jean and waved him through. The last was a four-by-five hole dug in the rubble. Two grunts jumped up when they heard the truck approach and looked at us as if we were ghosts. We left the Range Rover with them and walked.

We were in no-man's-land now, only about a hundred yards from Hizballah's pickets. This was the sector Mughniyah fought in, for Fatah, in the 1970s. Although I wasn't supposed to know about it, we were following a route the Lebanese Forces used to supply Hizballah with weapons and ammunition. Earlier that year when a war broke out between Hizballah and its secular rival, Amal, the Lebanese Forces backed Hizballah on the theory that Syria was supporting Amal. Only in the Middle East could a radical Christian group ally with a radical Islamic group.

We waited for about twenty minutes, sitting in some high grass, listening to the thump of a heavy machine gun and the occasional explosion from a rocket-propelled grenade. I noticed that Jean was unarmed, but what good would a pistol do if Hizballah decided to jump us?

Out in the darkness a shadow began making its way toward us, zigzagging across the open space to navigate a minefield. In time, the shadow turned into a man with a neatly trimmed beard. He wore a polo shirt, jeans, and cowboy boots. I'll call him Isam.

Isam and Jean hugged. Jean asked the man about his children; he knew all six by name. This went on for about five minutes before Jean told him why we came. By then we had done all the beating around the bush I could stand. I told Isam straight on that I wanted to grab someone who lived in 'Ayn Al-Dilbah.

"Do you know anything about 'Ayn Al-Dilbah?" Isam asked. I don't think he was daunted by the prospect; he was just taking my measure.

I ignored him. "It's 'Imad Mughniyah I want."

The man looked at me more closely now. He turned to Jean and asked, "Is he serious?" Jean nodded.

Isam turned back to me and said: "I'll kill him for two thousand dollars. A thousand in advance."

"I want him alive."

"Then find someone else."

We listened to the gunfire in silence. It was closer now.

"How do I know you can do anything in 'Ayn Al-Dilbah, anyhow?" I asked.

Isam laughed. "Mr. Jean didn't tell you who I am? I've killed more people than your marines and the *New Jersey* put together."

"Isam once set off eleven car bombs—simultaneously," Jean said, by way of an explanation.

To the average reader, that might not seem like something to brag about, but for a terrorist in Lebanon, it was like winning three gold medals at the Olympics.

Shots were whistling over us now: It was time to

leave. I quickly told Isam we'd meet the following week. In the meantime, I said, go back and start collecting everything you can on Mughniyah—where he lived, the descriptions of his cars, the names of his closest contacts. I added that I needed pictures of Mughniyah's home. Before Isam could say anything, I put ten new hundred-dollar bills in his pocket. Money, I wanted him to know, was not going to be a problem.

I knew, of course, that Mughniyah didn't really live anywhere. With the CIA and just about everyone else after him, he never spent the same night under the same roof or exited a building the same way he came in. He changed cars more often than he changed his underwear. But I wanted to see what Isam brought back before I could begin to trust him.

THE NEXT WEEK Isam got to the meeting before we did. He was carrying a sheaf of notes and an envelope of pictures.

"Here is where Mughniyah spent two nights last week," he said as he handed me a picture. I recognized the two-story building, a religious school in the southern suburbs.

"What is this?" I asked.

"Mughniyah's sister-in-law lives there. Every few weeks he spends the night there. But he never announces when he's coming. He just shows up, usually alone."

"How do you know that?"

"My cousin works in the school. She's seen him

come and go. She lives in 'Ayn Al-Dilbah and has known his family since she was a child."

The next day I went through the stuff Isam had given me. When I finally deciphered his cribbed notes, it was obvious Isam was well plugged into the 'Ayn Al-Dilbah gang. He had it all—cars, addresses, telephone numbers.

Isam didn't show up for the next meeting, or the one after that. Jean was worried. Neither of us relished sitting in no-man's-land for hours on end. Finally, on the third night, Isam did show. He ignored me when I asked where he'd been.

"This week Mughniyah is going to be back at the school. He has to be. Someone from Tehran is coming to see him there," Isam said. "We may never have another chance."

"How could you possibly grab him there?" I asked.

"I told you before: I can kill him, but you're out of your mind if you think I will kidnap him."

I let Isam talk.

"In front of the school there is a parking lot, and in the back an alley. What I propose is to put a car on each side and detonate them simultaneously. I figure a thousand kilos of Semtex will tidy up your little problem."

It was what we call a muffler charge, and Isam was right. Two car bombs on either side of a two-story building would definitely bring it down and kill everyone inside.

"Can you be sure Mughniyah will be there?" I asked.

"My cousin will tell me."

"What do you need to start?"

"Two thousand up front and ten thousand afterward—after Mughniyah is dead."

It didn't take me long to decide. I'd joined the CIA as a prank. And yeah, somewhere along the line I was converted and became an information junkie. I was obsessed with finding out who bombed the embassy. But none of it meant I'd been handed the moral authority to decide who needed to be killed. I'd leave that up to the politicians in Washington.

I told Isam to go back and collect more information. I never reported the incident to headquarters, and I would never see Isam again. Do I regret it now? Sure. Whether 'Imad Mughniyah is in league with Osama bin Laden, I really don't know, but I am certain there's not a dime's worth of real difference between the two of them. If we had accepted back then that we were at war with terrorists, Washington might have been more inclined to approve the operation Isam proposed, and I would have been more inclined to force the issue with my superiors in Langley. But we didn't, and like so many other problems, we let this one fester in place.

11

SEVEN YEARS AFTER we declined to go after 'Imad Mughniyah with maximum lethal force, the man who had launched him so successfully on his blood-drenched career would be awarded the Nobel Prize for peace.

What a lot of people forget about Yasir Arafat, especially since the 1993 Oslo agreement and the 1994 Nobel Peace Prize that he shared with Shimon Peres and Yitzhak Rabin of Israel, is that he started out life as an Islamic fundamentalist. Even after he became chairman of the umbrella Palestine Liberation Organization, he never cut his ties with either Sunni or Shi'a fundamentalists. They were a reliable source of political strength for him.

Arafat was born Muhammad 'Abd-al-Rauf Arafat al-Qudwa in 1929. The Qudwas were a branch of the prominent Huysayni clan, famous for its religious scholars. One member of the clan, Mufti of Jerusalem, had supported Adolf Hitler during World War II. Arafat grew up in Egypt, studied civil engineering at the University of Cairo, and for a time headed the Palestinian Students' Union there. After graduation, he served in the Egyptian army as a second lieutenant. It was then that he joined the Egyptian

Muslim Brotherhood. Later, he was arrested twice for his Brotherhood activities. Eventually forced to leave Egypt, Arafat moved to Kuwait, a country more tolerant of extreme religious views. There he founded Fatah in the late fifties, mainly drawing on members of the Muslim Brotherhood and Palestinians living in the Gulf.

Even after Arafat rose to prominence with Fatah's first attack on Israel on January 1, 1965, Arab leaders remained suspicious of his fundamentalist ties. When Egyptian president Abdul Nasser received Arafat in Egypt for the first time, he insisted that his guest submit to a body search, apparently convinced Arafat was more interested in assassinating him than in liberating Palestine.

Arafat's interest in Islam remained dormant until 1977, when an Islamic current started to sweep across the Middle East. Always alert to shifting winds, Arafat ordered Abu Jihad, his principal deputy, to harness the Fatah believers into a single organization to be called the Committee of 77. Operational control was given to a convert to Islam, Munir Shafiq Asal. Asal's first task, in turn, was to recruit and indoctrinate young believers, both Palestinians and Lebanese, through an already existing organization called the Student Cells. The most capable members of the Student Cells were inducted into one of Fatah's intelligence organizations. That is how 'Imad Mughniyah, 'Ali Dib, and Salah first became associated.

Eventually, Arafat flew a little too close to the Islamic flame. Not only had he started recruiting young Palestinian and Lebanese believers into

Fatah's ranks, he also began providing important support to the Syrian Muslim Brotherhood. After the Hama insurrection in 1982, when the Syrian army sifted through the rubble, it came across American military communications equipment. Syrian president Hafiz Al-Asad at first suspected the CIA, but then he realized the equipment had come from Fatah, which had been training and supplying the Syrian Muslim Brotherhood with the purpose of bringing down Asad. Asad considered going after Arafat right away, then decided to wait and take his revenge at a time of his choosing. Asad understood that revenge is a dish best served cold.

It came on May 17, 1983. Syria encouraged two minor Fatah members, Sa'id Muragha (Abu Musa) and Nimr Salih (Abu Salih), to break away from Fatah and form their own organization. Five weeks later, on June 24, Asad formally expelled Arafat from Syria. Arafat was forced to set up in Tripoli, Lebanon, but in less than five months Abu Musa and Abu Salih, backed by Syrian forces, attacked Arafat all over Lebanon. It was all over on December 20, 1983, when, under a steady Syrian bombardment, five Greek-chartered ships evacuated Arafat and four thousand followers from Tripoli's port. The French navy provided an armed escort to protect them from the Israeli air force attack. Arafat ended up in Tunis, isolated and out of the mainstream of Palestinian politics. The lesson he learned was that while Islam is a potent force, it's not always a good idea to show your hand. Arafat would never again get caught in the Hama trap.

★

ANOTHER THING that has gotten glossed over in the wake of Arafat's successes in Oslo and Stockholm is that, in a large sense, the 1979 Iranian Islamic revolution was suckled on the Palestinian teat. In 1972 Ayatollah Khomeini and Arafat signed an accord in Najaf, Iraq, to train Islamic fighters at Fatah camps in southern Lebanon. Almost every leader of the Iranian revolution passed through these camps, from Khomeini's son Ahmad Khomeini to Mustafa Chamran, the first commander of the Iranian Pasdaran. When the Shah fled Iran on January 16,1979, and Khomeini returned to Iran two weeks later, it wasn't in the least surprising that the first telephone call Khomeini received in his new office was from Yasir Arafat.

Almost nine months later, on October 19, 1979— two weeks before Iranians seized the U.S. embassy in Tehran—Arafat flew there to congratulate Khomeini in person. Their discussions were more than cere-monial. On November 18, 1979, Arafat issued orders to all Fatah cadres to provide "any assistance" requested to "protect" the Iranian revolution. Although at the time the U.S. was in the dark about "any assistance," we weren't for long.

In February 1980, a Lebanese Sunni, Anis Naqqash, attempted to assassinate Shapour Bakhtiar in Paris, where the former Iranian prime minister was living as a political refugee. Naqqash fumbled the operation, killing an old lady and a policeman instead; he was arrested and given a life sentence. At first his participation made no sense at all. Why would a Lebanese Sunni attempt to kill an ex-Iranian prime minister? Then it became evident that Arafat had loaned Naqqash to Iran to assassinate Bakhtiar. After all, Arafat already had a functioning terrorist network in Paris. It would be years before Iran could put together one of its own.

Beyond the Bakhtiar attempt, it soon became clear Arafat had put his entire worldwide terrorist network at Iran's disposal. And when he was forced out of Beirut in 1982, he handed it over lock, stock, and barrel to the Iranians for safekeeping. Many of the cadres went to the Pasdaran. That's how Mughniyah and most of his underlings and associates found their way to the Iranians. In one of those reversals of fortune that affect even terrorist organizations, 'Ali Dib, who had been Mughniyah's boss in Force 17, started working for Mughniyah.

It would take years to understand the exact relationship between Mughniyah and Arafat. A key piece of the puzzle would fall into place with the hijacking of Kuwait Airlines Flight 422 on April 5, 1988. We first heard about the operation when Mughniyah told Arafat he intended to conduct a "spectacular" operation to free the seventeen prisoners in Kuwait on February 23. Although Arafat did not know what the operation was, he agreed to help, and on March 14, 'Ali Dib wrote to Arafat suggesting that he should start preparing himself for negotiations with Kuwait. Four days after Flight 422 was seized as it left Bangkok, Dib contacted Arafat again, this time to tell Kuwait that unless it released the prisoners, hostages would start dying. Arafat was furious when Mughniyah went ahead and killed two hostages, but he continued to relay demands to Kuwait and then to Algeria, where the plane was eventually taken.

For someone who isn't a student of terrorism or the Middle East, this may sound like inside baseball, but terrorist organizations operate like the most complicated interlocking directorate ever created by a white-shoes New York lawyer. And at the end of the day whether you're tracing 'Imad Mughniyah or seeking to unravel the Iranian revolution, a lot of the trails converge at the feet of Yasir Arafat. There may even be a trail to Osama bin Laden, but what you never look for, you are almost certain never to find.

I think of that when I see Arafat standing in the Rose Garden at the White House or when I hear that a CIA director has met privately with him at some desert tent, and I wonder sometimes if Arafat's example doesn't make Osama bin Laden consider that he, too, might become a statesman in time. This book isn't about Israel, but I should point out that many of its statesmen started out their political lives conducting what we would now define as terrorist operations against Britain. In the pursuit of realpolitik, apparently there is always hope.

12

AUGUST 1988. BEIRUT, LEBANON.

Chuck McKee walked me out to the helicopter pad to see me off on my last ride out of Beirut. I'd been reassigned to Paris and wouldn't be coming back to Beirut again.

Although it would be difficult to imagine two more different people, Chuck and I were close friends. We had sat in the same office for two years, backed each other up on the street, and gone out drinking together whenever we had some downtime. I enjoyed ribbing Chuck, who was a huge, gentle bear of a man. When he'd had enough of it, Chuck would come over to my desk, lift me up, turn me upside down, and hold me by my feet away from his body. I'm no midget: Very few men I've met have been strong enough to do that.

As I turned around to look at Beirut—a fire was burning near the port—I knew I'd left too much undone. I'd just picked up a picture of Hassuna, the presumed suicide bomber who drove the truck into our embassy. It still needed to be checked. But it really was time to go. I'd gotten too close to my work. I was starting to think like the people I was after. Another case officer needed to take up where I left off.

If he was interested enough, he could run down the leads I'd unearthed on the embassy bombing. And then maybe, one day, the CIA could finally solve the embassy bombing, close the file, and send it to the National Archives.

I didn't tell Chuck any of this because he was staying another year. He couldn't afford to look at the place with the same detachment. As we watched the two Blackhawks approaching low over the sea, we shook hands and promised to keep in touch. I offered him a couch to camp on if he ever passed through Paris.

I have no idea why, but for some reason I said jokingly, "If you don't leave here soon, Chuck, you dumb son of a bitch, the terrorists are going to get you."

Chuck laughed as he reached down and patted the Walther PKK—James Bond's preferred side arm—that he kept taped to his ankle. "They'll have a fight."

Six months later, on December 21, 1988, Chuck went down when Pan Am 103 exploded over Lockerbie, Scotland.

FEW THINGS HAVE LEFT ME feeling more frustrated than the Pan Am investigation. All the early signs suggested that the bombing was the work of a group based in Lebanon, acting on Iran's behalf. If I had still been in Beirut, I would have had my agents all over the case, running down leads, checking facts, looking for new sources. But I was in an office overlooking the Place de la Concorde, and while Paris

Here I am as a nine-year-old in California, dreaming of hitting one out of the park, before my mother and I flew off to Zurich. *(Courtesy of the author)*

Getting ready for another jump at the Farm in 1977. *(Courtesy of the author)*

The American Embassy in Beirut, bombed on April 18, 1983. *(Courtesy of the author)*

Muhammad Hassuna, the man believed to be the suicide bomber who blew up the U.S. Embassy in Beirut. *(Courtesy of the author)*

Muhammad Murad kidnapped four American professors at Beirut University College in 1987. This photo was taken from Lebanese government offices by agents. *(Courtesy of the author)*

From left to right: Muhammad Hammadah, who hijacked a TWA airplane in 1985, his brother 'Abd-Al-Hadi Hammadah, and two unidentified Pasdaran escorts visiting the Iraqi front in Iran. This picture was stolen from an IJO safehouse in Beirut by CIA agents. *(Courtesy of the author)*

Husayn Khalil, a master Hizballah terrorist, praying at a Beirut mosque in the early 1980s. He is third from left in second row, wearing glasses *(Courtesy of the author)*

Passport application of Talal Husni Hamiyah, head of external operations for Special Security in Lebanon. Agents lifted this photograph at the author's direction from Lebanese government offices.
(Courtesy of the author)

'Imad Mughniyah's passport photograph.
(Courtesy of the author)

Ri'Babl Khalil Jallul's passport application. He died during the hijacking of an Iraqi Airlines flight in 1986. Agents also lifted this photograph.
(Courtesy of the author)

After losing two embassies, the State Department finally built a fortress in Beirut. This photograph is from 1987. *(Courtesy of the author)*

'Imad Mughniyah (center with hands in his pocket) watching CNN coverage of the Iranian Airbus accidentally shot down over the Gulf in 1988. *(Courtesy of the author)*

Posing on Beirut's Green Line in 1987. *(Courtesy of the author)*

A C-140 landing to evacuate the U.S. Embassy in Dushanbe, Tajikistan, in 1992. *(Courtesy of the author)*

In ancient Soghdiana (the Yaghnob Valley, Tajikistan) with a Yaghnobi in 1994. *(Courtesy of the author)*

A "CIA Army" in the Pamirs in Tajikistan. They accompanied me into the remote Yaghnob Valley in 1994. *(Courtesy of the author)*

Yasir Arafat being awarded the Nobel Peace Prize in 1994 with Shimon Peres, center, and Yitzhak Rabin. When I see photographs like this I have to remind myself that Arafat spent years in terrorist organizations. *(Courtesy AP/Wide World Photos)*

Burning confidential documents in Salah Al-Din, Iraq, March 1995. *(Courtesy of the author)*

The Director of Operations Dave Cohen awarding me a Merit Unit Citation for my work in Iraq from January through March in 1995. *(Courtesy of the author)*

It took more than a decade to find out precisely who blew up our embassy in Beirut. I am hopeful that it won't take that long for the government to get to the bottom of who caused the horrible attacks on the World Trade Center and the Pentagon. *(Courtesy AP/Wide World Photos)*

had a few Arab agents, they were on the periphery of terrorism at best.

The theory that Iran was behind Pan Am 103 was based on a piece of information that surfaced in early July 1988. A few days after the U.S.S. *Vincennes* accidentally shot down an Iranian Airbus in the Gulf, a Pasdaran intelligence officer flew to Lebanon to meet two officials of the Popular Front for the Liberation of Palestine/General Command, Muhammad Hafiz Dalqamuni and someone we knew only as Nabil. The meeting took place at the Damur refugee camp in southern Lebanon. The Iranian's instructions to Dalqamuni and Nabil were crystal clear: Blow up an American airplane—in the air, in order to kill as many people as possible. Iran had decided to take revenge for the Airbus.

The Iranian hypothesis fit in with what we knew about the regime in Tehran. The Iranian hardliners, who controlled the government, never accepted that the Airbus was shot down accidentally. Revenge, for them, was a simple act of justice: an eye for an eye. And Iran's turning to the General Command for help made sense, too. Iran had developed a taste for letting surrogates do its dirty work, and the General Command was one of the best terrorist groups in the world when it came to blowing things up. Its expertise was in sophisticated mechanisms like barometric switches. The General Command made its air debut on February 21, 1970, when it blew up an Austrian Swissair flight. Two years later, on August 16, 1972, the Front exploded a bomb in an El Al plane, injuring four. In the years since, it had only gotten better.

Dalqamuni, too, was the ideal emissary for Iran's interests. As late as the mid-1980s, he had been living in Europe, where he would sit for long stretches in the local McDonald's, depressed that his fellow Palestinians were dying in the intifadah. Then one day he turned to Islam, joining a small group of Islamic fundamentalists in the General Command who looked to Iran for inspiration. Iran vetted Dalqamuni and determined he was a true believer who could be counted on to keep his mouth shut if caught. Still, he needed testing. At Iran's direction, Dalqamuni organized two separate attacks on U.S. military trains in West Germany, one on August 31, 1987, and the other on April 26, 1988. No one was killed, but Dalqamuni had shown he was prepared to take risks and follow orders.

Dalqamuni appeared to have an airtight alibi for Pan Am 103. He had been arrested along with most of his German cell on October 26, 1988, and was still in custody when the plane exploded two months later, killing all 259 aboard and eleven more on the ground. But that didn't exclude the possibility that the operation had been handed off to one of the cell members who got away and as the weeks went on, an avalanche of information began to point in that direction.

On December 23, two days after the bombing, an $11 million transfer showed up in a General Command bank account in Lausanne, Switzerland. It moved from there to another General Command account at the Banque Nationale de Paris, and then to yet another at the Hungarian Trade Development

Bank. The Paris account number was found in Dalqamuni's possession upon arrest. What's more, Muhammad Abu Talib, one of Dalqamuni's associates suspected of having a role in the bombing, received a payment of $500,000 on April 25,1989. Did that and the other payments originate in Iran? Were they success fees for Pan Am 103? Certainly none of those are illogical conclusions.

Abu Talib appeared to have visited Malta on October 3 through 18 and again from October 19 to 26,1988—a significant tidbit, since clothes bought in Malta were found amid the wreckage in the suitcase the explosive device was hidden in. Did Abu Talib buy the clothes, or did one of the two Libyans who were eventually tried in Zeist, the Netherlands, for the bombing? We also knew that Abu Talib was traveling in and out of Libya. Was he coordinating with the Libyans for Dalqamuni? Again, the logic seemed to fit.

FOR OUR PART, the CIA was able to identify with a fair amount of certainty that the mysterious Nabil who attended the Biqa' meeting in July 1988 was a General Command official named Nabil Makhzumi (Abu 'Abid), who at the time was serving as Dalqamuni's assistant. Perhaps because he spoke Farsi, Makhzumi was the GC's main contact to the Pasdaran. His Iranian case officer, we knew, was a senior Pasdaran official named Feridoun Mehdi-Nezhad. Had Makhzumi traveled to Germany? Was he the one who took the handoff from Dalqamuni?

The Germans had no idea. We also found out Mehdi-Nezhad had visited Frankfurt in July 1988. But the Germans again had no idea what he had done there or whom he might have met. Mehdi-Nezhad had visited Libya in early 1988. If he had met with Dalqamuni a few months later, it would have provided further evidence that the Pan Am bombing resulted from a broad conspiracy by Iran, Libya, and the General Command. No one could dismiss the possibility, although the Germans seemed to come close.

In truth, the German investigation was a joke almost from the start. In one instance, the Germans failed to disarm one of Dalqamuni's bombs, and it exploded in a German lockup, killing a forensic scientist. The released Dalqamuni cell members were madly traveling around Germany just before Pan Am 103 blew up, yet the Germans couldn't determine what they were doing. Nor were they able to track down another Dalqamuni bomb to see if its timer matched the mechanism that had been found on the ground in Scotland.

The German investigation was further complicated by the fact that its government was secretly courting Iran. In 1979, when the Shah fell and the U.S. was booted out, Iran became a tempting prize for the Europeans. The Germans particularly wanted a reliable source of oil, which many other European countries already had. They also looked upon Iran as a promising market for the Mercedes and other exports. To help woo Iran, Germany started training its intelligence service, the Ministry of Intelligence and Security. The relationship quickly evolved into a full-fledged liaison, with the Germans even providing surveillance training to the Iranians.

The French were no different. The way they looked at it, they had their interests and we had ours. And there was no way France was going to carry America's water, and the French were increasingly focusing intelligence resources on North Africa. In 1991 a military government in Algeria deposed a democratically elected Islamic government, kicking off a nasty civil war. France was concerned that civil war there would spill over into France's large immigrant Algerian population.

BUT ALL THE BLAME couldn't be put on the Europeans. The fact was, the CIA was in the process of closing up shop overseas. It was clear to me that we were disposing of agents faster than we were recruiting them. Bonn didn't have a single Middle Eastern agent to run down leads—neither an Arab nor an Iranian. For that matter, it didn't have a single Muslim agent in all of Germany's enormous Islamic community, a failing that would become painfully obvious in the wake of the World Trade Center and Pentagon attacks when trail after trail began to trace back across the ocean to Hamburg and elsewhere. In the case of Pan Am 103, Bonn didn't have a single source at the Frankfurt airport to say whether anything suspicious had occurred before 103's feeder flight departed. The CIA couldn't even obtain airline manifests on its own: It had to rely on the Germans.

This, mind you, was at the absolute crossroads of European air traffic.

Almost as bad as the absence of new agents was the superannuation of old ones. The agents already on our books had lost their access, and no one seemed to care. It was like a permanent work slowdown sanctioned by Washington. And if Washington didn't care, why should the case officers care? Trying to recruit an agent was likely to get you evicted from your cushy post where the government paid the rent and utilities, and sent back to Washington, where no one could afford the skyrocketing property prices on a CIA salary. And what was the thinking in D.C.? I would have to wait to be reassigned there to find out, but the anecdotal evidence was not cheering.

In early 1989 I took over an agent from a young woman I'll call Becky. Deciding she wasn't suited for the spy business, Becky had resigned and was heading back to San Francisco, where she had been hired. The turnover meeting was held in a motel outside Paris, in one of those hideous bastard Bauhaus concrete-and-glass suburbs. The motel room carpet smelled of puke and cheap wine. Becky ordered a pot of coffee and tea from room service, and we waited for "Jacques" to make an appearance.

An arms dealer by trade, Jacques had been an outstanding agent, but his production had fallen off sharply in recent months. As he pushed his way into the hotel room, I could see that he had once been athletic, but he'd let his body go to seed. His belly hung out of his shirt, which was missing a couple of buttons. Jacques mumbled something about taking a girl to the hospital for a postabortion checkup. Becky ignored him.

Jacques looked at the coffee and then at Becky. "I need a goddamn drink. Do you think there's a bottle of cognac to be found in this filthy bordello?"

After Jacques got his cognac, we settled down and began sorting through a packet of documents he had brought with him. It was good stuff. Nothing about Jacques's deals, but he'd managed to filch information about his competitors' business. One Swiss-British merchant of death living in Zug was selling boatloads of Iglas, advanced Soviet surface-to-air missiles, to Iran. Jacques had the prices, letters of credit, end users' certificates—everything. I couldn't figure out why Becky hadn't reported information like this in the past, but I didn't say anything. Technically, Jacques was still Becky's agent. He'd be mine from the next meeting on.

When it was time for Jacques to leave, Becky coldly shook his hand, then rolled her eyes once he was out the door. It wasn't your normal farewell between a case officer and an agent. Usually a turnover meeting is a bit more tearful.

I'd arranged to have the following meeting in a small town away from Paris. My plan was to take the train to Geneva, rent a car, and drive back into France through one of the dozen small border crossings used by French money launderers. Jacques and I met in the town's only first-class restaurant, in one of those small curtained rooms off the main dining room that the French use to entertain their mistresses. I don't know what the maître d' made of

Jacques and me, but I didn't want the nosy Direction de la surveillance du territoire (DST), the French version of the FBI, tripping over our meeting.

We started with Kir royales and quickly moved to a white Burgundy from a *terroir* I knew. By the second bottle, Jacques had decided I was okay.

"Do you believe in God?" he asked.

He was serious. My first thought was that he had some fatal illness and was looking for solace.

"Er, no, not exactly."

"That's good." He smiled. "That's very good."

"That was a strange question, Jacques. It's the first time an agent ever asked me that one."

"Tell me it's strange. Do you know what Becky has been doing the last year?"

He was reassured when I said no.

"She has been trying to convert me, lead me back to Christianity to join her church. That's all she talked about for a whole year. She refused to talk about business—all the documents I brought her."

As soon as I got back, I told the story to Chuck Cogan, the Paris chief. Chuck was old CIA—prep school, Harvard, polo, native French. He spent his free time riding in the Bois de Bologne with his French aristocratic friends. He winced as I went on and then confessed that he had no idea what to do with a proselytizing case officer.

Three or four other people in the Paris office had converted to Becky's New Age church. One was an administrative officer who now spent his days handing out church leaflets in Montparnasse. Chuck informally checked with headquarters only to be told that he couldn't do anything that might violate anyone's First Amendment rights. If case officers wanted to pump for God on the CIA's time, so be it.

WEIRD AS IT MIGHT SOUND, the Jacques and Becky story was symptomatic of where the CIA was heading. When we weren't choking on political correctness, we were hamstrung by our own new laissez-faire, anything-goes attitude.

In Paris, we once came across fragmentary evidence of a secret Iranian intelligence station located off the Avenue de la Grande Armée. I proposed going after it, but Paris's young case officers, many of whom had never run a serious operation, just laughed. There was no conclusive proof the station really existed, they said; hence, we shouldn't bother. I was stunned. Two years earlier, Iranian operatives had been setting off bombs all over Paris and killing our diplomats and agents. It was worth the candle.

Undeterred (okay, pissed off), I found a French government telephone technician who agreed to install a tap on the suspected Iranian station's telephone. A couple months of eavesdropping, I figured, and we could tell whether we needed a full-court press. The PTT tech failed his polygraph, but who cared, I argued. If it turned out the tech was working for the French, we would simply say that since they hadn't been doing their job policing Iranian terrorists, we had to do it on our own. The European Division was aghast. I was ordered to jettison the PTT tech immediately and forget the clandestine Iranian station.

Another, better opportunity soon came along. In November 1990, we discovered that France was secretly hosting three Abu Nidal students in Besançon. The French government paid for everything—tuition, food, lodging, apparently on the theory that it was better to have Abu Nidal inside the tent pissing out than the other way around. When I proposed going after them, or at the very least tapping their telephone, I was looked at as if I were deranged. "State will never let it happen" was the response.

To be sure, Paris went through the motions of spying, but it was only for appearances' sake. Case officers met their agents and wrote reports, but the information was poorly sourced, irrelevant, and often already public. A few case officers trolled receptions, but the only thing they really wanted to do was meet official contacts. No one was going to throw you out of a country for cooperating with a friendly government, and you were home by dinner.

Paris case officers spent most of their time fighting over housing, attending training seminars and rambling meetings in the secure "bubble," writing long-term perspectives, and whatever else occupies a government bureaucracy in midage. On Saturday morning most everyone in Paris drove up to the U.S. base in Mons, Belgium, to shop at the PX.

And then there was the language problem. The older officers spoke good French; the younger ones didn't. French agents, like their countrymen, hate slowing down for someone who can't bother to learn the language properly. French snobbery was another barrier: Hush Puppies, Brooks Brothers trench coats, and neon fanny packs offended the host sensibilities. Paris's case officers were frozen out of French society. All they could do at night was watch videos.

Something else I noticed: As the DO went into decline, satellites, not agents, became the touchstone of truth in Washington. Few things are more satisfying for a policymaker than to hold in his hand a clean, glossy black-and-white satellite photo, examine it with his very own 3D viewer, and decide for himself what it means. Not only could he do without analysts, he could do without agents, too. And thank goodness. Agents were messy. They sometimes got things wrong, even occasionally lied. And they definitely had the potential to cause ugly diplomatic incidents.

As a fatal malaise settled over the CIA, case officers began resigning in droves, and some of the best left first. In Paris—beautiful, bewitching Paris—the attrition rate was running about 30 percent. Convinced by all the outward signs that spying was no longer a serious profession for serious people, they went home to find a job in investment banking or any other profession America took seriously.

If I had stayed in Paris much longer, I would have ended up resignmg, too. I needed to go someplace the CIA still operated like it used to.

13

OCTOBER 24, 1992. DUSHANBE, TAJIKISTAN.

I STUCK THE HANDSET of the STU-III, a secure telephone, out the window of what passed for a CIA ███████ so the headquarters duty officer could hear the battle going on outside.

"Listen to it," I hollered just as a tank in the street behind the Oktoberskaya Hotel fired a round from its main gun. A long burp from a heavy machine gun and a couple of explosions followed in quick succession. Only a stone's throw away from the hotel, Dushanbe's main mosque kept belting out the same Koranic sura over its PA system. Every once in a while someone would break in and scream, "La Allah illa Allah"—there is no God but God.

I had been up for most of the last forty-eight hours, and fatigue was setting in. It didn't help that I'd been on the road the entire week before, including five days waiting in Kiev for a flight to Dushanbe that didn't exist. Every morning I went to the airport expecting to board the Dushanbe plane, which was advertised to leave on time. Every day the plane never left. Finally, on the fifth morning the airport manager took pity on me, pulled me aside, and spilled the state secret that the Kiev to Dushanbe flight had stopped flying six months before. "No airplanes, no gas," he said, shaking his head sadly. I made a mental note to tell the clowns back in the travel section to stop booking people on the Kiev to Dushanbe flight. I wasn't even going to think about why Aeroflot let me check in every day but I was starting to get an inkling why the Soviet Union had collapsed.

Without a Russian visa, I was forced to backtrack to Frankfurt, where I slept a few hours in a chair at the Rhein-Main Air Base, then rode into Dushanbe on top of a cargo palette in the back of a freezing U.S. Air Force C-141 Starlifter. The pilot came in low, below the twenty-five-thousand-foot peaks that cover nearly all of Tajikistan—the same mountains that so awed Alexander the Great that he turned south and marched east through Afghanistan rather than try to cross them.

There followed two long nights drinking vodka with a couple of Tajiks. My second day on the ground, I caught a bad cold. The only thing that could have awakened me at 6:09 on the morning of the third day did—the throaty growl of a ZSU-23 antiaircraft gun firing outside my window. At first I couldn't remember where I was, but when you think you're taking incoming fire, it doesn't really matter. My inclination was to take cover in the bathtub, except there wasn't one. Someone seemed to have stolen it, maybe while I slept. Only then did I fully remember where I was—Tajikistan: the remotest, poorest, most isolated republic in the former Soviet Union. The edge of the crumbling periphery.

Lying in bed as I listened to the gunfire, I wondered what exactly I'd gotten myself into this time. After Paris, I had been assigned to Rabat, Morocco, for a three-year tour. With its big houses, mild climate, clay tennis courts, and emerald-green golf courses, Rabat was a plum post. There was even skiing in the Atlas Mountains outside of Marrakech. I'd had a good job, too—deputy chief of ███████, the management track. Three years in Rabat, and I could take full command of a midsize ██████████ the next time around.

The fact is, though, that I was bored. The war in the western Sahara was over. Worse, everything important in Morocco went on inside the royal family and the only figure of any significance inside that closed circle was King Hassan II, a man who kept his own counsel. When Hassan II wanted access in Washington, he went through a K Street lobbyist, not the CIA. Essentially, we didn't know what was going on in Morocco until we read it in the newspapers.

That left the Soviet target, but in early 1992, Uncle Milty, my old Khartoum boss and now chief of the Central-Eurasian Division, informed Rabat that Russia would henceforth be treated like Germany, France, Italy, or any other friendly country. The cold war was over. Period. As for our old nemesis the KGB, we could just take it off our target list. If the KGB rezident in Rabat were to walk in and volunteer to tell us everything he knew, we weren't authorized to give him even a nickel to catch a bus back to his embassy. None of this squared, of course, with the subsequent arrest of dozens of Russian spies, from Rick Ames to

Robert Hannsen. To give another example, it meant the CIA had to turn away Vasili Mitrokhin, a KGB archivist who then volunteered to British intelligence and provided information that led to the identification of dozens of spies, including a U.S. colonel. You figure the logic in that.

The bottom line: If Rabat were to turn out the lights and close up, it would be a long time before anyone noticed. I wanted back in the action, and Tajikistan seemed to be the ticket. It was a country in the throes of an Islamic revolution, and it looked as if Islamic fundamentalism might spread from there to the rest of Central Asia and the Caspian Sea, maybe even up into Russia. Stingers and heroin were coming north across the border from Afghanistan, and all sorts of sophisticated weapons were going back the other way, mainly to Iran. The place seemed to offer everything: terrorism, drugs, and nuclear-weapons, the three demons the CIA could still use to justify its budget. Besides, my other career choices—a résumé-building desk job back in Langley or maybe, if I could dress myself up well enough, a staff position with one of the congressional intelligence committees—were seeming less and less like any me I wanted to be. If Tajikistan couldn't hold my interest, I figured, no country could. When I went back to Washington to volunteer, I was all but handcuffed to make sure I wouldn't get away. The ranks of adventurers in the CIA were thinning fast.

There was something to take care of first, though. I've been tightlipped, I realize, about personal matters. The CIA doesn't encourage a lot of openness where family is concerned, and I've had plenty of reason not to advertise the fine details of my life. Suffice it to say that I got married while working in a Middle East capital I'm not allowed to mention I ever lived in, to a woman I'm now divorced from. In the balmy days of our marriage, though, my wife and I brought three children into the world. When I was working in Beirut, my family lived at first in Cyprus but moved to Belgium when a couple of Libyan thugs started following me. This time around, I wanted to make sure they had a more permanent address, so before I started out for Dushanbe, my wife and I bought a postage-stamp-size vineyard on Burgundy's Côte d'Or in France. On it was a charming, dilapidated farmhouse that sat on the side of the hill, in the middle of the vines, with a sweeping view of the Saône Valley. The property caught my eye as I was driving back from an agent meeting. I didn't even know it was for sale until I saw it advertised in the next village. The same afternoon I called my lawyer in Paris to make the owner an offer. I figured it would be the perfect rear base to stash my family while I was on the frontier, serving in the armies of civilization.

THE HEADQUARTERS duty officer back in Washington whistled in appreciation as he listened to the fighting going on around us. When I got back on the telephone, I told him State was bringing in an evacuation flight to take everyone out, including the CIA. Problem was, I still had to call McDill Air Force Base to ask for the C-141.

"Dushanbe? Never heard of it," the duty officer at McDill said. "Is this some kind of joke?"

I read off Dushanbe's eight-digit coordinates from an air chart. When he found Dushanbe, he laughed. "You assholes really are out in the middle of nowhere."

"About our plane?"

"When the money's in the bank, you'll get your plane," he said as he hung up.

The standing agreement between State and the air force was that an evacuation plane was paid for in advance. The air force must have been stiffed in the past.

Assuming his masters would pony up, Stan Escudero, the ambassador—who by then had a pistol strapped to his side—deputized me to round up the Americans and bring them to the embassy. It wasn't going to be easy. The fighting hadn't let up; worse, we didn't know where all the Americans were. By the end of the day, though, we had managed to let most of them know they were to assemble the following morning at the Tajikistan Hotel. Luggage would be limited to one carry-on bag each.

To transport everyone to the airport, the ambassador borrowed three BTR-80 armored personnel carriers and their crews from the 201st Motorized Rifle Division, a Russian regular army unit that stayed on after Tajikistan got its independence in 1991. Lowering myself into the hatch of the first BTR, I couldn't help but chuckle. Ten years before, I would have paid an agent a lot of money for the plans to one of those things. Now I had one of my own.

The BTR driver didn't pay much attention to the rules of the road. He drove down sidewalks, rammed a couple of cars, and knocked down at least two iron fences before driving right up the stairs in front of the Tajikistan Hotel. I must have been a sight, nursing a hangover and disheveled, as I stood talking on a Motorola radio in the BTR's turret like I was Rommel in the Libyan Desert.

The Americans and about fifty other foreigners were waiting in the Tajikistan Hotel's dark, dreary lobby.

"I'm from the U.S. government, and I'm here to help you," I started. I admit it wasn't very funny but it was the best I could do at the moment. There wasn't a smile in the whole lot.

"I've got good news. A plane is on its way here to evacuate us. You're all welcome to leave on it, including citizens of the European Community."

Before I could finish, they started arguing with one another whether to stick it out or leave.

"Listen up," I interrupted. "I also have some bad news. Before we let you on the plane, you will have to agree to reimburse the U.S. government up to $10,000 to defray the cost of the airplane." In fact, it was State regulation that civilians had to pay for a seat on an evacuation flight. In practice, though, State rarely billed anyone, as I tried to reassure them.

Several Iranian diplomats in the crowd seemed to miss this last nuance. They eagerly took notes and kept asking me for my name. I finally threw them a scrap. "Mr. Bob," I said. That night Tehran Radio broke in with a news flash that a Mr. Bob was selling tickets to poor, stranded refugees in Tajikistan, making an obscene profit. My image in the press wouldn't improve in the years ahead.

We spent the rest of the day closing up. I'd received permission to go into a "phase three burnout," which meant everything was destroyed, from documents to the computer hard drives.

Right before destroying our crypto, I called the CIA's operations center to let it know we were going off the air. "This is Dushanbe. We're going tactical," I said, trying to make a joke of it. The young lady with the honey voice on the other end of the line didn't get it. Like the guy at McDill, she probably didn't know where Dushanbe was. Just then there was a crescendo of tank fire down the street. It sounded like the siege of Stalingrad. And then, right on cue, Jim Morrison's voice filled the air. We'd been playing and replaying our five office CDs all morning to drown out the mosque. Now Morrison seemed to be telling Dushanbe's story: *This is the end, my only friend, the end.* The woman at the operations center at least knew who Jim Morrison was. I heard later she sent a recording of our conversation to Tom Twetten, the director of operations.

WE MADE IT OUT SAFELY, the ex-communists recaptured Dushanbe back from the fundamentalists, and we were able to open again for business in January 1993.

I reclaimed our rooms on the third floor of the Oktoberskaya Hotel, but in our absence the Russian embassy had opened down the hall from us. We had to pass through its hallway to get in and out, which meant that the CIA's office in Dushanbe was located inside the Russian embassy. I bet Uncle Milty never imagined that when he decided Russia was a friendly country, but it worked out fine. I got along with the Russians, including the KGB rezident, who would come down to our offices late at night and pound on the door looking for a bottle of Scotch.

Truth is, the only real game in town was the Russians. The 201st Division was the thin khaki line holding back a wave of Islamic fundamentalism that threatened to sweep across the southern tier of the former Soviet Union. We were reminded of it every few weeks. Each time the fundamentalists tried to mount an attack on Dushanbe, you could hear the tanks at the 201st's cantonment start up their engines and head out into the mountains, the clattering of their treads echoing all over Dushanbe. From time to time you could see Russian bombers from Mery, Turkmenistan, pass over Dushanbe on their way to attack rebel positions in the mountains.

To me, it was clear that we needed a Russian source to tell us what the Russians were doing. Washington, for example, would need to know in a hurry if the Russians suddenly decided to pull back and leave Tajikistan to Islam. The Russians, though, had apparently never received Uncle Milty's ukase that we were all friends. There was nothing they could do about the CIA office located in their embassy—we'd paid our rent a year in advance—but Russians were required to report all contact with

Americans, especially with me, the CIA chief. And one report usually meant the end of the contact.

To find a way inside the friendly enemy camp, I took up skiing again. Russians love mountains just like Indian military officers love hunting. The conditions were primitive, a single rope tow. If you wanted a long run, you climbed a glacier. But I quickly became friends with several Russian skiers, and soon we were heading off almost every weekend to a pass with year-round snow.

It wasn't long before the ploy paid off. In March I met Colonel Yuri Abramov, a Russian paratrooper assigned to Tajik paratroopers. Yuri was a world-famous jumper, holder of something like forty-nine international records. One night he invited me over to his apartment in Dushanbe. Out came the vodka, and the last thing I remember before taking a nap on Yuri's couch was a toast to our mothers.

Early the next morning Yuri shook me awake: "We're going now." I didn't bother to ask where. It was still dark. An hour in a lumbering UAZ, a Russian military jeep, and we arrived at a military base in the mountains south of Dushanbe, about a five-minute flight from the Afghan border. In the middle of the sloped grass field was an ancient AN-2 biplane. Without saying a word, Yuri jumped out of the jeep, grabbed a parachute lying on the ground, and handed it to me. "Here, put it on." It was only then I remembered telling Yuri the night before that I had once parachuted.

A dozen Tajik and Russian paratroopers were already sitting on the floor of the AN-2. Judging from their AKS74Us (a short AK-47 with a grenade launcher under the barrel) and the ammunition magazines and grenades strapped all over their bodies, we were going on a combat jump. Into which war was the question. I also wondered about the parachute strapped to my back. Did it have toggles, or would I have to steer by pulling on the risers? Thanks to my big mouth, I would have a chance to find out, on the way down.

The plane took off and headed toward the Afghan border. But before we got there, we started to ascend in circles. As I waited for my inevitable turn in the door, I had to ask myself once again what I was doing. I didn't like small airplanes, parachute jumping, or even vodka, which I'd swilled most of the night before. I was forty years old, too old to be jumping with Russian special forces. And the reason I was doing it? It was the only way to get close to the Russian military. I was just doing my job, or at least the job I conceived I should be doing.

When we reached two thousand feet or so, Yuri emerged from the cockpit and motioned for me to hook up to the static line. The paratroopers were smirking at me like drunken apes, knowing what was in store as Yuri led me to the open door. The view wasn't reassuring. The clouds and rain were too thick to see the ground, and a heavy wind buffeted the AN-2, making it creak like an old wooden bed. For all I knew, we'd been blown off course and were actually over Kabul. Red, my jump instructor at the Farm, never would have let us jump into a storm like that.

"What about the wind dummy?" I yelled into

Yuri's ear. If we were going to jump, I at least wanted something nonhuman to go out the door first to show us which way the storm was blowing so I could steer my chute into it.

He either didn't understand or purposely ignored me.

"You're first," he shouted. He then added, as if it sealed the matter, "You're our guest."

As I plummeted through a cloud, I realized why Yuri didn't need a wind dummy. I was it.

TWO THINGS ENSUED from my little jump. First, headquarters sent a message to all the offices in the former Soviet Union, stating there would be no more leaping out of Russian military airplanes. Fine, I remember thinking, because there was no way I was ever going to get back in that damn sardine can again. Then, about a week after the jump, there was a knock at my door. I opened to find a Russian in Levi's and a plaid shirt. "My colonel would like to see you," he said, sounding like Boris Karloff. Without waiting for my answer, a Russian colonel in combat fatigues came out of the shadows and walked into our office. *Pretty gutsy,* I thought, *an officer showing up at my door right under the nose of the KGB rezident.*

The colonel had the self-possession of a cavalry officer. Probably because he was. One of the youngest full colonels in the Russian army, Grigor, as I'll call him, commanded an elite armor regiment. His father had been a very senior official in the Soviet Union. With nomenklatura credentials like that, it was no wonder he could just waltz through the Russian embassy as if he owned it. He probably could have had the rezident shipped off to the gulag if he'd wanted.

"Are you the American military attaché?" Grigor asked.

For a Russian buzzard colonel, I would be anything he wanted me to be. "Yes, I fill in for that position."

"Good," he said. With his blond hair, thick neck, and blue eyes, the colonel looked more German than Russian. He had a German directness about him, too. "Tomorrow there will be a car to pick you up at nine." He did an about-face and walked out, his aide following in his wake.

The next day things started out calmly enough. The driver dropped me off at the main Russian military range, about forty miles from Dushanbe. The colonel, his wife, and a dozen other Russian officers and their wives were already there. I was the first American most of them had ever met. I broke the ice by pitching in to pick mushrooms. While the women cooked them over an open fire, the officers and I drank vodka. We made at least four toasts to the hero of the Gulf War, General Norman Schwarzkopf.

Just when everyone was starting to feel good, two of the Russians brought out their miniature silenced assassination weapons. One looked like a derringer pistol; the other was disguised as a pen.

"This is how we deal with the Vahabis," a captain said, holding his pen up in the air.

Vahabis—or Wahabis as we call them—refers to

Saudi fundamentalists. It's a word derived from the eighteenth-century Saudi Islamic reformer Muhammad Ibn 'Abd Al-Wahab, the man responsible for Saudi Arabia's strict interpretation of Islam. I'd heard the rumor that the Russians were assassinating fundamentalists in Tajikistan. Suddenly, I suspected it was true.

The captain unscrewed the top of the pen and extracted a 7.62 subsonic bullet. It looked just like a standard AK round, but the captain noted that it was made of soft lead, which would explode on impact. "It's the perfect assassination round," he said. When he reloaded the pen and fired it into a small pond, the only sound was a splash. It was much quieter than any CIA suppressed weapon I'd ever heard.

More vodka followed. Just as everything was starting to get a bit hazy it was time to move to the next activity—the range. While the wives stayed behind, we piled into a couple of jeeps and drove half a mile to a pop-up range with about a dozen metal silhouettes. We got to pick our weapons from the back of a truck, anything from AK-47s to belt-fed .30-caliber machine guns to RPGs. There was even a 40mm chain gun.

Fortunately, no one picked the chain gun. The experience was hair-raising enough as it was. Every once in a while someone would accidentally hit one of the silhouettes, knocking it down, but since the control box used to raise it back up wasn't working, one of the revelers would have to walk downrange to right the silhouettes—and no one, except me, stopped firing.

GRIGOR DECIDED I'd acquitted myself well enough and invited me the following week to take one of his T-72s out for a test drive.

I'd never driven a tank in my life, let alone a Russian tank. The driver's compartment was a nice fit for someone about four foot two. Hunched over, I could barely see through the Plexiglas aperture, but I wasn't going to say no. I started off by driving it right through a mud hole about ten feet deep. Once I got my sea legs, I joined the other tanks as they raced around a valley, stopping occasionally to fire at cardboard targets in the shape of tanks. Grigor was so proud of me, he made me an honorary member of his regiment.

Headquarters took notice of my efforts with another message to all offices in the former Soviet Union: No more driving Russian tanks. I was sorry about that. Unlike the AN-2 biplane, I'd become attached to the T-72. But I was also earning Grigor's trust, enough so that he decided to show me the dark side of Russia.

GRIGOR HAD TOLD ME only that he wanted to show me something that would interest my country. Shortly after eleven at night, we headed off to the airport, taking backstreets to avoid patrols and checkpoints. Grigor entered the airport through the military side. The Mi-8 and Mi-24 Hind helicopters and transport planes were just shadows in the dark. We stopped about a hundred feet from an IL-76 cargo plane and sat without saying a word.

After about an hour the IL-76's cockpit lights came on. A soldier standing by the plane flicked on a flashlight and waved it in slow circles. A little while later an Mi-8 helicopter put down next to the IL-76, leaving its rotors turning. Someone started throwing heavy burlap bags out onto the tarmac. A half-dozen soldiers picked them up and threw them through the IL-76's cargo door. It was all over in ten minutes. The Mi-8 flew back in the direction of Afghanistan. The IL-76 started up its engines, taxied out onto the runway and took off.

"Heroin," Grigor said. "The weekly shipment."

On the way back he told me the story. The Tajik interior minister, Yaqub Salimov, and a few Russian generals were smuggling tons of raw opium from Afghanistan to Moscow on Russian military airplanes. After secret labs around Moscow processed the opium into heroin, it was smuggled into Sweden by boat and from there all over the world, including the United States.

I told the story to our ambassador. An old-school Foreign Service officer, Escudero believed in the mission more than his career. He agreed to go with me and make a call on Salimov.

Salimov was a thug. He had started out life as a boxing instructor at Dushanbe's agricultural college. On the side, he temped as an enforcer for a local criminal group. One time he put too much muscle into his work and ended up doing seven years for manslaughter. He never cut his ties to the ex-communists, though, and when they came back to power in Tajikistan in 1992, he was a natural choice to keep the peace.

"Let me do the talking," I whispered to Escudero as we walked up the two flights of stairs to Salimov's office.

Mustering all the authority I could, I explained to Salimov that the U.S. government could no longer tolerate Tajikistan's involvement in the heroin trade. I went on for about ten minutes. Salimov maintained a stony silence, all the while twirling a pen between his fingers, which were roughly the size of bananas. Sometimes he would put the pen down to crack his knuckles. It was as if he were limbering up for a big fight. Escudero never said a word until we were outside, and then only winked at me in appreciation.

Two weeks later, Salimov sent me his response. I was sitting in the office with Stephan Bentura, an Agence France Presse correspondent based in Moscow, when we heard a thunderous boom. In Dushanbe, a bomb in the middle of the night wasn't something to write home about, and this one had gone off about a mile away. No sweat; we kept talking. A couple minutes later, the embassy administrator burst through the door. "They blew up your house."

I'd just rented the place a month before, in a quiet residential neighborhood. I intended to use it as a place to meet my contacts, out of range of the KGB rezident.

Driving up, you could see the house was pitted from shrapnel. A deep crater had magically appeared in the front lawn. The night watchman, who was sitting in the living room at the time, said he saw two police cars drive up and a person leaning out. The next thing he remembered, a satchel charge was sailing at the front window. Fortunately for the watchman, the bars on the window stopped it, and he suffered only a concussion. I noticed the telephone wires to the house were cut.

When I told Grigor what had happened, he clucked his tongue in disapproval. It was time to raise the stakes: He offered me a T-72 to flatten Salimov's house.

As if I needed further proof of Mother Russia's capacity for corruption, Grigor introduced me to the aide of the Russian ground-forces commander during one of his visits to Dushanbe. As soon as we sat down to a dinner party in the officers' mess, the aide remarked without the least warm-up that he'd heard the CIA had a C-130 coming in once a month. I acknowledged it was true. "Then why don't we do some business," he said. "I'll fill it up with cigarettes and sell them to the army here, and we split the profits fifty-fifty." Even after all I'd seen in Dushanbe, I was astonished. I'd just met the man, and he was proposing I join him in some Russian mafia deal. I'm sure if I'd asked him, he would have sold me a stolen nuclear warhead.

GRIGOR SOON OPENED UP a new subject, one Washington hated hearing about: Russian nationalism.

Grigor liked to describe himself as an enlightened

Russian nationalist, but in fact he was just a Russian nationalist. He'd made up his mind that Russia badly needed a revolution, as profound as the October Revolution, to cleanse it of the corrupt politicians and drug-dealing generals.

One night I came over to his house with a crate of good German beer. Grigor liked his vodka, but the beer was a special treat. Halfway through the crate, Grigor let his guard down and talked about Boris Yeltsin's 1993 assault on the Moscow White House and how close it came to destroying the Russian army. When the elite Tamanskaya Division received the orders to assault the White House, the enlisted crews, to a man, refused to get in their tanks. Simply put, they mutinied. As a result, every tank that participated in the assault was officer-crewed, but that wasn't the end of it. Afterward the officers who had participated in the assault were all but drummed out of the army. Ostracized and passed over for promotion, many resigned in humiliation. "Yeltsin tore the army apart," Grigor told me. "He will never be able to count on it again."

I visited him at home again a week later. Grigor was in a particularly somber mood. Before I could sit down, he said, "Let's go for a drive." His UAZ was waiting in front of the apartment building, but he sent his driver away and drove himself.

We drove aimlessly for a while before he said anything. "What would Washington think if some honest Russian officers put an end to the farce in Moscow—get rid of Yeltsin?"

I looked at Grigor. He was serious.

Grigor didn't say anything for a full minute. "Look, Mr. Bob, I and a few officers have been talking. We're all serving on the borders of the former Soviet Union, places that those bastards in Moscow won't even visit. They don't give a shit that if it weren't for us, Russia would collapse. All they care about is stealing everything they can put their hands on to go live in southern France. You wouldn't believe it. Ammunition crates arrive empty—every last round stolen. I can't get radios for my tanks. The bastards are stealing them and selling them to Moscow taxi companies. Our kitchen gardens are the only thing that keep us from starving. It's the worst sort of treason."

"Grigor, who do you mean by 'us' ?" I asked.

"Oh, there are hundreds of officers who think like me. We're all on the frontier. Maybe ten percent of the military, but we're the fighters."

"Do you have a leader?"

"Alexander Lebed is the only one who can pull this off, but we're not talking to him yet. It's too early."

General Lebed, then the commander of the 14th Army in Moldava, was Russia's most popular general. Soldiers were deserting from all over the former Soviet Union to join Lebed's force, which was fully staffed. The rest of the army, meanwhile, was running about two thirds below full manpower.

"Isn't there someone else?"

"There's a general at the Staff College who knows us all—General ███████. But Mr. Bob, you ask too many questions. Let me ask you one. What would the United States do if we made a coup against Yeltsin?"

Grigor wasn't looking for a green light, but when I reported what he had told me, headquarters burned up the return lines with a message for Grigor: No coup; Washington fully backs the democratically elected government in Moscow. I'd already anticipated that response. I was just happy that headquarters let me keep meeting Grigor.

I did try to do a favor for him, though. I have no idea where he found them, but at one meeting he produced several brochures for Motorola communications equipment. He asked if I could help him procure a system for his regiment. The response from headquarters was unusually terse: "Inappropriate."

IT WAS A LITTLE AFTER NINE on August 9, 1993, and someone was pounding on our office door. It was Grigor.

"Have you heard the news?" he asked me, out of breath.

I'd been out all morning with the communicator. We still hadn't taken traffic.

"Your man in Tbilisi. He was assassinated."

███████████. Fred Woodruff was ███████████ ███████. He was temporarily assigned to the embassy in the Georgia capital of the former Soviet republic. Woodruff had been shot and killed the evening before.

"I know who did it," Grigor said. "Those bastards in Moscow."

Grigor, in fact, knew nothing about Woodruff's killing, but if his suspicions were paranoid, they weren't necessarily wrong. Fred Woodruff had been shot outside of Tbilisi while riding in the backseat of a Niva jeep driven by Eldar Gogoladze, the head of the bodyguard detail for Georgian president Eduard Shevardnadze. There were two female passengers in the car.

Beyond that, things got murkier. The Georgians arrested a soldier and charged him with the shooting. According to the Georgian police, the soldier, drunk at the time, had fired one round from his rifle in an attempt to flag down the Niva for gasoline. The Georgians, however, refused American investigators access to the soldier—at least not until he was on his deathbed several years later, by which time he had recanted his confession.

Other inconsistencies in the Georgian story went unexplained. A militia checkpoint, only a hundred yards from where Woodruff supposedly was shot, heard and saw nothing. Gogoladze said he passed the checkpoint after the shooting but didn't stop. He couldn't explain why or why he hadn't at least alerted the militiamen about the shooting. Nor did Gogoladze seem to be in any hurry: It took him more than two hours to get to the hospital, normally a twenty-minute drive. Gogoladze explained that he had gotten lost but couldn't remember where. This was a man who'd spent his life in Tbilisi.

Not only did Gogoladze's Niva disappear during those crucial two hours, it stayed gone for more than thirty-six hours after Gogoladze delivered Woodruff to the hospital, and when it did reappear, it had obviously been cleaned up. The embassy security officer found a dent in the Niva's ceiling, right above the driver's seat, where the bullet hit after it exited Woodruff's head. Clearly, the bullet had not left the car, but it was nowhere to be found inside and thus couldn't be matched to the confessed shooter's AK-47. There was also no sign of how the bullet entered the car. The rear window was intact, and there was no hole in the metal skin. When the security officer pointed this out to the Georgians, they went away. The next day they came back and announced that they had discovered a small puncture in the seal that held in the rear window's glass. Indeed there was one, but the embassy security officer was almost certain it hadn't been there when he first checked the car.

There were other odd details that didn't add up. Based on the autopsy, Woodruff had been shot with a dumdum bullet—an assassination bullet like the Russian officers showed me that day at the range— yet the shooter had no reasonable explanation why he had loaded his AK-47 with hard-to-come-by assassination rounds.

The FBI spent days going over the gunman's supposed position but couldn't find the spent shell casing until the Georgian investigators showed up. One of them grabbed an AK, positioned himself where he believed the gunman had stood, and fired a round in the air. He then followed the trajectory of the spent casing into some bushes. There he found not only the casing from the bullet he'd just fired but a second one as well. "Here is the casing," he said triumphantly. The FBI agents were incredulous.

Another part of the mystery was that the Russian

mole Rick Ames had met Woodruff in Tbilisi shortly before the murder. According to eyewitnesses, they got into an ugly argument, but no one ever found out exactly why. Did Woodruff accuse Ames of being a mole? And what had been in Woodruff's camera? The female passenger in the front seat said that when Woodruff was shot, she turned around to see the woman in the back opening up the camera to take out the film, but the trail went stone cold from there. None of these anomalies proved a conspiracy, but I found it curious that no one was interested in running them down.

Long after the investigation came to a standstill, rumors and leads surfaced that complicated the Woodruff case still more. The most intriguing came when a Russian military intelligence officer was arrested in a neighboring country carrying a flash suppressor for an assassination rifle. Under interrogation, the Russian claimed he was a member of the team that had assassinated Woodruff. He was released and disappeared before his story could be confirmed, but that wasn't the only potential link. Although she denied any connection to the murder, one of the female passengers in the Niva was married to a Russian military intelligence officer. Again, no one followed these leads.

Woodruff's murder was like Pan Am. Part of the problem was that there was no solid proof of a bigger conspiracy. The larger part by far, though, was that Washington didn't have the stomach for a thorough investigation. Even after it was determined that Russian intelligence had fired a rocket-propelled grenade into the side of our embassy in Moscow on September 13, 1995, the Clinton administration wasn't interested in confronting Russia or even acknowledging that Russian nationalism was a problem. Incidentally, the FBI agent who hypothesized the Russians were behind Woodruff's murder was quietly reassigned to a bank-robbery squad in Atlanta.

GRIGOR'S TUTORIALS were convincing me that the lash-up replacing the Soviet Union wasn't going to work. Now he wanted me to take a deeper look by making a trip to the Pamirs. Although a few embassy officers had visited Khorog—the Pamirs' capital—by helicopter, no American official had ever driven through them. "If you want to see what will become of Russia one day, drive along Tajikistan's border," Grigor told me. "It's the best preview of hell you'll ever have."

I could only imagine. The Pamirs, which covered about three quarters of Tajikistan, were maybe the most lawless land in the world, ruled by a patchwork of Islamic guerrillas, warlords, bandits, smugglers, and Russian deserters. The only way to make a living in the Pamirs was by trading in weapons and narcotics. Not surprisingly, the ever opportunistic Iranian Pasdaran was having a field day. It had set up a base right on the other side of the border, in Taloqan, Afghanistan, to fuel instability in central Asia. It had even gone so far as to buy a couple of U.S. Stinger surface-to-air missiles and turn them over to the Tajik fundamentalists. The Russians maintained several outposts along the border, but the poor bastards defending them were lucky just to keep their heads. Every now and then, of course, their luck would tail out and the rebels would overrun one of them. The next day the newspaper would feature gruesome pictures of heads detached from bodies.

The danger was certainly part of the lure, but I had other reasons for wanting to spend time in the Pamirs. Ever since I had arrived in Dushanbe, I'd heard rumors about the remnants of an ancient civilization tucked away in a valley high in the mountains. The people who lived there were said to be descendants of the ancient kingdom of Samarkand, which had produced Alexander the Great's wife, Roxane. Although they now called themselves Yaghnobis, their language hadn't changed significantly in the last twenty-five hundred years. It was very close to ancient Soghdian, an Indo-European tongue in the Iranian family. The Yaghnobis' way of life apparently hadn't changed, either. They lived without electricity or running water. And if the wild rumors were true, the Yaghnobis had even reverted to worshiping fire.

Joseph Stalin had unsuccessfully attempted to efface the culture by scattering the Yaghnobis across the Soviet Union. After the regime fell in 1991, Harvard professor and Iranian scholar Richard Frye—a veteran of the World War II-era OSS—was the first American to hike up into Yaghnob. The window slammed shut again the next year, with the start of the civil war. If I managed to make it up there,

I'd be on a very short list of Americans who had ever visited the ancient kingdom of Samarkand.

Basically, I decided to combine two trips in one. The first half would be a drive through the Pamirs, following a two-lane road that ran along Tajikistan's border with Afghanistan and China. On the way back to Dushanbe, I'd return through the Garm Valley and see if there was a way to walk into Yaghnob. At best, it was an iffy proposition. A fifteen-thousand-foot pass stood between the Garm and Yaghnob valleys, and there was no way to learn from Dushanbe either who controlled the pass or whether it was clear of snow.

The first hurdle was to get through rebel lines. To figure that out, I needed to make a reconnaissance trip to Tavildara, the last town under government control. Since it was safer to travel in pairs, I persuaded the embassy's economic officer, whom I'll call Maggie, to accompany me. A newly minted Foreign Service officer, Maggie was looking forward to putting a little war reporting under her belt.

Maggie and I brought along a linguist, an attractive young Iranian girl I'll call Nell. Nell not only spoke native Farsi, of which Tajik is a dialect; she had also picked up a few East Iranian dialects, including Soghdian, while she was a student at Oxford. But Nell's talents weren't limited to languages. She had helped pay her way through Oxford, she told me, by dressing up in a heavy set of clothes wrapped with flashing lights and dancing as a kind of come-on during raves at abandoned airfields. Having never attended a rave, I had to take her word for it, but even though her university dancing days were over, she still didn't mind dressing the part.

Driving into Tavildara reminded me of the final sequence in *Apocalypse Now*, when Martin Sheen reaches Marlon Brando's lair at the river's end. Tavildara, though, was a hot battlefield. You could see it as soon as you drove into town, or what had once been the town. The only sign that anyone had ever lived there was mounds of rubble. The road was missing, too, replaced by huge craters strung together like a pearl necklace. We stopped to hear if there was any shooting going on, but it was absolutely quiet. If the rebels were in the surrounding mountains, we couldn't see them.

A burned-out T-72, still smoking and with a tread thrown across the road, marked the entrance to the army's camp. Shirtless and holding a sniper rifle, a soldier sunned himself on a nearby rock. He shrugged when we asked where his commander was. Ten minutes of poking around the camp finally led us to his billet, in the basement of what must have previously been a house. You had to pull away the camouflage netting and climb down a hole the size of a toilet to get in. Inside was a warren of sandbags, crates of grenades and ammunition, racks of RPGs and light antitank rockets, and stacked assault rifles. If the place took a direct hit, half of Tavildara would go up with it.

A private was sitting on the floor, loading an ammunition belt. The commander, Colonel Sergei, was "taking his bath," he informed us. The private showed us into Colonel Sergei's room, which was the size of a big rabbit hutch. He closed the door and left us alone. We sat down on a pair of cots to wait. Nell put on her Walkman and tuned out.

Maggie and I heard Colonel Sergei before we saw him. Drunk as a Siberian pickle, he was belting out some old Volga boatman's song. I looked at my watch. It was just about noon. Apparently informed by the private that he had guests, Sergei stopped singing. Now we could hear him giggling as he tried to sneak up on us. All was going fine until he bumped his head on the low ceiling and cursed under his breath. The next thing we knew, he had knocked the makeshift door almost off its hinges with his rifle butt and burst into the room. As soon as he saw us, though, Sergei froze. The orderly apparently hadn't told him his visitors were Americans. I, for one, was every bit as surprised to see him. He couldn't have been more than twenty-eight or -nine. With his full blond beard, emerald-green eyes, and sheepish grin, he wasn't my idea of the commander of the farthest outpost of the former Soviet Union.

Once we were all seated, Maggie, who had good Russian skills, asked about the recent fighting around Tavildara, but Sergei ignored her. Instead he shouted at the private through the wall, "I curse the eyes of your whore of a mother. Why is there never a goddamn bottle of vodka when I need one?" The private found a bottle, and the day went into a tailspin from there.

Sergei's second in command, an Uzbek major, showed up with two more bottles of vodka. We were into the first of those when the Uzbek got up, went

out, and came back with an American land mine he'd
captured from the rebels. No one had bothered to
remove the detonator. "Here," he said, handing it to
me. "This is a present from the great Soviet Union to
America." Not to be outdone, I went out to the Niva
and brought back a surplus U.S. military flak vest.
The major loved it. He put it on, grabbed me by the
arm, and dragged me back outside. Handing me his
Makarov pistol, he said, "Shoot me." Fortunately, I
was sober enough to say no. I finally persuaded him
to hang the vest on a pole. The major emptied a clip
into it and was so delighted when not a single round
penetrated the vest that he grabbed an AK-47 and
emptied a magazine into it. This time the vest
shredded. The major didn't mind, though. He put the
vest back on and wore it for the rest of the party.

By the time we had polished off bottle three, it was
time to go out on the range. Although Sergei was
completely plowed by then, he still had enough
presence of mind to tell us to shoot down the valley
not up into the mountains where the enemy was
perched out. No point in irritating the rebels if you
don't have to, he said.

Things went just fine, at least at first. It was a
beautiful cool day. Nell and Maggie got to fire an AK
for the first time. Mercifully, there was no more vodka.
I'd retrieved from the Niva a CIA-issue twelve-gauge
folding-stock riot gun and showed it to the Uzbek
major, who by now had presented me with a box of
hand grenades. The riot gun proved to be a mistake.
The major insisted on trying it out and fired off a
couple rounds—in the direction of the mountains.

In theory, it wasn't a threatening act: A twelve-gauge shotgun is useful only at close quarters. But the rebels were in no mood for fine distinctions. The first incoming round pinged off a tank only twenty feet from us. Several short bursts of fire followed and then a constant staccato of automatic rifle fire that seemed to be coming from everywhere. It wasn't long before a mortar round whistled over the camp and exploded about fifty yards beyond the perimeter.

I looked over at Maggie. She was wheezing. She'd bargained only to cover a war, not to start one. "Let's go," I said, putting my hand on her arm. It reassured her that someone had a plan. "I'll get the shotgun and you get Nell," I said.

Maggie ran toward Sergei and Nell. "We're leaving!"

Sergei, who had taken a liking to Nell as the day wore on and now had his arm around her, shouted back at Maggie in his broken English, "Good. You go. Woman stay here with me."

Not one to be messed with, Maggie ran over, grabbed Nell, and pushed Sergei backward. We all ran for the Niva.

As we drove out of the camp, crews were scrambling into their tanks. I noticed they were all Tajiks. Their Russian officers were too drunk to do anything but watch. It was something to hear a dozen T-72s starting up their engines simultaneously, I turned around one last time and saw the camp covered in a heavy pall of diesel smoke.

We stopped about half a mile beyond Tavildara to listen to what sounded like a fierce battle. I threw the land mine and the box of grenades into the river, and we continued back to Dushanbe.

THE NEXT SPRING, when the snow melted off the passes, I dusted off my project for a trip through the Pamirs. This time I persuaded Henry, a visiting State Department officer, to accompany me. Henry spoke near-flawless Russian. What's more, he'd been in the special forces. He was the perfect traveling companion for the Pamirs.

We packed the Niva with military rations, water, and some twenty jerry cans of gasoline. Our only communications equipment was a hand-held radio that linked us up to Washington via a low-altitude navy satellite. I left the shotgun behind, but I did bring along two grenades, which I hid up behind the dashboard. To Henry's astonishment, I also strapped a pair of skis to the roof of the car. "It's good cover," I explained. "The bad guys will think we're just adventurers."

When we came to Tavildara, we didn't even slow down. Sergei was likely to still be sore about Nell. In the mountains above Tavildara, the road had disappeared beneath a massive landslide. There wasn't a single vehicle on the road. We didn't even see any rebels along the way but at the top of Kaborabad pass, we came across the remains of a fresh battle. The side of the mountain was pockmarked with black craters—probably from SU-27 fighter-bombers—and burned-out tanks and armored personnel carriers.

We were starting to wonder if the Russians were fighting a war with themselves when two scarecrows cradling AK-47s stepped out from behind a rock and blocked our way. When they put us in the sights of their rifles, stopping seemed only politic. They asked us for a ride to Kalai-khum, the first town on the Afghan border.

It didn't take long for the chitchat to lapse into an uneasy silence. I watched in the rearview mirror as the two mujahadin cased the Niva to see what was to be had. When they switched into Tajik, which they assumed we didn't know, the situation took a menacing turn. As best as we could tell, they were debating what to do about us. Taking us home and introducing us to their families wasn't an option they were considering.

Before our passengers could come to a decision, we came to Kalai-khum. An Afghan flag fluttered over a mud-and-wattle border-post hut on the other side of a shallow stretch of the Panj River. In front of us, a sandbagged .50-caliber machine-gun position blocked our entry to the town. Our muj hopped out and were in the middle of an animated conversation with two of their colleagues manning the machine gun when one of the hitchhikers came back and stuck his head in the window: "We need you to come with us to take care of formalities." That wasn't a good sign. "Fine," I said. "We'll go right to the police station." Instead I slammed the Niva into first and peeled out. When I looked in the rearview mirror, the four muj were running behind us.

We drove out the other side of the Panj as fast as

we could. Afghanistan, across the river, suddenly seemed a lot more civilized than the Tajik side. We were making good time until a tire started to go flat. Fortunately, a Russian border post sat just ahead, protected by high berms, walls, and razor wire. I drove through the front gate without giving the sentry a chance to stop us. Immediately, a knot of Russian soldiers gathered. With their hollow eyes and filthy uniforms about to fall off their backs, they looked like they'd been on strict rationing for a long time. Even their rifles were rusted. I offered them some of our rations, but no one accepted.

While I changed the shredded tire, Henry went to look for the commander. The soldiers just stared at me. No one offered to help.

I was tightening up the last lug nut when Henry came back following a Russian lieutenant who looked to be about sixteen years old. They were arguing loudly in Russian. The lieutenant kept repeating that it was forbidden for foreigners to visit this part of the Soviet Union. He ignored Henry's reminder that there was no Soviet Union. Finally, the lieutenant walked over to the Niva and stuck his face in mine. "You and your friend get the hell out of here. Now."

Henry made one last try. "Can't we at least sleep outside the gates?" It was dusk now. Khorog lay at least eight hours away—along a road the Afghan muj used for target practice.

"No," the lieutenant shouted. I could see he was more scared than angry. "It will give the bastards something else to shoot at. You've got one minute to get out, and I don't care where the fuck you go." He nodded at the guards, who started fingering their triggers. It was then that I noticed the base's main defense amounted to a half-dozen antiaircraft guns, all facing across the river toward Afghanistan. The gunners were starting to feed in ammunition belts, preparing for another night on the frontier.

We made it to Khorog by the next morning, stayed a day and then continued along the Chinese border, hard by some of the most beautiful mountains in the world. At each border post we stopped at, the Russians were totally mystified by our presence. Every time they asked if we had Moscow's permission to drive through the Pamirs. It was as if they hadn't heard the Soviet Union no longer existed. We stayed at the border post at Murgab. (The Russians told us it meant "dead chicken" in the local dialect.) For dinner we ate Marco Polo steaks, from the stately and vanishing Marco Polo sheep, about all the food there was to be had at Murgab. The commander said he hadn't received supplies in a year. Then he added that he was finishing up an *eight-year* tour. Had Moscow changed much, he asked?

Although Henry and I didn't make it to Yaghnob, I eventually found a guide to take me there. We entered the valley from the western side, then walked for two solid days along a narrow trail perched precariously above a two-thousand-foot cliff before we came to the first settlement. The rumors were right. The Yaghnobis really weren't of the last two millennia.

At the next village, we ate around a table that used a carpet for its top. Even though it was the middle of summer, it was cold, and a little boy kept placing fresh burning embers under the table to keep us warm. Thanks to sleeves in the carpet, we could stick our arms through the tabletop to warm our hands as we chewed. The village was without running water or electricity but the setting—a combination of mountains and glacier covered by year-round snow—was spectacular and intricately tied to the ancient culture. Instead of praying to Mecca, as most Muslims do, the Yaghnobi prayed to the highest peak, which they considered the jumping-off point to heaven.

AFTER ALMOST TWO YEARS of turning on the tap and seeing mud spurt out, taking ice-cold showers, and living off military rations, I'd had enough of Tajikistan. It was time for someone else to come out and share the fun. In January I started to nudge headquarters to find a replacement. After two months of silence in response, I got on the telephone to the division's personnel office. I was apologetically told the Russian speaker who was supposed to replace me was going to the Army War College instead. An alternate would be found right away. But that guy ended up going to some midcareer management-training course. The third alternate simply dropped out of the assignment. Dushanbe "wasn't a good career move," he'd told the division. I was starting to feel like I had died, gone to hell, and would spend eternity in Dushanbe when headquarters proudly informed me it had found a replacement. I was ecstatic, at least until I started reading the guy's bio. He was a paramilitary officer who spoke neither

Russian nor Tajik, had never recruited an agent or even handled one. It was as bad as sending an analyst out to replace me. The one thing he apparently knew how to do was crimp a blasting cap, which would be helpful only if headquarters decided to relocate our Dushanbe office to Tavildara.

Even after all my years in the CIA, I was stunned. The CIA had no agents in the Russian military and apparently didn't care, at least not enough to send someone to Tajikistan to recruit one. It also didn't care that my replacement wouldn't be able to talk to Grigor, who didn't speak English. The CIA had apparently written off the Russian military despite the fact that it still possessed missiles that could deliver a nuclear warhead to anywhere it wanted in the U.S.

I shouldn't have been surprised. As the civil war in Afghanistan started to boil, I repeatedly asked for a speaker of Dari or Pashtun, the two predominant languages in Afghanistan, to debrief the flood of refugees coming across the border into Tajikistan. They were a gold mine of information. We could have even recruited some and sent them back across the border to report on Afghanistan. I was told there were no Dari or Pashtun speakers anywhere. I was also told the CIA no longer collected on Afghanistan, so those languages weren't needed. Headquarters instead offered to send out a four-person sexual-harassment briefing team. Another black mark was put up against my name when I declined the offer.

I was beginning to seriously wonder what the CIA did care about these days when a cable landed on my desk, informing me that Claiborne Pell, the chairman of the Senate Foreign Relations Committee, was coming out to Tajikistan and wanted to talk to me. *Finally*, I thought. Pell was a former Foreign Service officer and a veteran of the cold war. Surely he would want to hear what I had to say about the Russian army.

The week before his arrival, I organized my thoughts on a stack of three-by-five cards. I especially wanted to tell Pell what I'd learned about the Russian officers plotting against Yeltsin. How could he not be interested in the possibility of a coup? I secretly hoped he might go back and pound on headquarters until it sent a real case officer to Dushanbe to replace me, someone who could at least keep meeting Grigor.

It seemed less important than the Russians at the time—as it still might prove, since missiles will always be a better delivery system for mass destruction than jumbo passenger jets—but I also wanted to tell Senator Pell what I was learning about Islamic fundamentalism in Tajikistan and Afghanistan.

I had resumed my Islamic studies when I got to Dushanbe. Almost every day, I read the Koran and the other canons of Islam with a Muslim scholar. Apart from improving my Arabic and Persian, I wanted to see what the Islamic texts said about holy wars and suicide. There was no consensus. You could pretty much read what you wanted into them.

Along the way I also had recruited a ███████, ████████████ who was close to the Tajik Islamic chieftain Abdallah Nuri. Nuri operated out of

Afghanistan, where he waged a relentless war against the Russians and their local allies. The connection was important: Russia and Tajikistan were begging the U.S. for help against Nuri. They were convinced the U.S. knew more than it was saying. Nuri received a lot of his funding from our closest ally in the Middle East, Saudi Arabia. Independently we tracked large clandestine subsidies and weapons shipments from the World Islamic League of Saudi Arabia, an organization protected by the Saudi royal family, going to Nuri. Since our offices in Islamabad, Pakistan, and Riyadh, Saudi Arabia seemed incapable of providing intelligence, the ██████████ was almost all we had to go on.

Incidentally Russia's and Tajikistan's concerns proved to be well founded. In July 1996 Nuri brokered an alliance between Osama bin Laden and Iranian intelligence. At least one meeting took place between bin Laden and an Iranian intelligence officer. Although we never found out what happened at the meeting, we knew bin Laden intended to propose to Iran a coordinated terrorism campaign against the U.S. Perhaps if I'd been replaced with a case officer who could talk to the ██████████, we might have found out if bin Laden's proposal was ever acted on.

Again, and I can't emphasize this often enough, there is no silver bullet that, all by itself, would have prevented the horror of September 11. But not meeting agents like the ██████████ I recruited, or using him as an access agent to get to people who knew still more about bin Laden, ensured we wouldn't. The fact was, bin Laden took advantage of a constellation of factors to forge his network, and any number of groups or sources might have told us what he was up to.

America is at war as I write, and the enemy's recruits are like water. Arrest or kill hundreds of them, and hundreds of others will flow into their places. We can't kill them all, but we can figure out what their plans and intentions are by talking with them. We can figure out the direction of their war by infiltrating people in the mosques who might tell us how bad things are and how many young men are devoted to taking their own lives. That's what we didn't have. That's what we were forfeiting all over the CIA and the intelligence community generally, in the pursuit of goals I still can't fully understand. And that's what I wanted to say to this senator who had dared to come to the front lines in Tajikistan.

CLAIBORNE PELL'S air force C-20 put down in the early afternoon on March 31, 1994. I didn't have a chance to speak with him until that evening, at a dinner at the presidential dacha. Pell was holding up remarkably well, especially for a man of his age who had been on a plane all night. After dinner Ambassador Escudero introduced us, and Pell and I walked the grounds and talked.

I started by telling him about the ground-forces commander's aide trying to recruit me into his criminal enterprise. Pell didn't say anything and just kept walking. Figuring I had him hooked, I moved on to what I had learned about the attack on the Duma in 1993 and how it had affected the military. I was building up a head of steam that would carry me into Islamic fundamentalism, the lack of a Tajik-speaking case officer to meet my cleric, and more.

"The ambassador told me about your trip to the Pamirs, to Soghdiana," Pell interrupted. "Tell me about it."

For the next twenty minutes I talked about what I'd seen in the Yaghnob valley. Pell was fascinated, and I never got back to Russia. It turns out I had been expected to deliver a travelogue instead of intelligence. Maybe, I remember thinking, it was time to rename the CIA the Central Itinerary Agency: "Out-of-the-world trips to out-of-the-world places." Hell, they wouldn't even have to change the monograms back in sunny Langley.

The cold war truly was over, I finally realized—dead and buried. I just hoped our capacity to spy hadn't died completely with it.

PART III
YOU'RE ON YOUR OWN

14

MARCH 3, 1995. SALAH AL-DIN, IRAQ.

"GET UP HERE and take a look at what just came in," Tom yelled down the stairs.

He was pulling the morning traffic in the second-floor bedroom we'd converted for communications. An ex-special forces major, Tom was working on contract to the CIA, helping us fight our covert war on terrorism. Using contractors was yet another indication of what the agency had come to. But I didn't care. Short and dark, Tom could have passed for an Iraqi. He was also seasoned and unflappable. He rarely yelled about anything, especially an incoming cable. As I headed up the stairs, all I could think of was that a rocket had come in from headquarters, ordering us out of the north.

Headquarters never was comfortable having a team in northern Iraq in the first place, operating solo. For that matter, no one was ever really comfortable with Iraq. For all the ballyhoo in the press, the 1991 Gulf War had been at best a limited engagement by coalition forces against Saddam Hussein, meant to drive his army out of Kuwait and punish him for the incursion but not to expel him from power. That prospect made our Arab allies, who understand about power vacuums in the region, distinctly uneasy. When Iraqi Kurds and the majority Shi'a rose up against a weakened Saddam in March 1991, the Kurds begged for our help. Instead we stood idly by as Saddam put up his helicopters and strafed the opposition. It was only when the fleeing Kurds began to flood into Turkey and Iran that President George Bush imposed his no-fly rule that allowed the Kurds to regain Kurdistan, the unrecognized state that occupies roughly the northern third of Iraq, which the Kurds call home. (The Kurds, an Indo-European people who speak a language close to Farsi, are the largest minority in the Middle East without a nation of their own.)

The operating idea seemed to be that the CIA could take care of our unfinished war: Clean it up, find some way to get rid of Saddam, and stop the always fractious Kurds from killing one another. Back in Washington, such thinking was apparently au courant. Out in the field, there were certain facts that didn't fit Washington's preconceptions. For a start, no one could be sure Saddam wouldn't try to kidnap or assassinate us. Then there were the Kurds, our hosts. After they threw Saddam's army out of the north in 1991, they unexpectedly found themselves with their own virtual country at the end of the Gulf War; but with no central authority they quickly waltzed themselves into a civil war. Mostly it was intermittent skirmishes and sniping, but from time to time they would haul out the heavy artillery and shell each other for a day or two.

In mid-February the fighting had turned nasty. A car bomb went off in a crowded market, killing more than a hundred people. A woman wrapped with plastic explosives blew herself up in a building around the corner from our house in Salah al-Din, in the same room where we met one of our Kurdish contacts. Not long after, the two main Kurdish factions fought a pitched battle less than a mile from Salah al-Din. Some stray 155mm shells fell near us, about the length of a football field away.

In the last few days, it wasn't just the Kurds who seemed bent on annihilation. Iraq, too, looked like it was about to go up. Saddam had put his army on full alert on February 28, canceling all leave and calling up reserves for the first time since the end of the Gulf War. The next day, on March 1, Iran followed suit, sending armor to the Iraqi border. And if this wasn't enough to get Washington's attention, a Turkish division moved up to the Iraqi border, probably squaring off for a counterinsurgency campaign against Turkish Kurdish guerrillas based in northern Iraq.

With the three largest armies in the Middle East on a collision course, Iraq was starting to look like a runaway train—and the four of us, my three-man team and me, were standing in the middle of the tracks. If Washington had lost its nerve at this point and ordered us out of the north, I wouldn't have been surprised. It had become corporate policy to close up at the first crack of a rifle. No one with any say-so seemed to even remember our dirty wars in Vietnam, Laos, and the Congo.

I'd done what I could to beef up security. I sent the communicator home—Tom knew how to operate the satellite transceiver. One officer had gone to Qalat Cholan, a Kurdish camp near the Iranian border; a second went to Irbil to live in the Kurdish parliament. Both were fortresses out of reach of Saddam's assassination teams. Tom and I probably should have moved out of the Salah al-Din house, where we had been living through most of February. Although it was identical to all the other mouse-colored, flat-roofed, poured-concrete houses in the village, Saddam's agents almost certainly knew we were there. But things were happening too fast to take the time to move. We'd just have to rely on our Kurdish guards to protect us.

"They're pulling us out, aren't they?" I asked Tom when I joined him in the communications room.

Suddenly, the failure of nerve back in Langley and elsewhere in Washington seemed inevitable. I hoped we'd be brought back only as far as the Turkish border so we could keep meeting our contacts. Pulling us back to Washington would punch a gaping hole in the morale of the Iraqi dissidents at a time they were finally serious about going after Saddam.

Tom had a look of wild amazement on his face. "Like I said," he told me, "you're not going to believe it."

It was a rocket, all right, but it had nothing to do with pulling us out. The cable Tom handed me was something I'd never seen in my nineteen years in the CIA: a message from the White House, sent by the president's national security adviser, Tony Lake, and transmitted through CIA channels. I was supposed to deliver it that morning to the Iraqi dissident leaders in the north.

It has to be really bad news, I told myself as I started to read. In fact, it was a catastrophe.

THE ACTION YOU HAVE PLANNED FOR THIS WEEKEND HAS BEEN TOTALLY COMPROMISED. WE BELIEVE THERE IS A HIGH RISK OF FAILURE. ANY DECISION TO PROCEED WILL BE ON YOUR OWN.

In the second and only other paragraph, I was instructed to cable Washington as soon as I'd delivered the message.

Standing less than nine miles from the Iraqi front lines, with Kurdistan's snow-covered and impenetrable mountains at my back, I found myself focusing on the word "compromised." If Saddam really did know how close he was to being overthrown, he would defend himself like a cornered rat, more than likely sending an armored column north of the Zab River to look for us. The first T-72 tank would be in Salah al-Din, poking its 125mm cannon through our front door, before we could get our boots on.

I reread the cable, hoping to wring some sense out of it. The "action" Lake's message referred to was a coup d'état against Saddam Hussein, timed to go down in less than thirty-six hours. Washington had known about it for more than a month, since the end of January—more than enough time to postpone or stop it. That much I was certain of; I had outlined the coup, chapter and verse, for the folks back home.

Washington had known, too, that the coup wouldn't go down quietly. A very noisy diversion was supposed to precede it. We expected—indeed, we *wanted*— Saddam to put his tanks on the street in the hours leading up to it. But Washington had simply ignored everything we'd reported, letting preparations go forward as if there was a green light. Only now, after the officers behind the coup couldn't turn back, did the national security adviser finally react.

Why, I kept asking myself in those first stunned minutes after I had read the cable. Why this? Why so late? It wasn't as if Tony Lake could credibly distance himself from either the coup or the CIA. I wasn't running a rogue CIA operation that the National Security Council didn't know about. Lake's assistant for the Near East, Martin Indyk, personally authorized the CIA to set up a clandestine base in northern Iraq, the one I now headed. When the State Department tried to veto the base, Indyk peremptorily overrode it. And Indyk, like everyone else in the NSC who followed Iraq—including Lake—knew the reason for the base was to ███████████ the Iraqi dissidents overthrow Saddam. If the NSC hadn't liked the idea of the coup, it should have called it off in late January when it was first proposed. Calling it off now, in this way, would doom forever any chance we'd have to get rid of Saddam.

It crossed my mind to call Indyk on our secure satellite phone, but even if I'd had his number, he wouldn't have answered. NSC staffers don't take calls from CIA bases in the field. What's more, there was bad blood between Indyk and me. Half a year earlier,

I'd told him that the NSC and everyone else in Washington could forget about a bloodless coup getting rid of Saddam. That's not the way Iraq worked. The meeting, incidentally, hadn't done my career much good. But the point was that Washington's fantasy about a nonviolent overthrow of Saddam helped the big thinkers there get to sleep at night, and since we had no human sources inside or even near Saddam's circle—none—there was nothing to bring them back down to earth. Now I just had to accept that I was 6,192 miles and eight time zones away from the capital of the free world and wasn't going to find out what had gone wrong until I got back there.

"Was there another cable that came in with this? Like what exactly was compromised?" I asked Tom.

He shook his head.

I called the Iraqi Operations Group, my office in Washington and the headquarters component responsible for ▆▆▆▆▆▆ Saddam.

"Don't you know the Iraqi army is on a full alert?" the duty officer asked, irritated.

"The army is supposed to be on alert," I stammered. "That was part of the plan. But what about the other part, the secret part?"

I didn't want to be any more specific about the coup; I wasn't sure if he'd been read into it or not.

"Well, apparently another war with Saddam wasn't part of Lake's plan. He's made up his mind, and he doesn't want to hear any more about it."

I hung up and took a look around the gloomy second-floor bedroom, our war room: the blanket tacked over the window, air charts tacked on the wall, AK-47s and boxes of rations stacked in the corner, the LST-5 tacset, and the generator humming out on the balcony—we hadn't had any electricity since Saddam cut it off to the north on February 28. It looked theatrical now. I found myself thinking that for the last month and a half, we had been nothing but boys playing war.

"A walk?" I asked Tom. I needed some fresh air.

As soon as we stepped out the door, we were almost overwhelmed by the silence. Since we had arrived in Salah al-Din in late January, we had gone to bed and awakened to the sounds of the Kurds shooting at each other on the Irbil line. Even after the truce on March 2 that officially brought the fighting to an end, sniping went on throughout the day. Now nothing.

Down the street from our house, three Kamaz trucks—the Russian version of a U.S. military deuce and a half—were parked in front of a barracks belonging to the Iraqi National Congress, the main Iraqi dissident group. Three young men in uniform, shouting and laughing, loaded them with ammunition and supplies. They were preparing to move to the Iraqi lines for the planned diversion.

Salah al-Din's main street was deserted, its only café empty. The old men who spent their days sipping sugared tea, their rusty Chinese SKS and Enfield rifles stacked against the wall, had returned to their villages in the mountains, the only safe place to be when things went to hell in Kurdistan. The waiter—who, like everyone else in Salah al-Din, knew we were CIA—watched us warily, then disappeared behind a rug that made do for a door. Even if you didn't know about the coup, you could tell something was in the air.

No doubt about it, I thought. *This isn't going to be an easy message to deliver.*

15

JANUARY 21, 1995. NORTHERN IRAQ.

WHEN MY TEAM and I walked into northern Iraq on January 21, 1995, we had no idea anyone was making plans to move against Saddam. I'd volunteered to take a team into the north because I knew it was the only way the CIA could get a heads-up if Saddam was about to invade another neighbor. I also knew it was the best place to recruit Iraqi military officers.

Our first task after crossing the border was to meet an Iraqi major general, in Zakhu, a small town the Kurds had seized in the March 1991 uprisings. Until he defected to the north in November 1994, the general had been an adviser in the Iraqi presidency. The hope was that he might know something about where the Scuds were hiding and, even more important, about Saddam's biochemical warheads.

The general must have found the group of us an odd sight when his driver pulled up in front of our house at exactly eleven A.M. We had spent the last two days in the back of trucks getting into the north, only to discover the house we were to live in had no electricity water, or heat—this on a night so cold the water in our canteens froze. Unshaven and unbathed, wearing surplus military cold-weather gear and cradling automatic rifles, we looked more like stragglers left behind by a routed army than representatives of the United States.

Nonplussed, the burly general rolled out of the car, straightened himself up, and offered me a hand of tempered steel. He was wearing an unremarkable suit, scuffed penny loafers, and a paisley silk tie, but his tar-black regimental mustache, squared shoulders, and stiff gait gave away the soldier underneath. Besides, I recognized him from a press photo, sitting next to Saddam in a bunker during the Gulf War.

We sat down in our living room as the cook served us tea, but the general found it difficult to start. He kept asking whether we were comfortable, how we liked Iraq, and whether we needed anything. It was a polite ritual I'd gotten used to working in the Middle East.

"General, could we talk a little about Saddam's strategic weapons?" I asked, cutting him off.

My question surprised him. "I don't know anything about them," he said. "Only Saddam, Saddam's son-in-law Hussein Kamil, and a few people around Saddam know where they're hidden."

We sat without saying anything for a minute. I was about ready to thank him for the meeting when he cleared his throat and asked, "Does the U.S. want Saddam to remain in power?"

Here we go again. The general was alluding to a vintage conspiracy theory that dogged everything we tried to do in Iraq—the myth that the U.S. secretly kept Saddam in power. I'd heard it from just about every Iraqi I'd met. Some even believed Saddam was a paid CIA agent. The theory dovetailed nicely with the Iraqi belief that dark, unseen forces ran the world and history could be reduced to a series of conspiracies, interconnected by an overarching design known to only a few. It followed, then, in this twisted scheme of things, that a foreign policy of any consequence had to be scripted according to a secret plot. As one theory went, Saddam and the U.S. had struck a secret agreement in 1980 for Iraq to invade Iran. The sole objective was to take Iran down a peg. Then, when Iraq emerged from that war as a menacing giant in the Gulf, the U.S. conspired with Kuwait to *lure* Iraq into invading Kuwait—only so the U.S. could smash Iraq's army. It was Iraq's turn to be taken down a peg. Imperialism couldn't work any other way.

The theory explained a lot of otherwise inexplicable mysteries, such as why the U.S. Army didn't hunt down Saddam at the end of the Gulf War, and even permitted him to put up his helicopters so he could crush the popular insurrections. It explained why the U.S. allowed Saddam to smuggle oil through countries allied with the U.S., like Turkey and Jordan. It also explained why after Saddam's attempted assassination of ex-president George Bush during his visit to Kuwait in 1993, President Bill Clinton fired a couple of cruise missiles into empty buildings in Baghdad rather than go after Saddam.

The theory got still nuttier in 1993 when the son of a former Iraqi prime minister living in London, Sa'd Salih Jabir, started the rumor that the CIA had deliberately betrayed a coup against Saddam, even giving him the list of the plotters. Although the lie was cut from whole cloth, many Iraqi military officers accepted it as the truth. It made our job of recruiting them nearly impossible.

And what was our motivation for keeping Saddam in power? He was our surrogate, bogeyman, and neighborhood bully rolled into one. The U.S. needed Saddam to keep the peace in the Gulf. Whisper Saddam's name and the Arab Gulf states would huddle around the U.S. like pups around a bitch. And the price the Gulf Arabs paid for American protection was not raising the price of oil. It all made perfect sense to Iraqis.

There was only one way to deal with a conspiracy theory like that: Take it head-on. "We want Saddam out. It's the Iraqi people who've kept him in power all these years," I said.

The general considered my answer for a moment. Deciding he had no choice except to trust me, he said, "Let's go outside."

We had gone about twenty yards down the street when the general turned to face me.

"I've been dispatched to the north by a group of military officers who intend to get rid of Saddam," he said in a hoarse whisper, looking around to make sure no one could overhear us. "We need to know whether your country will stand in our way or not."

He looked me in the eye for what seemed like a full

minute, to make absolutely sure I understood. I didn't say anything. It was no time to interrupt.

"And there's a second request we make," he continued. "The moment we take power, we need the U.S. to grant us immediate diplomatic recognition—otherwise there will be a fight for power, a civil war."

The general stopped talking. It was clear that this was all he was authorized to say. It was a lot for him, to be sure, but not nearly enough if he expected U.S. support.

"Washington will need to know the details, like who's involved," I said.

The general held up his hand to stop me. "Please get an answer from Washington first, and we will talk about details then."

We came to the edge of town and turned back. The general had a meeting with the Turkish general staff in Ankara. A Turkish military helicopter was waiting for him on the other side of the border. He intended to tell the Turks about the coup.

"I know you would like to ask the question, but maybe you're too polite," the general said as we walked back. "Yes, we know what we are doing. And we know what the penalty for failure is.

"I've seen firsthand how good Saddam's security is. During the war I briefed Saddam three or four times. Do you know how I—and everyone else—met with Saddam then? You were told to go to a certain street corner in Baghdad and wait, sometimes for up to two or three hours. Eventually a car would approach and stop. You were told to get in the back and lie down on the floor. A blanket was thrown over your head so you couldn't see anything. The car would drive around Baghdad for at least an hour. You had no idea where you were. Then the car would stop. And there Saddam would be, waiting in front of a very ordinary house, probably commandeered for only that one meeting. When the meeting was over, the same car took you back in the same way. You never knew where you were. Saddam's security is very, very good, but we know its vulnerabilities. Please trust us that we know what we are doing."

As the general was ready to leave, he rolled down the window to say one last thing.

"All that we ask of Washington is that it be frank with us. We must know whether it wants Saddam out or not. Nothing more. I'll be back from Ankara in two or three days. I hope you will have our answer by then."

As soon as I got back inside, I sent a report to headquarters about what the general had told me.

I KNEW THE GENERAL'S MESSAGE wouldn't go very far without any details, but I hoped Washington would at least take his defection seriously. Not only was he the first general to break ranks since the end of the war, but he also was from a politically prominent upper Euphrates family. Even more important, he was a Sunni Muslim, the same sect Saddam belonged to, the one that kept him in power. Although the Sunni Arabs made up only 20 percent or so of Iraq's population, they controlled the armed forces and the security services with an iron grip. No tank, airplane, or unit larger than a company could move without authorization from a Sunni officer who had unquestioned loyalty to Saddam. Without the support of Iraq's Sunnis, Saddam couldn't last a day in power. Moreover, the signs were mounting that the general's departure had rattled Saddam's cage.

In the past, Saddam had made a point of ignoring defections, but on November 8, in addition to dispatching assassination teams to hunt down the general, Saddam took the unprecedented step of ordering the senior cleric for the general's clan to publicly denounce him—a Muslim version of excommunication. Saddam wanted to make sure the rest of the Sunnis understood there was no place for apostates in the congregation. Clearly, he feared that the general might be the first frayed thread in an unraveling mantle of power.

Even if Washington decided not to support the coup, I figured we would have to take a fresh look at the stability of Saddam's regime. Was his Sunni core of support headed toward meltdown? We couldn't accept the general's word at face value, but the CIA should have been in a position to check the general's information with clandestine sources in Iraq—Sunnis still living inside and serving military officers. And there, of course, was the snag. By 1995, three years after scores of nations and more than half a million coalition forces had gone to war against Saddam Hussein, the CIA didn't have a single source in Iraq who could back up or refute what the general had told us. Not one.

Not only were there no human sources in the

country, the CIA didn't have any in the neighboring countries—Iran, Jordan, Turkey, and Saudi Arabia— who reported on Iraq. Like the rest of the U.S. government, its intelligence-gathering apparatus was blind when it came to Iraq. The general's credibility would have to be established in other ways, and his information painstakingly vetted.

Ideally, we would have met face-to-face with the officers preparing the coup and heard the story directly from their mouths, but even that wasn't possible. Iraq was what the CIA called a "denied" area. All communication had to be by go-betweens, because no CIA personnel could visit any part of the nation controlled by Saddam. In effect, the designation created a catch-22, since Iraqi military officers were not permitted to travel outside Iraq, including the Kurdish north. Getting caught earned an officer a ticket to an acid bath, a good excuse to stay home. That meant the only way to communicate was through a cutout, a courier, who could travel back and forth across the lines without being noticed. It wasn't a perfect system—imagine watching a play in which all the action takes place in the wings, relayed by an intermittently onstage narrator—but it was all the choice we had.

A week after I sent off word of the general's intentions, headquarters came back with a snappy five-word reply: "This is not a plan."

I recognized the prose as belonging to a CIA officer who had worked for me in the Iraqi Operations

Group. He'd spent only one year overseas, in Vietnam, twenty-five years earlier. He'd never set foot in the Middle East. Even still, headquarters' reaction struck me as bizarre. It didn't ask for additional details or even offer encouragement. It was as if the CIA had hundreds of agents on the ground and no sparrow fell in Iraq without our knowing about it.

I went to see the general the next day, at his house in the middle of Salah al-Din at the end of a tangle of narrow, muddy streets. Sparsely furnished, the place looked as if he'd fled to the north with his family and only what they could carry. We sat cross-legged on the floor while his wife served us tea and their children peered at us from behind a door. I'd already made up my mind that it was pointless to tell him about the message from headquarters. He wouldn't have understood; and, not understanding, he would have been even more reluctant to confide in me. Anyhow, the way I read the message, Washington hadn't rejected the coup; it just needed more details, such as the names of the officers involved.

When I told the general that I hadn't yet received an answer about the coup, a flicker of foreboding passed across his face. The secret committee had hoped for a twenty-four-hour turnaround on their message, he said. Couriers were crossing the lines every night, expecting to return with an answer. It was incomprehensible to the general that Washington couldn't decide on a matter of this importance within hours.

I tried to turn the conversation in a different

direction. We talked a little about the situation in the north, the problems he was having with his children out of school, the shortage of food.

As I was standing up to leave, the general motioned me to stay. "Tell Washington this."

I sensed the general was about to open a door he would have preferred not to—to give me the details of the coup. If I was right, there would be no going back for him. The general and his colleagues, his secret committee, would be putting their lives in our hands, accepting on faith that the story about the CIA betraying a 1993 coup wasn't true. I suspected they had decided to take the risk because they knew it was the only way to get Washington's attention. They were still convinced they needed America's permission to move against Saddam. And I was right. To win the CIA's support, the general sang like a canary.

THE BACKBONE OF THE COUP was three seasoned combat units—the 76th Brigade, the 15th Infantry Division, and the 5th Mechanized Division. Among them, the general said, they had enough firepower to hold off any single combat unit loyal to Saddam, including an elite Republican Guard's division, the military units responsible for keeping Saddam in power. Admittedly, they couldn't defeat a combined Republican Guards force, but they expected to move on Saddam before loyalists had the time to organize and deploy. The plan would start like lightning, arrive like thunder, and be over before anyone could do anything about it.

There was also a fourth unit, one absolutely crucial to the coup's success: a tank-training company attached to the Salah al-Din Armor School, which was located just outside of Tikrit. Its commander, a colonel, would spearhead the coup. As soon as he received the go from the secret committee, he would commandeer twelve tanks and their crews from the school, drive them to Saddam's compound in 'Awjah, and box him in long enough for the other three units to arrive and deliver the coup de grâce.

A small village east of Tikrit, 'Awjah had been chosen as the venue to corner Saddam because everyone knew, in the inner circle at least, that 'Awjah was Saddam's bolt-hole, the place he took refuge when anything went wrong in Iraq. Saddam had been born in 'Awjah and had a strong sentimental attachment to it. After coming to power, he built a sprawling, moderately well-defended compound at the village's edge. The committee's plan was to create a diversion away from 'Awjah, perhaps in Baghdad, and wait for Saddam to arrive there before the colonel put his tanks on the road. Although the committee could pretty much count on Saddam's heading to 'Awjah when the diversion started, it sought to leave nothing to chance: A source inside Saddam's security detail would notify the plotters as soon as Saddam had left for 'Awjah.

The key to the coup's success was maintaining its integrity right up until the first shot was fired—Saddam couldn't have the slightest suspicion he would be targeted at 'Awjah—and the way to do that was to limit knowledge of the coup to family members. Everyone on the secret committee and the commanders of the four units were related by blood. Most were first cousins.

"That's the only kind of conspiracy that can survive in Iraq today without being immediately betrayed," the general told me. Moreover, most of the troops who would participate in the attack on 'Awjah were from the Shummar tribal confederation. With Iraq disintegrating under the UN embargo, old tribal bonds were replacing loyalty to the state.

The committee figured that as long as the secrecy of its plan held, and if there were no other competing troop movements, the colonel's tanks would need about twenty minutes to get to 'Awjah. Another ten to twenty minutes for the other units to arrive, and Saddam, surrounded, could either give up or the tanks would level his compound. It would all be over in less than an hour.

OVER THE NEXT TWO WEEKS the general gave me the names of the four commanders and their unit designations. He drew family trees for me and explained the relations among the officers. He also named the officers who would be in the transitional military government. Three of them knew nothing about the coup or even that they had been chosen to serve. They wouldn't be told until the colonel's tanks were on the road. It was all part of compartmentalizing information and keeping the coup secret.

After each meeting I sent a message to headquarters. The names of the key participants checked out with the databases at CIA headquarters, but Washington still hadn't said what it wanted to do about the coup.

IN LATE FEBRUARY the general came over to our house, discouraged by my masters' silence. At our last meeting he had asked if one U.S. fighter, on a given date at a given time, could fly over central Iraq as a signal to the committee that the U.S. supported the coup. I hadn't even bothered relaying that one. If Washington wasn't going to acknowledge the coup, it would ridicule the idea of an air force flyover.

After tea was served and we lapsed into our customary silence, the general finally turned to me, putting his hand on my arm.

"The Kurds are about to wreck everything. Please arrange a truce between them. A truce will signal that the U.S. is serious about removing Saddam."

16

THE GENERAL had a point. Although the Kurds had no role in the coup, at least in the beginning, they definitely had the potential to spoil it. By mid-February their civil war had spread all over the north. Iran and Turkey were about to intervene, and the temptation for Saddam to stick his snout under the Kurdish tent was quickly becoming irresistible.

The origins of the Kurdish conflict go deep into time, history, and character. By late February 1995, though, the ancient rifts had come down to two main factions: the Kurdish Democratic Party, or KDP; and the Patriotic Union of Kurdistan, or PUK. They had fought each other to a near standoff, but rather than just call a truce as any group in its right mind might do, they continued to battle on. Worse, as their desperation grew, both were separately considering inviting Saddam and his despised army to intervene in the north—the same Saddam who had gassed the Kurds in 1988, killing thousands of civilians.

Any appeal to Saddam would be a disaster for the coup plotters. Committed troops couldn't refuse orders to go into in Kurdistan: Saddam would immediately and ruthlessly crush even the hint of a mutiny. The general made it clear to me from the beginning that the committee needed the status quo to hold up until the last minute, but it was more than just the committee's coup at stake. The Iraqi army back in the north, even for a day, would be an irreversible symbolic victory for Saddam. Steeped in conspiracy theory, Iraqis would immediately assume that the United States had secretly given Saddam the green light to go in and that they had been right all along in believing that the Americans wanted to keep Saddam in power.

Forget the truth of the matter, or even the logic that undergirded the assumptions. If Saddam was ever going to be thrown out, the Iraqis were going to have to do the job and not us. It was their perceptions that counted, not ours. If they were convinced the U.S. secretly kept Saddam in place, they would conclude that it was futile to act against him.

THE KURDS weren't the only desperate ones. Ahmad Chalabi understood as well as anyone just how fragile the situation was.

Chalabi was head of the Iraqi National Congress, the Iraqi opposition umbrella group based in Salah al-Din. When I first met him in Washington one muggy August afternoon in 1994, it was difficult to imagine someone less likely to unseat Saddam. Marching across the lobby of the Key Bridge Marriott in his Savile Row suit, $150 Italian silk tie, and hand-stitched calfskin oxfords, he looked more like the successful Levantine banker he once had been than like someone who was going to ride into Baghdad on the top of a tank. Short and overweight, his body showed the side effects of too many long business lunches at first-class European restaurants. When he shook my hand, I picked up the faint smell of scented soap.

As incongruous as Chalabi's appearance was, his résumé offered even less promise that he might one day lead a successful Iraqi opposition. First, he was a member of Iraq's lowest caste—the Shi'a Muslims, who had never ruled Iraq and weren't about to anytime soon. Second, Chalabi's family had been forced to flee Iraq for Lebanon in 1958 when the Hashemite monarchy fell. Thirteen years old at the time, Chalabi had grown up abroad, exchanging his Iraqi accent for a Lebanese one. Chalabi was further tainted when he attended graduate school in the U.S. While picking up a master's degree at MIT and a Ph.D. in numbers theory at the University of Chicago, he had learned to speak American idiomatic English. No matter what Chalabi said about his Iraqi nationalist credentials, Iraqis looked at him as a stateless exile. Finally, a bank that Chalabi had owned in Jordan, the Petra Bank, collapsed in 1989, losing hundreds of millions of depositors' dollars. Although no one was sure who ended up with the money, Chalabi was blamed, and a Jordanian court convicted him in absentia of embezzlement.

Outside Iraq, Chalabi was a felon; inside, he remained almost completely unknown. But what he lacked by way of credentials, he made up for in brains, energy and a practiced political touch, all qualities that were tested daily by the Iraqi National Congress. The capos of the opposition who made up the congress were a sack of fighting alley cats. Shi'a clerics, Bedouin chiefs, royals, communist apparatchiks, ex-military officers, ex-Ba'th Party officials, Kurdish chieftains—they hated one another as much as they hated Saddam. What's more, each one of them thought he was more qualified to head the group than Chalabi.

Chalabi had been elected president of the INC at a 1992 meeting in Vienna, and for two years he had managed more or less to hold it together. By the time I met him in mid-1994, though, his authority had come under serious challenge. The main Shi'a Muslim groups had dropped their anchor in Tehran, where Chalabi was seen as a tail-wagging CIA dog. A more serious threat came from the Iraqi National Accord. One of the important constituent groups of the congress, it was threatening to bolt from the organization even as it was trying sub-rosa to unseat Chalabi. By early 1995 Chalabi was running what was in effect a rump INC—the Kurds. If Saddam invaded the north, Chalabi would lose even the Kurds, not to mention his base of operations. Most likely he would be forced into exile again, and Chalabi knew better than anyone that Saddam wasn't going to be overthrown from a European café.

For a guy with virtually no internal support in Iraq, Chalabi knew how to get things done and especially how to nudge people where he wanted them to go. He had produced a lengthy position paper entitled "End

Game," on how to jump-start the March 1991 uprisings, when the Shi'as and Kurds had taken advantage of the end of the Gulf War to try to wrest power from Saddam and his Sunni supporters. The paper had been well shopped around Washington by the time Chalabi presented me with a copy—at a sushi restaurant in Georgetown, two days after our first meeting—but if the thinking wasn't particularly new, "End Game" did help him stand out in the crowd. Besides, it wasn't like we were being overwhelmed with other plans to get rid of Saddam.

Chalabi would call me occasionally on a secure telephone from Salah al-Din, where he spent about half the year, to entreat me to set up a CIA base in the north. The Kurdish fighting was getting out of hand, he would say; only an official American presence there could stop it. Since the State Department still refused to establish its own mission in northern Iraq, the CIA was the next best thing. I thought Chalabi had a good point, but it wasn't until the general defected from Saddam's army and crossed into the north that I was able to convince my bosses to let me put together the team and head to Kurdistan.

I HAD BEEN PLANNING to keep my team in Zakhu, along the Turkish border. The general who had defected would be returning there after his meeting with Turkish authorities, and at least for the moment, Zakhu was out of the way of the warring Kurds. Headquarters wasn't anxious for us to venture to Salah al-Din in the middle of the fighting. Chalabi, though, would hear none of it. About an hour after the general finished telling me about the coup, Chalabi was on the telephone, urging us to move forward to Salah al-Din.

"You absolutely must be here for Litt's visit," Chalabi hollered over the static on the line one morning. "Don't wait in Zakhu for the general. The Kurds won't understand why you're not in the Litt meetings."

Litt was David Litt, the director of the State Department's North Gulf Affairs and the de facto ambassador to Iraq. He traveled to the north once or twice a year, staying no more than a few hours each time. Unlike CIA personnel who had to drive to the north, he traveled in U.S. military Blackhawk helicopters, which cut the trip from days to hours.

I'd briefly met Litt in Washington and found him humorless. I had the further impression that he disliked the CIA. Still, after I started working in the Iraqi Operations Group, I called him and offered to drive down to State to brief him on what the CIA was doing about Iraq. He never returned my call. I tried a few more times before giving up, but I did learn before we left Washington that Litt intended to visit the Kurds about the time we were due to arrive, so I called up State and asked what was on his agenda. The State desk officer wouldn't even tell me what day Litt was supposed to visit the north. Now I was being invited to the party albeit from the other side.

Chalabi must have sensed my hesitation over the phone. "Don't worry. The shelling has stopped. I've just talked to the Kurds. They've promised to be on their best behavior."

WE ARRIVED IN SALAH AL-DIN a little after one and went straight to Chalabi's house. The street was jammed with vehicles and guerrillas toting AK-47s and rocket-propelled grenade launchers. Chalabi's aide told me that Litt had already met the Kurdish leaders and was just finishing up with Chalabi.

Litt was speechless when he saw me walk through the door. Without even a nod in my direction, he turned to a distinguished man in a charcoal-gray suit sitting next to him and whispered in his ear. They both stood up, shook Chalabi's hand, and headed for the door. A few seconds later I heard their cars start up and leave in a blare of horns, and the shouting of the Kurdish fighters, known as *pech merga.* Not long after, the whirr of Blackhawk rotors passed above the house.

Chalabi walked back into the room, smiling.

"Who was the suit with Litt?" I asked.

"A Turk. He's in charge of Iraqi affairs at the Turkish Ministry of Foreign Affairs."

Chalabi was savoring the irony: The Turkish government was privy to what the State Department was doing in Iraq, but the CIA wasn't.

"Well?" I said.

"Mr. Litt had a splendid pair of meetings, first with Talabani and then with Barzani."

Jalal Talabani was head of the PUK; Masud Barzani the KDP.

"I suppose Litt demanded they knock off the fighting or we pull our air cover," I said. In Salah al-Din, it almost passed for humor.

Chalabi laughed. "Litt told them—you're going to have to sit down for this—the U.S. intends to pay for a force to separate the Kurds. He promised two million dollars."

"Whose money?" I asked, knowing State didn't have it.

"Yours. The CIA's."

Chalabi was nearly beside himself with joy. There was nothing he liked more than watching the U.S. government trip over its own feet.

That night I got on the telephone to Washington. No one had heard about the $2 million. An hour later, headquarters called back. Not only had the CIA never agreed to fund an interposition force, doing so would be flat-out illegal. The damage, though, was already done. The Kurds didn't distinguish between the State Department and the CIA. Litt had made the promise. I was the one who would pay the price.

WHEN IT FINALLY BECAME CLEAR in a few weeks that there would be no money for Litt's army, the fighting picked up. Talabani's PUK was down to the bottom of the barrel. It could either launch one final offensive against the KDP or spend its last nickel on a call to Saddam in Baghdad. Something had to be done.

"The clock is running out," Chalabi said over dinner one night. "Litt has destroyed your credibility. The Kurds will never listen to you now. Only a preemptive strike can save the situation."

Chalabi was right. I considered telling him about the general's secret committee and its coup, but knowing about it would have frustrated Chalabi more.

"What will Washington do if I organize an uprising?" he asked. "It's the only way to stop Talabani from attacking."

I knew that no one in Washington would put credence in Chalabi's uprising, just as no one really cared if the Kurds quietly shelled each other into smithereens. PUK and KDP were acronyms that the national security cognoscenti threw around to keep the uninitiated off-stride. Washington's only real interest was to keep the Kurds out of the front pages of the leading newspapers. In the dank swamp that Iraq had long since become, no news was very good news. Still, I thought, why not let Chalabi propose his uprising? At the least, it might force Washington to deal with the secret committee's coup.

"Schedule one and then ask," I answered.

Chalabi did just that. The next day he asked me to inform Washington that he would lead an uprising on March 4, to begin exactly at ten P.M. Boiled down to its bones, it called for Talabani's and Barzani's combined guerrillas to launch small-scale, simultaneous attacks along Iraqi army lines in the north. A Kurdish fifth column would provoke disturbances in Kirkuk and Mawsil and sabotage government facilities all over Iraq. The Shi'a groups in the south would start attacking the Iraqi army at the same time. Within twenty-four hours, Chalabi predicted, the army would revolt and join the uprising. It was pretty much the same plan Chalabi had described in his "End Game." Although neither Talabani nor Barzani had agreed to participate, Chalabi felt that once he threw down the gauntlet, they would—especially if the U.S. were to offer some sign of support.

I wrote a message to Washington about Chalabi's plans, specifying the day and hour. Knowing Washington's opinion about Chalabi and his shopworn "End Game," I was fairly convinced that a message would come back with the return mail ordering him to call it off, or at least postpone it. Silly me.

WHEN IT CAME to convincing the Kurds to join the uprising, the hardest nut for Chalabi to crack was Masud Barzani.

Barzani was the son of the noted Kurdish rebel Mustafa Barzani, or the Red Mullah, as he was popularly known in the U.S. Mustafa had led a sporadic guerrilla war against Saddam in the early 1970s, but after the Shah of Iran and Henry Kissinger pulled the plug on him in 1974, Mustafa was forced to give up. He moved to the United States and died a broken man in his bed in McLean, Virginia. Not without reason, perhaps, Masud distrusted the U.S. government and, in particular, the CIA. Only grudgingly did he allow the U.S.-backed Iraqi National Congress to keep its headquarters in Salah al-Din, a town under Barzani's control.

To make matters worse, Barzani was doing fine with the status quo. After spending most of his life in exile, he enjoyed having his own country even if it was only a virtual one. Operation Provide Comfort, the air protection provided by American planes, came free of charge—the U.S. almost never attempted to interfere in his affairs—and by late 1994 Barzani had a nice little business in smuggled Iraqi oil.

In the months before the Gulf War, the United Nations had imposed a total oil embargo on Iraq, cutting off all exports, including oil. Almost immediately, though, the embargo had sprung leaks. First it was barges in the Gulf, running the blockade at night. Soon an overland route to Turkey opened up. Vegetable trucks transported the oil from Kirkuk in jerry-rigged tanks welded to their undercarriages. By 1995 some estimates put the quantity as high as a hundred thousand barrels a day crossing into Turkey. To get there, the oil had to pass through a large tract of Kurdistan controlled by the KDP and Barzani took his cut from each truck. The smuggled oil was also a lifeline for Saddam, who used the money to fund his intelligence services and Special Republican Guards —the forces that kept him alive. Indeed, everyone seemed to profit from the smuggling except Talabani, who wasn't getting a penny because no part of the smuggling route passed through his corner of Kurdistan. With Barzani accumulating money in his war chest, smuggled oil began to dangerously destabilize the north.

You only had to drive a few miles into the north to understand the dimensions of the smuggling operation. Trucks carrying oil were lined up bumper to bumper, often for as long as twenty miles, waiting to cross into Turkey. One Kurd told us that when there was a spike in Turkish oil demand, the trucks stretched all the way to the Iraqi lines beyond Dahuk, about seventy miles. Over the months upon months of smuggling, so much oil had leaked from the trucks that the road was dangerously slick to drive on.

Washington knew all about the smuggling but pretended it wasn't happening. As far as I know, neither the State Department nor our embassy in Ankara ever challenged Turkey, which could have shut down the whole operation with a single telephone call. Part of the problem was that the Turks were already unhappy about the Gulf War's aftermath. We'd promised Turkey a quick, decisive war but never mentioned the possibility of an open-ended embargo and the long-term damage it would have on Turkey's economy. But there was also a bureaucratic roadblock to enforcing the embargo: Our embassy in Ankara fell under the State Department's European Bureau. Smuggled oil, Saddam, Iraqi dissidents, the fractious Kurds—they were the Near East Bureau's problem. All our Ankara embassy cared about was keeping the Turks happy and if the Turks said they needed cheap oil for their refineries, well, that was good enough for Ankara.

What I couldn't understand was why the White House didn't intervene. All it had to do was ask Saudi Arabia to sell Turkey a hundred thousand barrels of discounted oil. Turkey certainly would have stopped the smuggling for the right price. It was almost as if the White House wanted Saddam to have a little walking-around money.

For Iraqis, of course, the arrangement made perfect sense. By turning a blind eye to the smuggled oil, the U.S. managed to turn the Kurdish opposition against itself even as it helped Saddam pay for his praetorian guard, just what you'd expect of a clever superpower that was secretly supporting the local despot.

MY OWN RELATIONS with Masud Barzani went sour from the start. Whenever I met with him at his Sar-i Rash office, a former government guest house about a five-minute drive from Salah al-Din, Barzani would begin to shift uneasily in his seat as soon as I raised the subject of the ongoing fighting between the Kurds. It wouldn't be long before he would sit bolt upright, straighten himself to his full height (his feet still wouldn't touch the floor), and start cursing Talabani. This would be my signal that the meeting was over. Once, when I told him the U.S. was fed up with the Kurds and would abandon the north one day, Barzani lost his temper. He walked over to where I was sitting, pointed his index finger at me, and hissed through clenched teeth: "Don't threaten me."

It didn't seem possible, but as the fighting picked up, my stock with Barzani sank even lower. On February 17 I asked him about his relations with Iran. Angry as ever, he flatly denied that he even had a channel to Iran, let alone the ability to attack the PUK from Iranian soil. The next day when I visited Talabani at Qalat Cholan, his camp near the Iranian border, he told me that he'd just learned Barzani had

cut a deal with Iran that would allow him to transport
artillery across Iranian soil so he could attack the
PUK from the east. The axis of the assault would be
Panjwin, a PUK-held town on the Iranian border.

A little before six A.M. the next morning, Talabani
woke me to tell me that, just as he had predicted,
Barzani's forces were shelling Panjwin from the
foothills on the Iranian side of the border. If true, it
had the makings of a catastrophe for the U.S.: Iran
had to be kept out of Iraq at all costs. When I called
Barzani on the satellite telephone, he swore his troops
were not in Iran and he wasn't shelling Panjwin, from
Iran or anywhere else. Someone was lying. I decided I
had to take a look myself.

Talabani loaned me four Toyota Land Cruisers
and a Toyota pickup with a .50-caliber machine gun
bolted on its bed, and we drove about four hours
through snow-patched mountains. Descending the
valley into Panjwin, I saw no immediate sign of a
bombardment. At the town's edge, I was met by the
local PUK commander and the mayor, who showed
me around. On foot, you could see the smoking
craters. I picked up the fragment of a 107mm base
plate. It was warm. The mayor explained that the
shelling had stopped once the rumor circulated that
the "American ambassador" was on his way.

As we walked through the town, the villagers
slowly started to come out of the ruins and follow us.
One man was so furious that he picked up a boulder
and threw it at an unexploded shell, cursing Barzani.
I sped our little inspection tour on, right up to the
Iranian border. By now I was close enough to clearly

see that the gunners manning the 107mm rockets on the far side of the border were Barzani's *pech merga*. Behind them stood khaki-clad soldiers from Iran's Pasdaran, the Islamic Revolutionary Guard Corps.

As soon as I got back to Talabani's camp, I called Barzani to tell him what I'd seen at Panjwin.

"You betrayed me" was his only response.

Granted, I had gone to see for myself what was happening, and I'd used Talabani's equipment and men to get there, but only in the Middle East could you betray someone by refusing to accept the lie he had told you in the first place.

BARZANI'S KURDISH NEMESIS, Jalal Talabani, was not only genial and urbane; he was also a first-rate actor and a world-class politician. Built along the lines of a double-wide fireplug and with a smile as broad as the Euphrates, Talabani enjoyed the role of a likable rogue. When I would confront him after he'd made some unprovoked attack on one of Barzani's positions, he'd laugh, hand me a cigar, and promise not to do it again. And the next day, of course, he'd start attacking all over again. Truth suffered with both men, but at least with Talabani, there were some good times in the bargain.

Talabani was an Iraqi nationalist. He believed that the Kurds should have a degree of autonomy, but he didn't want to see Iraq partitioned among its ethnic groups. Unlike Barzani, Talabani seemed to genuinely want Saddam gone and was ready to make any sacrifice necessary to accomplish that aim.

Talabani even had his own plan for getting rid of Saddam.

He first told Tom and me about it at a meeting in Kui Sinjaq, his native village, on March 2. Talabani ushered us into his bedroom, out of earshot of the political bureau and military commanders who waited in his cramped living room. Books and papers were everywhere—on the bed, under the bed, stacked against the walls. With the lights off and curtains drawn, the room smelled of sleep. The three of us sat on the edge of Talabani's unmade bed.

"I am at a fork in the road," Talabani said in his fluent but heavily accented English.

There were two choices staring him in the face, he said, neither of them safe. He could continue fighting Barzani, as he had for the last year, but it had become a war of attrition and he was unlikely to be able to inflict a decisive defeat. In the meantime, the dirty oil money was giving Barzani an insurmountable cash advantage. At the present level of conflict, Talabani wouldn't have anything left to fight with in a week or two. Or, he said, he could launch an out-and-out offensive—a do-or-die effort against Barzani and his KDP before the PUK's stocks of weapons and ammunition ran out completely. Apart from its finality, the latter plan ran the risk of sucking in an outside power, like Iran or Turkey, or encouraging Saddam to step in from the south.

"And that is what is worrying me now," Talabani said.

He had received information from a spy inside the KDP camp that Barzani was panicking and ready to make common cause with Baghdad. Using the same channel he employed for his oil business, Barzani had promised Saddam that if Talabani were to launch an uprising, he wouldn't participate in it. In return, Barzani expected Saddam's help in expelling Talabani from Irbil, the administrative capital of Kurdistan, which the PUK had seized the year before.

"He's a weak man," Talabani said of his rival, "prey to a narrow tribal view of the world—someone who doesn't give a damn about the opposition or Chalabi's uprising or even overthrowing Saddam. He cares only about the Barzan clan and would make a pact with the devil to protect it.

"So I could do nothing, keep my fingers crossed, and hope Barzani and Saddam don't make a deal. But I have another choice. Simply turn over the card table."

Talabani spread out a map of Iraq on the bed, pushing a stack of books onto the floor.

"Look here. This is the V Corps line," he said, running his finger along V Corps positions south of Irbil. V Corps was the main Iraqi force in the north facing PUK and KDP lines. "What do you see?"

"A reinforced Iraqi army corps," I answered, refusing to believe he was about to propose attacking it.

"That's what it says on your Pentagon's maps, with all of those little flags standing for divisions and brigades. But what I see is a demoralized, vulnerable, beatable army."

Talabani grabbed my hand to make sure he had my full attention.

"What I'm going to do is simply pull back my troops off the Irbil line—just abandon it—then march them south and hit V Corps here, here, and here," he said, jabbing his thick finger at three V Corps divisions. "And you'll see. Entire companies, even divisions, will surrender at the first shot."

"And if Barzani attacks you from the rear?" I asked.

"If he does, everyone will know him for the traitor he is, and he will not survive a day. His own people will squash him like a bug."

"And what happens if you defeat V Corps?"

"That's where you come in. We'll see how badly Mr. Clinton wants to get rid of Saddam."

On the face of it, a band of Kurdish irregulars attacking an Iraqi army corps head-on was like jumping out of an airplane without a parachute: a thrill ride destined to end in a splat. V Corps wasn't the finest fighting unit in the Iraqi army but it had plenty of armor and artillery and its forward positions along the Kurdish lines were dug in behind berms, razorwire, and concrete bunkers. In addition, it was backed up by a fully manned and equipped elite Republican Guards Division, and it was positioned well below the thirty-sixth parallel, where Saddam's Mi-24 Hind gunships were allowed to fly. Harassing V Corps was one thing; engaging it in a battle, quite another.

As for his own forces, Talabani had no more than two thousand lightly armed *pech merga* to throw against V Corps. The few tanks he had captured from Saddam in 1991 had been sold to Iran. While he had some artillery, he was critically short of ammunition. Toyota Land Cruisers, his troops' only transportation, gave him speed and mobility but nothing else. The Land Cruisers would be sitting ducks for Saddam's gunships.

But Talabani was neither crazy nor reckless. He had fought Saddam's army before, and he understood its vulnerabilities as well as anyone. If Talabani thought he could take on V Corps, there had to be something to it, at least to my thinking. The critical question, as I saw it, was just how bad off the Iraqi army was, and bits and pieces of evidence suggested it was in real trouble.

Handfuls of Iraqi defectors had been slipping into the north ever since the Gulf War. Now the trickle was turning into a river, and they carried tales of a defeated army: scarce rations, no ammunition, no fuel. The elite Republican Guards were only slightly better off, the defectors said. In late 1994 Saddam had ordered the ears of captured deserters cut off, another sign of rising discontent. Every night Iraqi television ran grotesque pictures of young men with missing ears, blood running down their necks.

In short, the stars seemed to be aligning against Saddam, even if no one could be certain his army was on the brink of collapse. The problem was that no one—not I or Chalabi or Talabani, certainly not anyone back in distant Washington—could tell what and whom the stars were aligning around. Talabani's war plan threw a third ring into the circus, along with the general's coup and Chalabi's "End Game" attack. Could attacking V Corps work? Was Talabani serious about pulling the trigger, or was he just playing politics with me and, through me, with Barzani and all the others? I really didn't know. The only beacon I had to go by was what I understood American policy to be: that we would support any serious movement to get rid of Saddam Hussein. Those were my orders as I understood them, the reason I had brought my team into northern Iraq. And I took my orders seriously.

"So, what should I do?" Talabani asked when he finished. "What choice do I make? Fight Barzani or Saddam?"

"Make a truce with Barzani."

"It's too late for that. Barzani is desperate. At any minute he will sign an agreement with Saddam, and when he does, we will all be finished—the Kurds, the opposition, and you."

"What about his promise to join Chalabi's insurrection on March 4?"

"Barzani is sitting up on his mountain just itching to betray it," Talabani said. "If he really cared about the opposition and uniting the Kurds, he would have agreed long ago to share the money from the oil."

I hesitated before speaking. I wanted to choose my words carefully. "Jalal, if the choice comes down to Saddam invading the north or you attacking V Corps—and those really are the only alternatives— you know which side I come down on."

"I knew that was going to be your answer." Talabani laughed, crushing my hand in his iron grip. "Let's go tell the others."

There were just enough chairs in Talabani's dining

room, the largest room in his house, for everyone to sit on. I looked at Talabani's field commanders as they filed in and took their seats around the table. They were an odd lot. Half were unreconstructed Marxists who had spent most of their lives in Europe and came back to Iraq in March 1991 only to fight Saddam. The rest were hard-as-nails guerrilla fighters whose sole interest was slitting the throats of Saddam's soldiers.

Standing at the end of the table, Talabani waited patiently for the room to go quiet. Even after it did, he stood silently for a good minute. Then, with *"It's time to turn our guns on Saddam,"* the room exploded into clapping and shouting. Talabani went on for another fifteen minutes in Kurdish. By the end, his commanders would have run through the wall if he'd asked.

As soon as Talabani sat down, his *pech merga* swept into the room bearing enormous platters heaped with lamb, rice, and Persian nan, the waiters handsomely accented by bandoliers and sashes.

When it was time to go, Talabani walked Tom and me to our car. Just as I was about to climb in, he took me by the elbow and pulled me aside so no one could hear us.

"You know, I can't do this alone. What is Washington going to do when I attack?"

"Washington wants Saddam out." That wasn't the answer he was looking for, but there was no point in telling him that Washington was simply ignoring him, me, and Iraq. It hadn't even responded to the message I had sent in mid-February on the day and hour

Chalabi's uprising would begin.

No question, I was operating on the edge of my orders, out where the bright fires burn, but so far as I knew, I was telling Talabani the truth. ▮▮▮▮▮▮▮▮
▮▮▮▮▮▮▮▮▮▮▮▮▮▮▮▮▮▮▮▮▮▮▮▮▮▮. And I hadn't yet seen Tony Lake's cable. Even after I did, it would take some time for all its implications to sink in. I had no idea that while I was running around Kurdistan trying to find some way to help Saddam Hussein's enemies drive him from authority, Washington had forgotten to care whether he stayed in power or not.

"Jalal," I said again, by way of emphasis, "I assure you Washington wants Saddam gone."

17

CHALABI READ Tony Lake's message and collapsed on the sofa.

"Does this mean we have to stop everything?" he asked me, almost inaudibly.

"Ahmad, you read English as well as I do. It says it's up to you to go ahead or not."

"Have you given it to Masud?"

I knew where Chalabi was heading. He was right, too. The major general who had defected from Saddam's army was forced to fold his plans into Chalabi's as best he could thanks to Washington's refusal to respond to his coup proposal. Even though Chalabi wasn't to be trusted with the fine print, the two had made common cause. Barzani, though, had watched Chalabi's preparations for the March 4 uprising with undisguised anger. He couldn't simply refuse to participate—doing so would cost him too much face with the Kurds—but he expected me to stop Chalabi. It infuriated him when I stuck to the position that the U.S. believed all Iraqis would be better off without Saddam and that we would thus encourage any opposition group that was serious

299

about changing the government in Baghdad. Chalabi and I both knew that Lake's message was a heaven-sent excuse for Barzani to sit out the action.

"Has Mr. Lake never heard of the Bay of Pigs?" Chalabi asked, standing up, his face a bright scarlet. "As soon as Masud sees this message, he's going to screw everyone. I guarantee you that." He wadded Lake's message up and threw it in the corner. "Fuck Lake. He might be able to scare Masud into not doing anything, but not me. I'm going through with it."

Chalabi walked me to my car and opened my door.

"Lake could not have picked a worse time to pull out," Chalabi said, now brooding. "I'm just afraid that at the end of the day it's going to be our blood on the floor rather than Saddam's."

Just as Chalabi predicted, Barzani dropped out, even before I could show him Lake's message.

When I pulled up in front of Barzani's Sar-i Rash palace—the eagle's nest above Salah al-Din where I had met him so many times during the last month—it was obvious he had decamped. The windows were shuttered; the cars, gone. The two guards at the front gate said they had no idea where he could be found.

I went to look for Nicherwan Barzani, Masud's nephew and second in command, to give him Lake's message. Nicherwan invited me over for dinner, and I was able to get a good look around his house. The Italian designer furniture, the Persian rugs, and other finery screamed money. Clearly not all the revenues from the smuggled oil were going into the KDP's war chest. The Barzanis, Nicherwan and Uncle Masud, certainly had come a long way from their dirt poor, one-mule village hanging on the side of Kurdistan's barren scarp to their Sar-i Rash estates and virtual country in the north. The oil business was good. The last thing they needed was a dustup with their business partner, Saddam.

"Masud already knows," Nicherwan said sulkily, speaking through the grille of his door. "He already heard from our guy in Washington."

He only shrugged when I asked him what his uncle was going to do about the March 4 uprising, but I had a bad feeling we were in for trouble. Later that afternoon, Chalabi confirmed my suspicion: Barzani was on the Turkish border, in Zakhu, ready to hop across and take refuge with the Turks if things turned out badly. I just hoped it wasn't too late for the colonel to pull back and try another day.

CHALABI DIDN'T CHANGE his mind overnight. As reliable as a Swiss clock, the show started on March 4. By about eight that evening, the former school that served as the Iraqi National Congress headquarters was lit up like an amusement park. Somewhere Chalabi had found an enormous generator. Trucks filled the parking lot, waiting to load up INC recruits and head to the Iraqi lines. Toyota Land Cruisers pulled up in front, collected messages, and left with a squeal of tires. Inside, it was pure circus: ringing telephones, shouting aides waving paper in the air; everything, it seemed, but the one thing the Kurds needed most—the support of the United States.

The general was sitting alone in an empty office

when I walked in on him. He wore a newly pressed major general's uniform. A shiny officer's saber lay across the desk in front of him. He stood up and weakly shook my hand. In another hour, he said, an escort would take him to the Iraqi army lines, where he would be met and taken to Tikrit to link up with his colleagues. The general's arrival in Tikrit would be the signal for the coup to start.

The general didn't mention Lake's message, even though I had given it to him the day before. Like Chalabi, he felt it was too late to turn back. The colonel from the tank school who was to lead the assault had already armed his tanks with stolen shells; there was no way to return them and not be found out. I could do nothing to help. The general was either going to make it across the lines or he wasn't; his uprising was going to succeed or fail. I shook his hand, figuring I would never see him again, and set out for home. As I walked back, someone in the distance fired an illumination flare into the night sky.

I WENT TO BED expecting Chalabi to wake me with news, but the night passed without a word from him. At around nine the next morning—by now it was March 5—I set out to the INC headquarters. Even if the fight was going poorly, I thought, the place was sure to be a beehive of activity. Wrong. The building was completely abandoned. The generator was gone. There wasn't a car in sight, not even a guard to tell me where everyone had gone. The front door was banging open and shut in the wind. Inside, the offices were bare, stripped clean—computers, file cabinets, furniture. I remember being half surprised that the radiators hadn't been unbolted and taken off the walls.

As I trotted back to the CIA house, I started to compose in my head the message I would write to headquarters. *Dear Langley: I write with the sad news that last night I carelessly misplaced the Iraqi opposition.*

One of Chalabi's aides was waiting for me at the house when I got back. Barzani had had the general arrested a little after midnight, just as he was about to cross the lines to go to Tikrit. Although Barzani released him six hours later, the Iraqi army had used the time to seal its lines in the north. About the time of the general's arrest, Barzani called Chalabi to say that not only were his troops not going to participate in the uprising, but no one else was, either—at least from his critical patch of Kurdistan. The message delivered, Barzani's troops, under Nicherwan's command, promptly arrested every INC member it could find who carried a rifle. Barzani, the aide told me, placed the blame squarely on Washington's shoulders. The intent of Lake's message was clear: He wanted the general stopped as well as Chalabi. Faced with such massive betrayal, Chalabi had pulled up stakes and moved on to Irbil. Talabani, who controlled the city, hadn't moved on March 4, but at least he still was paying lip service to action on Saddam.

The following morning, March 6, I awoke to see the

general's car pulling up in front. He'd exchanged his major general's uniform for a cheap plaid sport coat. Even his mustache seemed to droop.

"Sir," he said quietly as soon as he sat down on the sofa. "I must leave now. I must go to Damascus to put my children in school."

And why not, I thought? His couriers, the secret committee, the colonel had all been arrested. There was no way Saddam was going to spare them. The general saw no point in keeping a morbid vigil in the north, waiting for an assassin's bullet.

I could tell he wanted to say a lot more. He had put everything on the line—his country, his family, his life. He had trusted us, trusted the CIA, and we had let the coup go forward, right up until the very end when the White House pulled the plug without warning or a decent explanation. He kept his own counsel, though, and the two of us sat in silence, finishing our tea. In truth, I still don't know what I might have said. That Washington in the end just hadn't wanted to commit? That even though I had kept my masters fully informed, they had dithered and dithered and, in the end, finally decided that too much was at stake to upset the status quo in Iraq? That, faced with a choice between sins of commission or omission, Washington had chosen the latter and left good and brave men twisting in the wind thousands of miles across the ocean? All of it seemed beyond expression. Instead I walked the general out, shook his hand, and waited until his car disappeared around the corner at the end of the street.

Back inside, I told Tom to raise the CIA's relay station in northern Virginia. The debacle was looking more and more complete, but I wasn't ready to give up yet. I wanted to see if the satellites had picked up anything, like a division, a company or even a single tank out of place.

The news was about as bad as it could get. By noon on March 5—on what was supposed to be D Day for the dissidents—the Iraqi army was off high alert. The armor that had been patrolling the streets in Mawsil and Kirkuk since February 28 was gone. There was no sign of movement in the garrisons of the 76th Brigade, the 15th Infantry Division, and the 5th Mechanized Division, the three units that were to have joined the coup. But what I was really interested in was the colonel's garrison near Tikrit. *Shit.* Nothing out of place. If his tanks had moved out of their sheds on March 4, they were back now.

AT 10:22 THAT NIGHT, the secure telephone rang. It was Bob ██████████, my boss in Washington. Since I had been in the north, he'd called me only once.

"What's happening out there?" he asked.

"Nothing. We're just sitting here around the pool sipping frozen daiquiris."

"Cut the crap. What I'm going to tell you, you can't repeat to anyone. Do you understand?" he said. His voice had gone cold.

After I assured him I did, he asked, "Is anyone on the team using the alias Robert Pope?"

"Never heard the name." Everyone on the team

was using an alias except me, but no one was using Robert Pope.

"You'd better be right, because you're skating on thin ice. I can't tell you what's going on. I shouldn't have even asked you about Pope. So this conversation never happened. Copy?"

There was no point in asking what he was talking about, because Bob would have told me if he could have. A retired marine colonel who had joined the CIA in his late forties, Bob followed orders. He may not have liked or agreed with them, but he followed them. If he said he couldn't tell me, I knew he wouldn't.

"You're to come back to Washington as soon as you can. When you pass through Ankara, don't tell anyone anything. They could be potential witnesses. And when you get home, don't call anyone. Especially don't call anyone from Iraqi operations. They could be witnesses, too."

Witnesses? The word definitely had a bad ring to it, but it was something else I couldn't do anything about from 6,192 miles away.

"Bob, I can't come back now. The opposition's in the toilet, but it's not hopeless. Give me a couple weeks and I can put things back together."

"You didn't hear what I said. You're being pulled out. End of story."

"I've got people spread across the north. I can't pick up and leave just like that."

"Okay. You can take up to four days if you have to. But not a day longer."

Only when Bob hung up did I realize that he hadn't

said a word about either the diversion or the coup. It was all the confirmation I needed that Washington intended to label both frauds. I knew enough about the way Washington worked to know that when it didn't like some piece of information, it did everything in its power to discredit the messengers, which in this case were Chalabi and the general. So the corporate line in Washington was that nothing had happened in Iraq on March 4, nothing at all. Frankly, at that point, I wondered if Washington wasn't right.

18

I FOUND TOM on the roof of our house, looking through binoculars toward the south, in the direction of the Iraqi lines. He listened silently as I told him about "Robert Pope" and our recall. Even as I spoke, I was running through a mental checklist of what we had to do to leave the north.

"I can feel it," he said when I finished. "Talabani's going to attack tonight, and Washington's going to have a lot more to worry about than someone named Pope."

Tom handed me the binoculars. All I could see were a few shimmering lights in the plains below Salah al-Din. Then, toward the south, the faint tail of a flare shot up into the sky. It burst and hung there, giving off a spectral glow. A few seconds later there was a single, bright flash, maybe from an artillery cannon, although I couldn't be certain at this distance. A minute, maybe more, passed in silence before an artillery battery opened up and explosions began reverberating through the foothills around Salah al-Din. Suddenly the night sky turned into a light show of artillery flares, and tracers.

My first thought, to be honest, was an old one: *Damn, the Kurds are at it again.* But the explosions were all coming from south of Irbil, nowhere near Talabani's and Barzani's lines. Tom was right: Talabani had decided to attack V Corps.

Taking two steps at a time, I ran downstairs to call Paul, the paramilitary officer I had stationed at Talabani's command center in Irbil. Paul managed to shout over the confusion that about two hundred of Talabani's guerrillas had just encircled a brigade from the 38th Division at Guwayr and were about to overrun it.

Paul called in reports all night. With only two wounded, Talabani's *pech merga* annihilated the 38th Division's 848th Brigade, capturing its headquarters. They also captured the attached 601st Battery. About eighty Iraqi soldiers were taken prisoner, including the brigade commander, Colonel 'Abd-al-'Aziz Namuri. Talabani's men dynamited the battalion's bunkers and destroyed its 152mm and 130mm artillery, looting what ammunition and small arms they could carry back in their Toyotas. Then they turned back a relieving force of Republican Guards, destroying an armored personnel carrier and several troop transports. The ferocity of the Kurds' attack stunned the Republican Guard's commander. He abandoned any attempt to relieve the 848th and ordered his forward units to take up defensive positions. It was a crushing victory—the first time the Kurds had inflicted this much damage to the Iraqi army since the March 1991 uprising.

As soon as Washington was awake, I called Iraqi operations.

"Yeah. We've read your report." It was the pasty-faced reports officer with stringy matted hair who thought I was a cowboy. Before I left Washington for the north, she had made a point of telling me she believed it was silly for the CIA to have a base in Iraq. "We picked up some collateral intelligence," she went on.

"Some?"

"It looks like there may have been some sort of fighting in the V Corps area last night. Rocket-propelled grenade and machine-gun fire. It stopped about oh-six-hundred this morning, your time. There was a report of about thirty prisoners moved to Irbil. But we can't confirm it."

"What do you mean you can't confirm it? We watched an artillery battle go on all night."

"We don't have any imagery to back it up."

"Yeah, of course. The attack went down at night."

"I'm just telling you what they think back here."

"You mean you think Talabani faked the whole thing—*all that artillery*—just to amuse us."

I hung up. I should have known better than to argue with headquarters. You never got anywhere. Worse, it was considered bad form, possibly even a sign of warped objectivity. As far as Washington was concerned, if the big eye in the sky didn't see it, it didn't happen.

I had more faith in my own eyes and wanted to see the war for myself. "Tom, pack up," I told him. "We're going to the front to look for Talabani."

A dozen jerry cans of gasoline and water, two AK-47s, a couple boxes of rations, a compass, a ground positioning system, an air navigational map of Iraq, and our LST-5 tacset were about all our old two-door Nissan Patrol pickup could hold. I decided not to bring our bodyguards. A convoy would attract too much attention.

Between Salah al-Din and Irbil we didn't see another car. Even the fields, normally dotted with brightly dressed Kurdish women planting spring seed, were deserted. As we crossed the Irbil plain, we could see that Talabani's trenches, artillery emplacements, and bunkers had been abandoned. Irbil was wide open to an attack if Barzani dared.

In Irbil we picked up an escort to take us to Sulamaniyah, a good-size Kurdish town near the Iranian border in northeast Iraq. Along the way we ate lunch in Dukah, at a shish kebab stand on the lake. A rusted sign hanging by one nail advertised sailboats for rent. I wondered what had happened to the boats and how many years it would be before anyone would sail there again. We were below the thirty-sixth now, fair game for Saddam's gunships.

It was dark when we drove into Sulamaniyah. The streets were deserted, and there wasn't a light on in the city except at Talabani's headquarters. A mob of young and old men surrounded it, trying to push their way in.

"Volunteers," said the guard as he cleared a path for us.

The Sulamaniyah commander showed us into his office and served us tea. He pointed at a map behind his desk with a ruler and attempted to explain what was happening on the front. But he seemed to know only where the Iraqi army was. Finally he gave up, shrugged, and suggested we leave right away for Talabani's camp. A guide sent by Talabani was waiting to take us there.

We drove up into the mountains south of Sulamaniyah, following a packed-dirt, unmarked road with our headlights off. Saddam's gunships were firing at anything that moved. A little after midnight we turned off a side road and descended into a clearing. In the middle of it was a squat, one-story cinder-block building, seemingly deserted, but as soon as we pulled up in front and turned off the engine, a dozen *pech merga* materialized and silently helped us unload the car. They wanted it moved away from the building as quickly as possible.

Talabani came barreling out of the building like a bear out of his cave, grabbed me around the waist, and lifted me off the ground. "It's about time you got here. You've been missing all the fun," he whispered. "And in your honor we will not sleep in the fields tonight but in my palace."

He hooked his arm through mine and guided me into the pitch-black building, a school that had been abandoned during the 1988 fighting between the Kurds and the government. Only Talabani, Tom, and I would sleep there. The *pech merga* were scattered in the surrounding hills and caves, where Saddam's helicopters would have trouble finding them. Talabani's room at the end of the hall was empty except for a half-dozen boxes filled with papers and books and a few blankets on the floor. The only light was from a single battery-powered camping lantern.

We sat down on a rug on the cement floor.

"We're going again tonight," Talabani said as he rooted around in a huge humidor for three fresh Cuban Cohiba cigars. "We are going to hit Karablakh tonight. My guys should be infiltrating across the lines as we speak." Since I had never heard of Karablakh, Talabani rolled over to get a map and show me where it was.

Stoked on his own adrenaline, Talabani ranted about how bad off the Iraqi army was; about his plans to capture Kirkuk, the center of Iraq's oil industry and, he assured us, the rightful property of the Kurds; and about the democratic future of Iraq. He would have gone on all night if my eyes hadn't started to close.

"Go to bed," he said. "But first, where is the cavalry?"

"It seems to me you're doing fine without any help."

"I'm running out of ammunition."

"Don't worry, Jalal. Washington is just waking up to what you are doing. It's the same game plan: Get rid of Saddam." That much, at least, I still thought to be true. ███████████████████████████. And Tony Lake's cable hadn't ordered Talabani or any of the others to scrap their plans to overthrow Saddam. It had simply advised that "any decision to proceed will be on your own." Talabani understood that, and he knew as I did that Iraqis would never be able to live in peace as long as Saddam was in power.

Talabani fished two more cigars out of his humidor. "Here, take this and go call Washington."

"Jalal, there's one other thing."

He looked at me.

"We're leaving, but a new team is going to replace us."

Talabani handed me my cigar without responding.

"Go to bed. We're all tired," he finally said.

About ten minutes later he tapped on my door, came in, and handed me a faxed report on Karablakh. His troops had just overrun a battalion there.

"See," Talabani said, his mood brighter. "The army is crumbling."

I got Bob's deputy in the Iraqi operations group on the tacset and told him about Karablakh. Unimpressed, he asked, "Where are you?"

"Singaw."

"Where?"

"It's a little village south of the thirty-sixth— Indian country. I'm with Talabani."

The deputy gasped. "You're out of your mind, and they're going to string you up as soon as you get back."

I pretended I hadn't heard him and told him, as I hung up, that I would be joining Talabani's *pech merga* in an attack on Kirkuk.

I was just falling asleep when Talabani knocked on the door again.

"Saddam's panicking. He's started shelling all along our lines." He closed the door gently. I could hear him chuckling back to his room.

Talabani was clearly going to be up all night, reading reports coming in on the fighting, but for me there was nothing like numbing exhaustion to induce sleep. I didn't care that there was only a thin wool blanket to sleep on, or that Saddam's helicopter gunships were out there somewhere in the night looking for us.

About six the next morning, Talabani woke us to inspect the troops. They were clustered all over the fields around the school, cleaning their weapons, loading up their Toyotas, preparing for more raids that night. As Talabani moved among them, they surged around him, bowing and kissing his hand. An aide brought us a tray of sweet tea to drink while we walked around.

Talabani pressed me to stay with him, but time was running out. We had to be in Ankara in a day and a half. A lightning tour of the front was all Tom and I had time for. Talabani hugged us good-bye and we promised to meet soon.

"In Baghdad." Talabani laughed.

The road to Chamchamal, a town a few miles east of Kirkuk, was paved and in good shape. Again we were the only car. It was a clear day, and we expected to be in Chamchamal in less than an hour. Then we saw it—an Iraqi Mi-24 gunship hovering over a ridge about three miles away. It wasn't moving or turning. It was fixed in the sky, watching. We could only hope that it hadn't seen us—there wasn't a rock, tree, or hollow to hide behind—and that Talabani's *pech merga* had splashed enough Kurdish mud on the Nissan to camouflage it. In less than a minute, the Mi-24 could have turned, flown into easy range, and vaporized us and the Nissan. We waited for what seemed like hours until the helicopter dipped behind the ridge, and then we drove away as fast as the Nissan could go.

Chamchamal was oddly quiet. People were shopping at the open-air market, but as soon as we turned off the engine, we could hear the boom of heavy incoming artillery. In the foothills east of Chamchamal, puffs of gray-white smoke hung in the air.

We continued right up to the front lines, to one of the crossing points between Kurdistan and Iraq. A group of Talabani's fighters milled around the makeshift border post. They didn't have any idea what was happening on the other side. All they knew was that the Iraqi police had abandoned their post and the border was wide open.

Our last stop before going back to Salah al-Din was Irbil. As soon as we cleared the gates of Talabani's main military garrison, we drove into a sea of Iraqi prisoners: maybe four football fields of them, standing, sitting, lying down. Outside the compound, alongside the road, were captured artillery pieces, Kamaz trucks, rocket launchers, crates of AK-47s, anything the *pech merga* could carry back to Irbil from their raids. The line of equipment stretched as far as we could see.

The PUK officer in charge met us at the duty room, assuming we'd come to interrogate his prisoners. I didn't have the heart to tell him that we didn't have the people—and wouldn't ever—to interrogate his prisoners, but I did want to talk to at least one. He brought me into a room where a dozen Iraqi officers sat on benches along the wall. I picked a captain at random. He looked to be about thirty years old and exhausted. Early that morning, a little before two, he told me, he got up to check on his company's pickets and was surprised to find the first position abandoned, as well as the ones on each side. He was on his way back to the company's command post to find out what had happened when automatic gunfire exploded all around him. He waited for his troops to respond, but no one did—not a shot. Almost simultaneously Talabani's *pech merga* were everywhere. It was as if they had dug a tunnel and just popped out of the ground. He had no choice but to surrender. I thanked the captain and gave him my last pack of military rations.

Before leaving, I saw the Irbil commander. He briefed me on the latest attack. His troops had overrun the 847th Brigade. Kirkuk was now vulnerable, and Talabani could take it if he had enough ammunition.

On the drive back to Salah al-Din, Tom described the Iraqi equipment he'd examined. There was little doubt, he said, that it had recently been captured. Based on long experience, he knew the guns could have come only from Iraqi units.

Back at the house, I sent a message to headquarters about the 847th and followed up with a call.

"We're still not picking up anything from overhead about the attacks." It was the pasty-faced reports officer again.

"You can't be serious. Do you really think there's a phony war going on up here? I've just come from

Irbil. We saw thousands of Iraqi prisoners with our own eyes. And there's the captured artillery."

The prisoners, the artillery, Tom's assurance that it was real, my assurance as the senior officer in the field that this wasn't a game—none of it made any difference to her.

"Fine," she said. "I believe you, but the rest of the community doesn't—especially the Pentagon."

I knew she was talking about the CIA and had mentioned the Pentagon only to deflect my annoyance, but none of that helped my mood.

"Well, tell those jerks to put up their platforms and they might see something other than the martinis planted on the bar in front of them."

"I'm just telling you what they're telling me."

"Yeah, I'm starting to get it. If it's not in *The Washington Post* or *The New York Times*, it's not true. Should one of their fancy Washington byline correspondents get on the wrong airplane and end up in Kurdistan, I'll be sure to point him to the front."

Silence.

"Give me Bob," I said, *"please."*

She did, but he wasn't impressed. "Give it a break," he said as soon as he got on the telephone.

"Bob, listen to me a second. There's a real live war going on up here. In another week there will be no V Corps."

"No one here gives a shit about the Kurds. You got it? The next thing I want to hear from you is that you've crossed the border into Turkey."

"You've got to understand that at least in the opposition's mind, I'm personally associated with what is going on—*the collapse of V Corps.* If you pull me out, the offensive will stop."

"And sir, you had better understand that Tony Lake wants your scalp. You have an appointment with Fred Turco at oh-nine-hundred on March 15. You'd better fucking be there."

AS PREDICTED, Talabani's offensive petered out and V Corps did not collapse. Talabani survived, though, with enough of his *pech merga* intact to go back to fighting Barzani in what seems to be a never-ending Kurdish civil war. Chalabi, for his part, wandered around for a while, then returned to Salah al-Din. Barzani, probably under Saddam's orders, eventually evicted him. The general whose defection had brought me to northern Iraq did go on to Damascus, and from there to London. And Saddam Hussein was only moderately discomforted by it all.

Not long afterward, Saddam started trading oil for food, which eased the suffering inside Iraq just enough to stem the tide of defections from his army. So if we want him out now, it will probably take a war, not a coup.

As for me, I had orders to report to Langley, Virginia at 0900 on March 15, and so I did.

PART IV
A POLITICAL EDUCATION

19

MARCH 1995. WASHINGTON, D.C.

I WASN'T THRILLED when Fred Turco shipped me upstairs to the general counsel's office that first morning back at CIA headquarters. The two FBI guys who were waiting for me didn't do much to add to my mood, especially when they informed me I was the subject of a criminal investigation. I had been yanked back from what I still consider a historic opportunity to unseat Saddam Hussein and dropped into a vipers' nest, but in all honesty, I wasn't really worried.

Whatever Tony Lake might have believed—or conveniently allowed himself to believe—there never was a rogue "NSC team" headed by one "Robert Pope" (aka Bob Baer) in northern Iraq. That was all Chalabi's work, a wonderful invention that Lake had swallowed whole. I don't claim to be a Boy Scout, but I hadn't violated Executive Order 12333, either, or federal murder-for-hire statutes. I still had enough confidence in the system to believe that the truth would prevail, and in fact it did.

On March 22, 1995, I passed an FBI polygraph test and drove a stake into Lake's investigation. FBI agents were rooting around in CIA files, but they weren't going to find anything for one simple reason: There was nothing to find. Eventually, on April 4, 1996, the Justice Department would send a "declination" letter to the CIA, an official notice that there wasn't enough evidence to prosecute. The CIA was about as apologetic as it knew how to be. It awarded my team a citation.

But neither a declination nor a citation was a get-out-of-jail-free card. I'd upset the national security adviser and sent the political seismic needles quivering at Langley. That meant two to three years in the penalty box: no overseas assignment until new management came along and memories faded. If I could keep my nose clean and mouth shut, I'd probably be able to get back in the field eventually. One more overseas tour, I figured, and I'd be able to retire. (Overseas years count extra in the Directorate of Operations; with enough of them, you can retire at fifty.)

To be sure, I'd never be promoted because someone would always vaguely remember that I'd infuriated the president's national security adviser and taken a joyride in a Russian tank. A couple of sniggers around the promotions board table and my file would end up on the "not management" stack. But the point was, the CIA was going to leave me alone if I didn't get into any more trouble.

My new job as deputy chief in the Central Eurasian Division's South Group was just the place for lying low. Although South Group oversaw eight posts in central Asia and the Caucasus, my job had nothing to do with running agents or coups. All I really had to do was keep the paper flowing and the in box empty and I had a lot of help with that. Some twenty-five people worked under me. If a thorny problem came up, like whether we should buy a new car for the chief in Bishkek, I could always buck it up to the group chief, Len, who could then buck it up to the deputy division chief, and so on. Headquarters was like slipping into a warm bath. Relax, and nothing much bad could happen. Or so it seemed at first.

It wasn't long, though, before I began to realize just how lost I was in the current culture of Washington and the CIA. Some of the signs were obvious. When I had last spent time in the nation's capital, it was still possible for a case officer to enjoy some of life's little luxuries. In the interim, housing costs had spun out of control, and restaurant prices had swollen so much that only the expense-account class could afford to eat out with any regularity. After putting my life on the line for two decades in places few people would choose to live, I was earning the same salary as a midlevel career civil servant who never leaves his desk. Worse, I seemed to be carrying around a set of job skills that were constantly diminishing in value.

That was the bigger shock: not that I was relatively poor but that my professional worth had dropped so sharply and that I was so ill equipped to deal with this new world. I knew more about the Popular Front for the Liberation of Palestine/General Command than I did about my own country, more about the Saudi Wahabis than I did about the House and the Senate. For decades I had unpacked my bags in places like Tajikistan and the Sudan and begun learning the ins and outs of the local culture, and that's what I did now. I needed an education, and no one was going to hand it to me, so I created my own graduate curriculum in American politics and set out to fulfill it. I did what professional intelligence officers are trained to do: I started talking with all sorts of people, anyone who could teach me how Washington works, intentionally or otherwise. And the lessons came pouring in. I would eventually learn far more than I had bargained for.

To my wonder, I would see how committee hearings and press leaks can be almost as effective as suicide bombers in promoting narrow, parochial causes. To my dismay I would find that the tentacles of big oil stretch from the Caspian Sea to the White House. And to my anger, indeed to my rage, I would also see how money not lives or national security skews so much of what takes place in the very places most charged with protecting us all.

It was like *The Odyssey*, I finally figured out. While we were off fighting Troy, the people back home were drinking and whoring. They didn't give a damn what those of us on the front had gone through, and they sure as hell didn't want to hear what we had to say now.

But I'm getting ahead of my story.

MY FIRST and in some ways most enduring lesson in the politics of Washington arrived a little before noon on May 17, 1995, in the form of the smart, bespectacled, but not unattractive South Group reports officer. She was holding a single piece of paper between her thumb and index finger. With her other hand, she held her nose.

"This one stinks like shit," she said. The South Group reports officer had a sharp tongue to go with her sharp mind.

The paper was a "tasker" from an NSC staffer named Sheila Heslin, who wanted to hear what the CIA knew about three American citizens: Georgetown University professor and prominent Maryland Republican Rob Soubhani; a doctor living in California, Sahag Baghdasarian; and oilman Roger Tamraz.

I didn't know Soubhani or Baghdasarian, but I'd heard a lot about Tamraz from my days in Lebanon. He was a business partner of Amin Jumayyil, the Lebanese president who had released the suspects in the 1983 bombing of the U.S. embassy in Beirut. The two had done well together, but in 1989, after Jumayyil's term ended, Tamraz's bank in Beirut failed, and a Lebanese prosecutor indicted him for defrauding his depositors. Tamraz blamed Syria for the bank's failure, claiming it was engineered to punish him for serving as Jumayyil's emissary to Israel. Whatever the truth, Lebanon registered Tamraz's indictment with Interpol, turning Tamraz into an international fugitive, a big enough black mark to prevent him from doing business in a lot of Middle Eastern countries. Always resilient, Tamraz moved on to the Caspian Sea. He was one of the first oilmen to show up in Turkmenistan after independence. Soon he had parlayed a suitcase of dollars of unknown origin into two prime Caspian oil-reserve blocks. By 1994 he was back in the news, promoting a pipeline that would carry oil from the Caspian to the Mediterranean via Armenia.

Sheila Heslin had included a note in the margin of the tasker, asking for derogatory information on all three men. In Tamraz's case, that would be a snap. But there was a small problem. (Or as my reports officer so gently put it: "Is she nuts?") Whatever his faults, Roger was an American citizen, and ever since Richard Nixon and Operation Chaos, the CIA had stopped spying on Americans. In 1981 an executive order had outlawed it. In the CIA's rule book, spying on Americans was tantamount to assassinating a foreign leader, but maybe, I generously thought, the new crew at the White House was too young to remember Nixon.

"Why does Heslin want dirt on these guys so badly?" I asked innocently.

"How should I know? Maybe she's a jilted lover."

"So what do we have to do with it?" I asked. Heslin's tasker, I had noticed, was addressed to the Directorate of Intelligence, not to our Directorate of Operations.

"Heslin thinks Tamraz is one of ours—a recruited agent."

That put Heslin's request in a new light. According to a 1977 agreement between the secretary of state and the director of the CIA, the DO is obligated to inform policymakers when they are in contact with an agent. Since NSC staffers were considered policymakers and Heslin was due to meet Tamraz on June

2, we were obligated to tell her about his connections to the CIA. The 1977 agreement, in short, trumped the 1981 executive order.

It turned out Heslin was right about Tamraz's having a connection to the CIA. According to a file sent over from the Near East Division, he had been in contact with our case officers since the 1970s. At one point, he had even provided cover for two of our officers in one of his U.S. banks. When it later surfaced that the bank was affiliated with Bank of Credit and Commerce International, BCCI—the bank of choice for international narcotics dealers, money launderers, and other crooks—the CIA pulled out of the arrangement. Heslin was wrong, though, in assuming Tamraz was an agent. We had never paid him, and in our books, that meant he never worked for us. Nor was he the kind of person we ever felt entirely comfortable dealing with. Tamraz was always his own man. He helped the CIA only when it served his interests.

When the desk officer brought me the Tamraz memo that was to be sent in response to Heslin's request, I didn't even look at it. "Give it to Len to sign," I told him. Len was the chief of South Group.

I was still evading responsibility, but I admit I was curious. How did Tamraz find his way to Heslin? How did she know about his connections to the CIA? More important, why would an NSC staffer even bother meeting him?

At precisely 1:02 P.M. on May 19, South Group faxed two memos to Heslin, both classified secret. One memo outlined the CIA's relationship with

Tamraz. The other explained that Soubhani, who was an oil consultant to Amoco as well as a professor, was an occasional contact of our chief in Baku. Although Soubhani probably had no idea he was even in touch with the CIA, we played it safe and let Heslin know about the connection. The DI sent its own separate memo on Tamraz to Heslin.

A week later the reports officer was back at my office. "Heslin's on the warpath."

I looked at her blankly.

"She's decided we're protecting Tamraz."

This time I read the Tamraz memo. It spelled out clearly that he was wanted in Lebanon for embezzling from his own banks and for other crimes.

"So what's wrong with that?" I asked. Embezzlement sounded derogatory to me.

"Heslin wants hard evidence to hang Tamraz, and we didn't give it to her."

Apparently, Heslin had gotten her dander up after comparing the memos from the DI and the DO. The DI sent along all the lurid Lebanese press reporting, which accused Tamraz of everything short of child molestation. Heslin had expected us to send over the same stuff—and more. Doesn't the DO keep track of American businessmen working overseas, Heslin had asked her DI contact.

I rewound the spool to those long nights waiting for my agents on the Green Line, hoping Hizballah wouldn't kidnap or kill me. Apparently I'd gotten it wrong. What the White House wanted all along was business intelligence, dirt on Roger Tamraz, rather than intelligence on the terrorists.

Still, I figured that Sheila Heslin might just need a little education. Probably she didn't know that a DO file was for contact reports and cables related to the running of an agent. It wasn't a place where we stuffed articles from the press or stored evidence against an agent, hoping one day to be able to indict him. To be sure, if we found that information on an agent broke American law, we made a record of it and turned the evidence over to Justice, but looking to indict our agents and contacts wasn't something we did as a matter of course.

I took the bull by the horns and called Heslin to explain all this. I also wanted to remind her, as we had on the cover sheet for the Tamraz memo we sent on May 19, that the rest of his files were in archives and it would take time to retrieve them for a complete summary.

Heslin was unimpressed. She grunted and hung up the telephone.

★

IN WASHINGTON, when it rains, it pours.

Bill ▆▆▆▆▆▆▆, the deputy chief in New York, stuck his head in my door. I think it was May 30. "You guys interested in running an American oilman doing business in the Caspian?"

Whenever another case officer offers you an agent, it's time to hold on to your wallet.

"No one in New York has the time to run this guy," he said. "Anyhow, the Caspian's too complicated for us."

Too complicated? Next thing I knew, Bill would be

telling me that the oilman was owned by a little old lady who drove him only on Sundays.

"Well, who is it?"

"Roger Tamraz."

That surprised me. Nothing in his file had indicated that New York was still meeting Tamraz.

Let me be absolutely frank here: Any sane Directorate of Operations case officer in my position would have run the other way. Red flags were flying all over the field. A wanted Lebanese middleman, a shady Caspian Sea oil deal, and an NSC aide on the warpath—it doesn't get much worse. Not to mention my track record with Tony Lake. But I'm always one to double my bet when I'm down.

"Sure," I said. I had no idea what I'd do with Tamraz, but the fact that a staffer at the NSC hated him was enough for me to meet him. Anyhow, the DO didn't have a single source in the Caspian. Tamraz was better than nothing.

"Tell him to call me at this number," I added as I scribbled my CIA unclassified line on a piece of paper.

Unclassified lines are publicly attributed to the CIA. If you were to call the operator and ask about the three-digit prefix, she could tell you the number belonged to the CIA. The other lines, the sterile ones, were registered at the phone company in someone else's name, like the Bureau of Engraving and Printing, Parkway Mortuary or something. I used the unclassified line because I didn't want Roger Tamraz to think from the get-go that we were going to play footsie.

★

As soon as Tamraz pushed his way through the Four Seasons' double doors, I recognized him from the photograph in his file. Slight and sandy-haired, wearing horn-rimmed glasses and a Brooks Brothers suit, he didn't look the least Lebanese. Ed Pechous was a couple of paces behind him. Lately the chief in New York and Tamraz's last case officer—the one who hadn't been sending in reports—Pechous had gone to work for Tamraz the day he retired from the agency.

Once we made eye contact, Tamraz sailed across the lobby as if he owned the place, just like the New York banker he had become. We were still introducing ourselves when he whispered something in Pechous's ear, handed him his briefcase, and turned his back on him as Pechous scooted away.

Nice touch, Roger, I thought. This had established him as just another Middle Eastern high roller who hired retired spooks, Secret Service agents, colonels, and ambassadors for the status: a bargain, too, less expensive than a private jet or a yacht anchored at Antibes, and easier to unload when budgets get tight.

After the waiter brought us coffee, I got down to business.

"How'd your meeting with Sheila Heslin go?" I asked.

"Wonderfully. She loves the idea of the Armenian route." (According to Heslin's version of the meeting, which I heard later, she all but threw Roger out of her office. It lasted a frigid twenty minutes.)

Tamraz pulled out a map of the Caucasus and

Turkey, which he slid across the table for me to look at.

"I'm going to connect the Caspian to the Mediterranean with an oil pipeline," he said, running his finger along a line that traversed Azerbaijan, Nagorno-Karabakh, Armenia, and Turkey. "It's the deal of the century."

For the next thirty minutes Tamraz droned on about his "peace pipeline." I think he sincerely wanted me to believe that a pipeline would bring Armenia and Azerbaijan to the bargaining table. It didn't matter to Tamraz that history had fairly well established that when political tensions rise, the first thing blown up is an oil pipeline.

"Seems like all this is going to cost a lot of money," I said, hoping to sidetrack him and bring the meeting to a quick end. "Who's going to pay for it, Roger?"

"The Chinese." He pulled out a press photo of Matt Steckel, the president of Tamraz's Oil Capital Limited, presumably at a signing ceremony commemorating the Chinese agreement to finance the pipeline. Since the caption was in Chinese, I had to take Tamraz's word that it wasn't a picture of his bankruptcy proceeding.

"Roger, this is all very interesting. We need to talk about it more. Is there anything I can do for you now?"

Roger paused and then said, "Yes, as a matter of fact, there is. I need the president to hear my proposal."

Clearly, Tamraz had a romantic view of my employer. He thought "CIA" was a kind of abracadabra that would magically open all the important doors in Washington, including the one at 1600 Pennsylvania Avenue. Somehow he had missed the press reports about Bill Clinton's turning away his CIA briefers when they showed up in Little Rock the day after he won the election.

"You know, Roger, we don't have the same juice we used to at the White House," I said, trying to clue him in to reality. "Frankly, it's difficult for even me to get a meeting at the NSC."

"What should I do?"

"Well, I think most people in your position hire a lobbyist."

Roger looked at me, all but begging for a name. I had just read something about Clinton's former counsel Lloyd Cutler in *The Washington Post*, and said that I'd heard he was good.

Roger gazed at me in awe, as if I'd just invented peanut butter.

"We'll keep in touch," he said as he shook my hand and rushed off to another meeting.

I LEARNED LATER that Tamraz knew more about lobbying the Clinton administration than many people. In 1994 he had hired the firm of Arnell and Hastie to buy access in Washington. The firm claimed to be especially close to Secretary of Commerce Ron Brown and did manage to broker a few meetings for Tamraz. Pleased, Roger sent a fat retainer to Arnell and Hastie for a ticket on Ron Brown's plane carrying a trade mission to Moscow. At the last minute, Brown got wind of Roger's Interpol warrant and disinvited him. What if Russia honored the warrant and picked up Roger on arrival? What if Russia seized Brown's U.S. government-issue airplane for transporting a wanted felon? International business was tricky that way.

Arnell and Hastie didn't care whether Roger missed the flight or not. The ticket was prepaid, nonrefundable, and nontransferable, and the firm wanted its money. It filed suit and won a judgment against Oil Capital Limited, Panama for $130,000— a pyrrhic victory since OCL, Panama had about 23 cents in its account.

Roger had also been lobbying the State Department hard. He'd won some converts and lost others. During his last visit to Turkey and Armenia, he started a fight between the U.S. ambassadors in Armenia and Azerbaijan that grew so nasty the two embassies stopped talking to each other.

WHEN I STARTED ASKING my contacts in the petroleum industry about Roger, the first reaction was invariably, Why would the CIA be asking about one of its own? Now I understood how Heslin had found out about Roger's connection with us— apparently he'd told everyone he ever knew.

I went to see an oilman who knew more about crooked oil deals than Tamraz, mainly because he'd been involved in even more.

"If you need to talk to the Mafia, why don't you go straight to it?" he asked.

I confessed I had no idea what he was talking about.

"Did you ever hear how Tamraz started in oil?"

No.

He smiled, pleased to be the one to tell me. Before he began, he poured himself a double chilled white Armagnac and clipped a cigar.

"Roger Tamraz was in Beirut working for Kidder Peabody on the IntraBank liquidation. He was going through one of Intra's safes and found a document concerning the former head of Saudi intelligence, Kamal Adham. Tamraz recognized its value right away. It was crucial to resolving a dispute in Adham's favor; so he called Adham for a meeting. When Tamraz handed Adham the document, he said only, 'You may need this.' Adham was stunned. 'How much do I owe you?' Tamraz replied, 'Nothing, but let's keep in touch.'

"Sometime later, Adham called Tamraz and asked him if he wanted to help with a deal in Egypt. It was a pipeline from the Red Sea to the Mediterranean, involving huge commissions that Adham didn't want his fingerprints found on. Tamraz agreed, the pipeline was built, and he got his cut as well as a reputation for being a savvy entrepreneur. It didn't matter that all he was doing was operating a shell game on Adham's behalf.

"Tamraz did so well with the Egyptian pipeline that he started nosing around for a new deal. It wasn't long before he found one in Italy."

The oilman stopped to relight his cigar and pour himself another Armagnac. "Do you remember Amoco's problems in Italy?"

"Come on," I answered, "let's get on with it."

"You'll love this. Amoco was at its wit's end, trying to solve its labor problems in Italy. It was about ready to shut down its Italian refineries and distribution networks—simply abandon them. No dummy, Tamraz saw an opportunity where others saw nothing at all. He persuaded Mu'ammar Qaddafi to buy all of Amoco's downstream facilities. With a buyer in hand, he is reported to have used some of his private contacts in Sicily to facilitate the deal. It worked like a charm. The labor problems went away, the deal was signed, and Tamraz got a five percent commission with an interesting bonus: When the Libyans decided it wasn't a good marketing strategy to have their name on Amoco's old gasoline stations, Tamraz loaned them his. That's why you see Tamoil stations all over Europe."

Next I called an oil trader who I thought might know something about Tamraz.

"Did you know that Ozer Ciller—the husband of the Turkish prime minister, Tansu Ciller—and Tamraz are business partners?" he asked me.

I didn't, although I did know that Roger had spent a lot of time in Turkey promoting his Armenian pipeline, and that he had met Prime Minister Ciller on at least one occasion. Our embassy in Ankara had reported that the Turkish ultranationalist group, the Gray Wolves, made the introduction.

As for Madam Ciller's husband, Ozer, he was said to keep bad company. Among others, he was connected to the Turkish narcotics baron Omar Lutfu Topal, who would be gunned down in a 1996 mob war in Istanbul. At the time, Omar had an outstanding arrest warrant in the U.S. for selling narcotics.

"So what business were Roger and Ozer in?" I asked.

"Oil. Tamraz is paying Ozer to front for him."

I checked the story in the files and found a reference to OCL's sharing an office in Turkmenistan with a Topal company named Emperyal that ran a half-dozen casinos in Turkmenistan involved in laundering drug money. The Turkish state pipeline company, Botas, was the third tenant in the building in Turkmenistan—a nice, cozy setup.

A week later the same oil guy called me back. "I can't confirm this, so take it with a grain of salt, but my friends in Turkmenistan tell me that Roger and Ozer were silent partners in Block I."

Block I was Roger's concession in Turkmenistan—an expensive piece of property with estimated reserves of 358 million barrels of oil and 3.7 trillion cubic feet of gas. CIA energy analysts had always wondered where Tamraz had found the money to buy it.

"Why would Ozer Ciller invest in Turkmen oil? It doesn't make sense," I said.

"Not if you don't understand the oil business. It wasn't Ozer's money. Lapis Holding fronted for him. It put up all the money for Block I, including a thirty-million signing bonus that undoubtedly went right into the pocket of Turkmen president Saparmurat Niyazov."

"Why would Lapis do that?" I asked.

"It wasn't Lapis's money either. The TYT [Turkish

Tourism and Investment Bank] loaned the money to
Lapis. After Ozer and Lapis bled TYT dry, it
collapsed. Both the liabilities and assets were written
off. So, to answer your question, it was TYT's
depositors who paid for Block I."

"Are you absolutely certain of this?"

"No, but that is what I hear."

"So who is bribing whom?"

"For the use of thirty million, I suppose Tamraz
could pay a little out of his pocket, don't you think?"

This was too good. I had to share it with someone,
so I called Sheila Heslin. Again, she grunted and hung
up the telephone without comment, but I found out
she made a note to herself shortly afterward. It read:
"Mon . . . Roger Tamraz . . . bribing Ciller's husband
. . . Sep 28 . . . Instructions: Bob Baer."

You'd think that the "instructions" Heslin had in
mind were to issue me a merit badge. If Roger
Tamraz was bribing government officials, he was in
violation of U.S. law, which meant she had him by the
short hairs. Without U.S. support, Roger would never
worm his way into the Caspian oil deal. Heslin did
have a hangman's noose in mind, as things unfolded,
but it was my neck, not Roger's, she wanted to fit it
around.

★

I ALSO PICKED UP another tantalizing lead: Roger
Tamraz may have been involved with Ozer Ciller and
Omar Topal in a coup in Azerbaijan, even though the
facts were murky.

In March 1995, about the time Roger was traveling

around Turkey and Armenia, Azeri president Heidar Aliyev had nearly been driven from office by an uprising led by the interior minister, Rawshan Javadov. After it failed, Javadov was killed, probably in an attempt to surrender. Those were the only facts we were certain of, at least at the beginning, but within weeks two Turkish intelligence officers working in Azerbaijan were arrested and tortured for their part in the coup. That made no sense at all—Turkey officially supported Aliyev—until it emerged that the two intelligence officers might have been working directly for Prime Minister Tansu Ciller; who paid them out of a secret slush fund. Soon the rumor mill was reporting that the Gray Wolves had been involved as well, along with Omar Topal. Since the Gray Wolves apparently had introduced Tamraz to Ciller, and since Tamraz and Topal were known business associates, it seemed prudent to be at least suspicious.

I MADE ONE LAST STAB at trying to pin down Roger. At one point he had waved in my face a fax from a Manhattan-based company he was associated with called Avis Capital. Roger said Avis Capital was going to help pay for his pipeline, so I had a friend in New York run down the company. The address on the fax Tamraz had shown me was real—a tenement in the Bowery—but there was no sign of Avis Capital. The building superintendent said he'd never heard of the company; nor had any mail ever arrived addressed to an Avis Capital.

I'd seen enough of how foreign hustlers had worked their way in Washington during Iran-contra to realize that Tamraz and the Clinton White House were an accident waiting to happen. The question was: How could I get out of its way?

IN THE MEANTIME, the CIA was circling the drain.

When the FBI arrested Rick Ames on February 21, 1994, I was in Dushanbe. Watching on CNN as Ames stood handcuffed by the side of his new Jaguar XJ-6, my first reaction was that no one at the CIA owns a Jaguar. The officers who once could have afforded one—the investment bankers and lawyers who fought with the OSS in World War II, and the few who'd stayed on to establish the CIA in 1947—were all gone. Ames's Jaguar must have been the only one in the CIA parking lot. How could security have missed it?

But the lapse in internal security was just the beginning of the misery. Rick Ames wasn't your average spy: When he gave away a dozen Soviet agents at one liquor-soaked lunch, he established himself as one of history's greatest traitors, in the company of Benedict Arnold, the Rosenbergs, and Kim Philby. Just as Britain's MI6 would never live down Philby, so the CIA would never live down Ames. He had ratted out our crown jewels, the reason we existed. The only difference between the two was that Philby sold out for ideology, while Ames did it for money, pure and simple.

When I got back to headquarters in August 1994, I

could see how Ames's betrayal was playing out. Then director Jim Woolsey was turning over the CIA's counterespionage to the FBI, an act that would be almost as destructive to the agency as Ames. In fairness, Woolsey didn't have much choice. The CIA had screwed up so badly with Ames that it could no longer be trusted to clean its own house. Congress was breathing down Woolsey's neck, and the press wanted its own pound of flesh. To appease everyone and atone for our sins, Woolsey turned the CIA over to its worst enemy in Washington—the FBI. Way back at the beginning of the cold war, J. Edgar Hoover had wanted to keep all national security operations, domestic and foreign, under his heavy thumb. Now it looked like his ghost was about to get its way.

The executioner the FBI picked for the task was Ed Curran, a serving FBI agent. From the day he took over the counterespionage group, Curran made it clear that he intended to run the place like a behind-enemy-lines commando unit. His first act was to fire anyone who knew anything, especially the little old ladies in tennis shoes—the CIA's institutional memory on Soviet espionage. He had to let them go: Smart people made Curran very nervous. Then, to let everyone know there was a new sheriff in town, he reopened every unresolved counterintelligence case on the books. Every single one. It didn't matter if the employee was retired or had moved on to a new nonsensitive job. The idea was to spread fear and paranoia throughout the CIA, and in that, he couldn't have been more successful.

When the CIA appointed Rod Smith as its own head of counterintelligence and thus Curran's nominal boss, Curran was in effect given free rein. A lawyer turned case officer, Smith never spent enough time in the field to learn the job, much less anything about counterintelligence. After an abbreviated six-month tour in Europe, he came back to headquarters, where he would stay moving up the bureaucratic ladder one dogged step at a time. In no time Curran had Smith feeding out of his hand. Blood soon flowed in rivers.

A casual friendship struck up, say, on an Italian vacation became a suspect foreign contact. Polygraphers were called in, and having been badly burned by Ames, who beat the lie detectors even while working for the KGB, they weren't happy. Anxiety turned to stress; stress, to a failed test. Soon Curran had a "new case," and as the witch-hunts went on new cases began to mount to the ceiling. Files were ransacked, police checks run. Then the FBI was called in because that was the deal Woolsey had made with Congress: The FBI investigates all suspected espionage cases. All over the FBI, well-meaning grunts were having CIA cases dumped on them, which they would then throw immediately on the floor, because, for all of Curran's exhortations, they knew they had a hundred stronger cases to work on. Back at Langley, though, the dirt was already down. Being under an active FBI investigation, no matter how flimsy the evidence, meant no promotions, no overseas assignments, no sensitive clearances. The cafeteria was filling up with people who might as well have been marked with scarlet "A"s, all of them eating alone.

The numbers tell the story. By late 1995 more than three hundred people were under suspicion, and that's not to mention the number of CIA employees terrified they would be caught up in the bloodbath through no fault of their own. One day you're at your desk, and the next you're a virtual prisoner in one of the security facilities out by Tyson's Corner. Everyone had a friend or colleague tied up in security purgatory.

Over at the FBI, director Louis Freeh couldn't wipe the smile off his face. He was dismantling the CIA piece by piece, while in the press, he was portrayed as Mr. Straight cleaning up the decadent, Jaguar-driving, rummy CIA. Congress showered money on him. He hired more agents but still had more money than he could spend, so he used it to open FBI offices abroad—offices that one day will displace the CIA. And the best part was that Freeh, who doesn't lack for a sense of irony, hired an ex-CIA officer—fired by Woolsey for his failures in the Ames debacle—to advise him on opening the new branches.

In the meantime, while the FBI was tied up eviscerating the CIA, Robert Hanssen was giving away the FBI's own secrets in trash bags.

AS YOU MIGHT HAVE GUESSED, I wasn't a dispassionate observer of Curran's purge. One day I was sitting in my office reading through the morning's traffic when the division's security officer and a young jackbooted sleuth from the counterespionage group fairly tumbled into my office. They were both breathless and made a point of slamming my door to underscore the seriousness of their visit.

"Why are you still in touch with a Russian from Dushanbe?" the security officer asked.

I'd been around too long not to know what he was doing. Start an interrogation with an accusation, throw the victim off balance, and you just might scare a confession out of him. In the business it's called an accusatory process.

I looked at him dumbly.

Seeing that this tactic wasn't getting them anywhere, he mentioned the name of a Russian woman I had known in Dushanbe. She had introduced me to the Russian skiers, but I was no longer in contact with her.

"We'll have to box you [polygraph] about it," the fascist from counterespionage said, summoning all the menace he could. He was wearing snakeskin cowboy boots, a sure sign of trouble inside the Beltway. "We'll find out the truth the hard way."

Two polygraphs in six months seemed like a lot, but I didn't have a choice if I wanted the CIA to continue to pay me.

About two hours later, I ran into the security officer in the hallway and gave him a what-the-fuck look. I knew the guy from before; we got along, so he told me the story. My colleague in Tashkent, ███████, had decided he wanted to ride the counterespionage wave for a promotion. He picked up a rumor about the Russian and me and sent it in, properly dressed up in the supersensitive ▮▮▮▮▮▮▮▮▮ channel cable. It was just the kind of lead the Curranites loved.

The only humor in the whole incident—and it was gallows humor at best—came when I filled out the prepolygraph security questionnaire. Had I had any problems with U.S. law enforcement since my last investigation? In the appropriate box, I neatly wrote in pencil: *Yes, investigated by the FBI for attempted murder.*

It worked like a charm. I was assigned the meanest, oldest, grizzliest polygrapher security had. He'd been around and knew how the game worked. He could tell the difference between a mole and someone who was in the business of meeting foreigners. I was in and out in an hour.

My colleagues weren't so fortunate. Too many of them ended up with twenty-three-year-old polygraphers plucked out of the hills of West Virginia—people who thought all foreigners were communists.

PREDICTABLY, Ed Curran's purge made the CIA even more risk-adverse than it had already become. People weren't just scared to meet foreigners on their vacations; they were scared to do it in their jobs as well.

You could see the results in everything we tried to do. There wasn't a single reporting agent in any one of the eight posts I supervised in central Asia and the Caucasus. No one was meeting anyone. There were no requests for even provisional approval of new agents, no contact reports. It was considered a lucky day if

South Group received an administrative cable from one of our posts on the frontier. As far as I could see, the other groups in the Central Eurasia Division were in the same sorry shape. Daily group-chief meetings were about budgets, projections, personnel changes, task forces, paper deadlines—anything but recruiting sources.

All over the Islamic world, cells were forming, ancient grudges were boiling to new surfaces, the infidel West was being targeted for destruction, and we didn't have a real ear to the ground anywhere.

Dave Cohen's appointment as the new director of operations did nothing to ease the situation. Cohen was a career analyst. Even though he had put in a cameo appearance as domestic head of the DO, he knew next to nothing about operations. Not only had he never met or recruited an agent, he apparently had no idea what an access agent even was. Among his first orders was to fire all of them. Remember the access agent in Madras who introduced me to Sami, the Arab officer on assignment to the Indian military? Remember all those agents in Beirut who ran down Mughniyah's networks? Under Cohen's new standards, I never would have been authorized to run them.

In the same spirit of antieffectiveness—and in accord with a new DO policy that desk jockeys were to be promoted at the same rate as field operatives—Cohen began handing ███████████-chief posts to people with virtually no qualifications for the job. Riyadh, Tel Aviv, Nairobi: I started to lose track. The only apparent qualification of the new chief in Riyadh was that he had been George Tenet's briefer when Tenet was at the NSC. Over my protests, the same thing happened in South Group. I was replaced in Dushanbe by someone who wasn't a case officer, and my reports officer with the sharp tongue was given an important chief's job in the Caspian. She was smart, but she'd never served as a case officer in the field, or run or recruited an agent.

Her last day at headquarters, she stuck her head in my office to say good-bye. "By the way, just to let you know, I don't recruit agents. That's not my job." She'd obviously picked up the new mantra going around that chiefs don't run operations—they "represented the director." It was crazy, like the local beat cop refusing to make an arrest because his job was to represent the chief of police.

Cohen, in turn, was replaced as the director of operations by a retiree. And the retiree's successor hadn't had an overseas assignment in more than a decade, and that to a backwater post in Europe. Did the agency even care about operations any more? If so, it was hard to see.

The effect on intelligence collection, not surprisingly, was devastating. I did my own investigation to see just how bad it was. In 1986 the Directorate of Intelligence had computerized all intelligence reports, putting them on a single server that I arranged to get access to. I started by searching for all reporting on the Islamic Revolutionary Guard Corps, the Pasdaran, from human sources—that is, agents, people on the ground. In the late 1980s, reporting on the Iranian Pasdaran started to taper off. By 1995 there was nothing—not a single report. It wasn't like the U.S. had lost interest in the Pasdaran, or should have. The Pasdaran blew up the Al-Khobar barracks in Saudi Arabia in 1996. It was more like we had voluntarily deafened ourselves and gouged our eyes out in the midst of an ongoing crisis.

I also looked into reporting on the Saudi royal family. ███████████████████████████████
██
██
██
██
██
██
██
██
██
██
███████████████████.

I'd seen the same thing with Iraq. Iraqi Operations was a Potemkin village. Of the thirty-five officers assigned to the headquarters component, at least 10 percent were documented alcoholics. Another 10 percent had been designated as low performers. Two in five were retirees who had come back to work on contract, and the rest didn't really care whether the CIA had a human source in Iraq or not. Congress dumped millions and millions of dollars on the CIA for Iraq, yet virtually none of it made it into Iraqi hands.

One American consultant in London was paid more than the director of the CIA and the president of the United States put together. She had an open first-class ticket to fly back and forth to the U.S. anytime she wanted. In London, she rented some of the priciest office space available. When the CIA went out to inspect, we found she had subleased the office, defrauding the government of even more money. In this one instance alone, I could account for $1 million just flushed down the toilet. It was out-and-out theft, and there were at least twenty other instances with other people that involved similar amounts of money.

Incidentally, the woman who had set up the payment to the London consultant resigned from the CIA on a Friday and went to work for the same company the London woman worked for the following Monday. The CIA inspector general's office found, to its horror, that the same woman, while at the CIA, had funneled two other equally large contracts into that consulting firm, the same one she now worked for. In the end it was too painful for the agency to bring the case to the Department of Justice's attention, and the London consultant continues today to successfully shake down Congress for money.

It wasn't only money the CIA lost control of. In 1997 British authorities were furious when they found out my old Iraqi friend Ahmad Chalabi had rented his studio on Barlby Road in London to a Saudi dissident, Dr. Sa'd Al-Faqih, one of Osama bin Laden's soul mates. Faqih's platform called for overthrowing the Al Sa'ud family in Saudi Arabia and expelling Britain and the U.S. from the Middle East. Chalabi had reason enough to fall out of love with us—we had, after all, abandoned him in his hour of need—but it was wrenching to see the people who wanted to be our allies making common cause with our enemies.

Nor was it just in the Middle East that the CIA seemed to have thrown in the towel. In 1996 a post in central Asia came in with a proposal to set up a secret site to monitor Lop Nor, the Chinese nuclear-weapons testing facility. The location was topo-graphically unique because it was at the end of a valley and served as a sort of funnel for emissions and electronic data from Chinese explosions. About the same time, the Department of Energy picked up indications that the Chinese were testing mini-aturized nuclear warheads, but it couldn't be sure since the tests were below the threshold of our current collection capabilities. The collection site would have remedied that.

"Sorry, the NSC turned the operation down," Peggy ██████, the head of Chinese operations, told us. "It does not want to risk irritating the Chinese by collecting information from platforms in Central Asia."

Eventually, we compromised and put a nuclear "sniffer" on top of one of our embassies, but it was hundreds of miles from Lop Nor and picked up nothing. Keep in mind the context of this decision: A Chinese official kindly sent us by overnight mail what appeared to be a Chinese government description of the W-88, our highly sophisticated, miniaturized nuclear warhead. Were the Chinese testing a weapon based on the W-88 design at Lop Nor? We'll never find out unless some other Chinese official sends us a postcard to let us know.

Worst of all, the CIA seemed to have stopped

caring about its own people, especially the ones who took the greatest risks. By the spring of 1996, I'd had enough of Washington and volunteered to go to Sarajevo on a counterterrorism operation meant to probe the depth and extent of the Iranian intelligence presence in Bosnia. I had a half-dozen people working for me, including a couple who paired up on a surveillance team. Since foreigners stood out in Sarajevo, I suggested they live outside of town and commute to their watching stations. The ride in was fairly safe because they drove an SUV with military markings, but one week, when I was out of town, their SUV was pulled for other duty and they were forced to make do with a small, locally plated VW. A few nights later, they were on their way home when a car cut in front of them, trying to force them off the road. They reacted according to the book. As soon as the woman saw the other car was armed, she yelled, *"Gun!"* Her husband, who was driving, sped up and swerved around the car, just in time to get sprayed with a machine gun. He survived, as did his wife, who was wounded in the back, but they almost didn't survive the bureaucracy back at headquarters.

"They should have just given up their car," the branch chief responsible for Bosnia said. "That's how we would have handled it in South America."

I was stunned. I knew the desk officer had spent only two years in some quiet post in South America doing administrative work. Worse, she knew nothing about Bosnia. She had refused to make a familiarization trip to Sarajevo. She spoke no Serbo-Croatian. I could have overlooked it all if later, she hadn't suggested the couple be put up in front of a Personnel Evaluation Board and reprimanded them for not giving up their car. No wonder that a headquarters staffed with officers so badly misidentified the Chinese embassy in Belgrade that we sent a missile into it.

20

AFTER MONTHS UPON months of listening to Roger Tamraz's many schemes to get rich quick, I finally learned why the CIA had kept up contact with him all these years: He could get to anyone, anywhere. He must have had a Rolodex the size of the New York City telephone book.

I had just walked into my office one morning when the telephone rang. It was Roger, even more ebullient than usual. The night before, he'd had dinner with Vice President Al Gore at Senator Ted Kennedy's house in McLean, Virginia.

"I sold the vice president on my pipeline," he said. "Your tip on Cutler really paid off."

What Tamraz didn't tell me, and I would find out only much later, was that he had put Senator Kennedy's wife, Victoria, on the payroll along with Lloyd Cutler. Victoria was supposedly helping to recover the money Tamraz had lost in Lebanon. His first check probably paid for dinner with Al Gore.

The former, and perhaps still active, international fugitive was not only pleased with his new dinner partners, he seemed to have suddenly become a

Friend of Bill. President Clinton, Tamraz informed me, had called Azerbaijani president Aliyev to press for "multi-pipelines." It didn't matter to Tamraz that Clinton no doubt had in mind the Turkish route, Baku-Ceyhan, not the Armenian route. Amoco and British Petroleum, Amoco's ally in the Caspian, had been openly dumping buckets of money on Washington lobbyists to persuade the White House to back the Turkish route. Any Washington insider—including, one would think, Lloyd Cutler—could have told Tamraz it was only a matter of time before their money prevailed and the White House specifically named Baku-Ceyhan. But Tamraz wasn't a man to accept defeat without a good brawl, and he certainly wasn't going to be intimidated by a pair of eight-hundred-pound gorillas like Amoco and BP. After all, who did Amoco come crying to when it wanted out of its problems in Italy?

"This lobbying thing is really paying of," he said before he hung up.

I learned later that President Clinton had indeed called Aliyev but that his call had been scripted largely by Sheila Heslin. Although I didn't know what the exact circumstances were that led to Clinton's call, I already knew for sure that Heslin didn't have Roger Tamraz's best interests in mind.

The way things worked on both ends of Pennsylvania Avenue would soon become a lot clearer, but to see what I was looking for, I would have to fly halfway around the world to the former Soviet republic of Azerbaijan.

★

IT WAS DUSK, and the snow-covered Caucasus were bathed in a radiant pink as the Gulfstream made a sharp right turn and dropped into Baku. A few minutes later, we were on the ground, taxiing up to an eerie, half-built, half-abandoned terminal that reminded me of a junked stage set from *Star Wars*.

We had a white-knuckle drive from the airport and dinner at a government guest house, then began the inevitable waiting. Around midnight, just when we were about ready to head back to the hotel, President Heydar Aliyev's gofer arrived to pick us up for our meeting.

Aliyev was one of the few Soviet leaders left standing after the collapse of the Soviet Union. Once a member of the Communist Party politburo and chairman of the KGB, he would have been a serious contender to rule the Soviet Union had it survived. Instead he had to settle for Azerbaijan, a backward Soviet republic that sat on vast oil reserves and occupied a strategic position on the western side of the Caspian. Aliyev knew exactly what he had, and he intended to make the most of it. Although he wasn't about to liberalize Azerbaijan politically, he threw open its oil industry to foreign investors, in particular the American majors.

Aliyev signed his first major oil contract on September 20, 1994, granting Amoco, Pennzoil, UNOCAL, Ramco, Statoil, Delta, and BP drilling rights for three offshore Caspian fields. The companies would work as part of the Azerbaijan International Operating Consortium (AIOC). With estimated recoverable reserves of about 4.4 billion barrels and a peak production of 700,000 barrels a day by 2010, AIOC's concession rivaled some of Saudi Arabia's mega fields. The oil companies' PR departments started calling it "the deal of the century." For Aliyev, AIOC not only provided badly needed cash, it also helped persuade the U.S. and Britain to lend him some necessary political support. With Russia on his north and Iran on his south, Aliyev lived in a bad neighborhood.

Although it was a little after one in the morning before we were ushered into Aliyev's Soviet-style office, he was wide awake. Comfortable in the corridors of power and with foreigners, he graciously went around the room and shook our hands. Although he was in his seventies, he still had a spring in his step.

Aliyev started the conversation with a rambling account of the failed March 1995 coup, the one the CIA suspected Prime Minister Ciller had a role in. According to Aliyev, just about everyone was involved, from Russia to Turkey. He even named some Azeri dissidents living in the U.S. I took notes for a while but lost interest as Aliyev waded deeper and deeper into the details; anyhow, I was half asleep. My interest perked up, though, when Aliyev brought up Exxon and Iran. I noticed Aliyev himself became more animated. There was even a trace of anger.

"You know, gentlemen, I am ready to help the United States and its oil companies, but I expect you to live by your bargains."

Aliyev looked around the room. It was clear no one knew what he was talking about.

Aliyev filled us in. In March 1995 he had received a call from the State Department's undersecretary for economic affairs, Joan Spiro. She said she was speaking in the name of Secretary of State Warren Christopher. In unmistakable terms, Spiro threatened that if Azerbaijan wanted to maintain good relations with the U.S., Aliyev would have to give Exxon its 5 percent. When Aliyev countered that he would face a lot of heat from Iran, Spiro brushed it off: "Don't worry, you'll get help." The next call was from Deputy Energy Secretary Bob White. White also insisted on Exxon's 5 percent. When Aliyev again mentioned Iran, White said, "We'll take care of it, just make sure Exxon gets its deal."

"So now that Exxon has its five percent, what are you going to do about Iran?" Aliyev asked. "I share a long, porous border with that country."

Listening to Aliyev I found it hard to avoid the conclusion that the Clinton administration was pimping for Exxon. Naïf that I was in the ways of the White House, I had assumed that the job of the government was to back U.S. business in general but never a specific company, especially when other American oil companies, including Mobil, gladly would have taken the 5 percent and probably paid even more for it.

After it broke in the press that Tony Lake and his wife had skirted the law by holding on to $304,000 in energy stocks when he was appointed national security adviser, I wondered if Lake had anything to do with Spiro's and White's calls. If so, the tension at home must have been thick enough to cut: Lake owned Exxon stock, while his wife held Mobil.

But the issue ran to more than money. It was about this time that the Sudanese decided they had had enough of hosting Osama bin Laden and offered him to us on a platter. Maybe if the White House and National Security Council had been spending less time thinking about Exxon and Mobil and Amoco and more time thinking about the implications of letting a known venomous snake slither away to Afghanistan, we might have all been spared a lot of future misery.

OIL SEEMED TO BE making bad bedfellows all over Washington. Jim Giffen was Mr. Kazakstan. If you wanted an oil concession in Kazakstan, you went to Giffen because his consulting company, Mercator Corporation, held all the keys to the kingdom. If you wanted to get out of your concession in Kazakstan because you'd been ripped off, you went to Giffen. He collected the commissions and distributed them, no questions asked, as long as the numbers on the check were right.

But Giffen did a lot more than business. He was Washington's de facto ambassador to Kazakstan. When Kazak President Nazarbayev wanted to come to Washington, he didn't phone Beth Jones, our ambassador in Alma Ata. He called Giffen, whose office in New York took care of all the arrangements, from travel to meetings to security. Giffen also arranged to do all the legal work and lobbying through his white-shoe law firm, Shearman and

Sterling. Nazarbayev poured millions of dollars into the firm, even though no one seemed to know where the money ultimately ended up.

In Washington, Giffen's preferred point of contact was Assistant Secretary of State Toby Trister Gati, the head of State's Bureau of Intelligence and Research. With a contact like Giffen, Gati quickly stopped calling up her own bureau or the CIA for anything on Kazakstan. She could get everything she wanted from Giffen. For instance, when the CIA found out that Nazarbayev was selling sophisticated arms to North Korea and Iran, including the S-300, one of Russia's most advanced surface-to-air defense weapons, Gati made the problem quietly disappear with a couple of phone calls to Giffen. (In the spirit of international cooperation, the North Koreans and Iranians simply found a new arms dealer.) It was all very chummy. Everybody walked away from the table a winner. The only unpleasantness was when Ambassador Jones found out that Gati had shown Giffen a top-secret CIA report on corruption in Kazakstan. He might have been the de facto ambassador, but he didn't have a security clearance. A nasty exchange of cables followed between Jones and Gati, but the State Department dropped the matter. Gati was a protected citizen and the potential embarrassment in Foggy Bottom wasn't worth it.

I myself found how deep Gati was into the oil business when I was called down to the NSC in December 1995 for an unscheduled emergency meeting on Georgia. When I walked into the NSC's stately conference room, I found the usual downtown nomenklatura: Dr. Coit Blacker, Sheila Heslin's boss; Rand Beers, head of intelligence programs for the NSC; and Jennifer Sims, who worked for Toby Gati at the State Department and was married to the dean of Georgetown University's School of Foreign Service. A few other people from Defense and State were there for decoration.

Sims didn't waste any time making her pitch: We absolutely had to give Georgia president Eduard Shevardnadze a Matador air-defense system to protect his planes and helicopters. (The Matador detects things like radar lock-ons and approaching missiles.) Shevardnadze was the only Caucasus leader who had committed to the main oil-export pipeline; America could not afford to lose him.

I vaguely wondered why, if he was so important, the oil companies didn't pay to protect his life. But I wasn't about to get into that one, and continued to doodle until Sims dropped her bomb:The money for the Matador would come from the CIA. At first I thought I'd fallen asleep and was dreaming. The State Department couldn't have forgotten already that after Fred Woodruff was murdered just outside of the Georgian capital, Eduard Shevardnadze had stonewalled the investigation at every turn. Now the CIA was being asked to reward Shevardnadze for his complicity by ponying up $2 million plus to protect his life—all so Amoco, Exxon, and Mobil could have some extra reserves for their yearly financial statement. Had the inmates finally taken complete control of the asylum?

At least I knew exactly how to drive a stake in this deal.

"Can't be done," I said, interrupting.

Everyone in the room stopped talking, surprised I'd said anything.

"Bob, what seems to be the problem?" Beers said, bracing himself for the worst.

"The man Ms. Sims proposes turning the Matador system over to is a murderer."

Dr. Blacker shoved back his chair. There was a big, gaping hole where his mouth had been. For a minute I thought he was going to come around the conference table and strangle me.

"Sorry, Bob, I'm not sure we all understand what you're getting at," Beers said.

"The head of the Georgian KGB—the head of Shevardnadze's security, the same man who is supposed to operate the Matador system—is a murderer. We have a video of him shooting six handcuffed prisoners in the back of the head. It's rather gruesome, but I'd be happy to go back to Langley and bring you back a copy. In any case, he's violated human rights. As much as we'd like to, there's nothing the CIA can do for you."

I wasn't making up the story, either—we really did have the video. No one asked to see it, and that was the last I heard about the Matador.

ALL OF THESE SIDE STORIES continued to stoke my curiosity about Sheila Heslin and the oil lobby, so I began calling around Washington to see what the deal was. Heslin's sole job, it seemed, was to carry water for an exclusive club known as the Foreign Oil

Companies Group, a cover for a cartel of major petroleum companies doing business in the Caspian. It was the same cartel that had wanted dirt on Tamraz and the others. The group particularly hated Tamraz because he was a lot more agile than they were. He had an absolute genius for getting to the best properties first and flipping them for huge profit, which drove up the majors' operating costs. As evidence, they cited Roger's purchase of Block I in Turkmenistan. He hadn't invested a nickel to develop it. His only interest was in reselling the field to one of them for a huge premium. There's nothing the majors hate more than buying off a middleman they don't have to.

Another thing I learned was that Heslin wasn't soloing. Her boss, Deputy National Security Adviser Sandy Berger, headed the interagency committee on Caspian oil policy which made him in effect the government's ambassador to the cartel, and Berger wasn't a disinterested player. He held $90,000 worth of stock in Amoco, probably the most influential member in the cartel and the one with the greatest reason to be wary of Tamraz. Another big oil alliance led by Chevron had lost serious time and money getting rid of a spoiler named John Deuss in a similar Caspian oil deal. Nobody intended to let Roger play the same role this time.

The deeper I got, the more Caspian oil money I found sloshing all around Washington. The Caspian Sea embassy fax lines were burning up with proposals from lobbying and law firms to sell access to the White House. Probably the most aggressive was

Berger's old firm, Hogan & Hartson, which put out the word that it could guarantee entrée into the White House. Anytime. Turkmenistan opted for the Israeli connection, hiring a firm called Merhav, which had good relations with the American-Israeli Public Affairs committee.

One thing was clear: Whether you were an oil company or an oil country, if you wanted to put something in play in the nation's capital, you had better be ready to pay.

NEVER INTIMIDATED by big oil, Roger Tamraz was putting his lobbying campaign on wartime footing, as I found out when my phone rang two days after I got back from Azerbaijan.

"I gave your name and telephone number to Don Fowler," Roger said without preamble. "He's going to call you. I told him about us, about our project."

I drew a blank. "Don Fowler?"

"The Democratic National Chairman. He's on our side."

"You gave *this phone number* to the Democratic National Chairman?"

Tamraz didn't see any problem, but then he rarely did. As for me, I saw a boatload. The number Roger had given Don Fowler was the unclassified one that marked me as CIA, and Washington had a long history that proved intelligence gathering and partisan politics were a lethal mix. As soon as I hung up with Roger, I called Fowler. He wasn't in, but I left my cover number and hoped he would tear up the other one.

A little after two, he called back on the CIA line.

"Don Fowler here." I could hear a PA system in the background. Fowler was calling from an airport telephone booth. "I'm a friend of Roger's. He tells me you're writing a paper about him for the White House."

In fact, I had told Roger about the memos we had sent the NSC in response to Sheila Heslin's little tasker. If the CIA was sending papers around Washington acknowledging a relationship with Tamraz that it had committed to keeping secret, the least I could do was tell him. It was his ass on the line.

"Son, I need a copy of that paper to show the president. He needs to know about everything Roger has done for this country. Let me know where I can pick it up."

Now, this called for some truly fast thinking. I could deny knowing Roger, but was it wise to lie to someone close to the president? Or I could admit knowing Roger but deny there was a paper, another lie but maybe just a tad more attractive. Then I realized there was a third way.

"Sir," I said, "I cannot talk about what Roger may or may not have done for this country. And if a paper exists, as Roger says, then it's at the White House. You'll be able to find it there."

I was proud of myself. I'd given Fowler a line of pure bureaucratic bullshit. As for the memo, let Heslin tell Fowler he couldn't have it.

Fowler, obviously annoyed that I wasn't going to play, snorted and hung up.

Suddenly the game was getting very rich. Right

number or not, Fowler knew he was calling the CIA, and I knew what he wanted: my help in overcoming Heslin's opposition to letting Roger in. That's what Roger had asked me for in the beginning, and I was certain that was what he wanted now from Fowler.

I also sensed that a cold call from the chairman of the DNC to a midlevel DO case officer under a very dark cloud had the makings of a *Titanic*-size disaster, so I called an FBI agent friend and asked his advice. He whistled appreciatively and then got down to business.

"What you do now is spread it all around Langley like manure," he advised. "Tell as many people as you can. Document it wherever you can. Because when this thing goes down, whatever it is you've managed to stick your nose into, no one is going to remember talking to you."

I started with my manager in the Central Eurasian Division. There was a look of pure horror on his face when I told the story. I couldn't find the lawyer for my division, so I went to see the one assigned to the Near East Division. To my eternal gratitude, as soon as I walked out of his office, he sent an e-mail summarizing our conversation to Bob Caudel, the CE Division lawyer; John Rizzo, the DO's lawyer; and Rob Davis, the same genius who told me the Iraq investigation would be a good thing for me. Later, when the whole thing exploded, that e-mail would save my skin.

I couldn't resist calling Heslin, hoping to get a rise out of her. By now I was learning to keep a journal to compare events and times and to help fill out the matrices. I placed the call on October 23. Here's what my notes say about our conversation.

Me: "You know Roger's going to make it into the White House. He's going to get his meeting with Clinton."

Her: "That's the stupidest thing I've heard in a long time. Roger's on the Secret Service blacklist. I know because I put him there. He can't get into the White House. Period."

Me: "He's going to do it through Don Fowler."

Her: "No, he's not. What do you people use for brains out there?"

I could almost see the phone slam down.

On October 25 my group finally finished the follow-up on Roger Tamraz. What with summer vacations and transfers, and ordering up the remaining volumes of Roger's file from archives, the memo had been lingering in the office since June. I would have preferred that the memo had been sent before Fowler's call, to avoid even the hint of any influence. But the memo spoke for itself. It included not only all the derogatory information we had sent to Heslin back on May 19 but newly inserted details about BCCI as well. It wasn't going to get Roger indicted, but it was an honest, accurate account of everything the DO knew about him.

The problems with the October memo came after it left South Group. Tamraz was starting to make a lot of people nervous. When the October memo landed on Dave Cohen's desk, duly logged in as DDO 95-3136, he didn't like the smell of things. The memo stated right on the cover sheet that Tamraz was rubbing elbows with the DNC and the White House crowd. So Cohen, who hadn't gotten to be director of operations because he lacked the political instinct for self-survival, bucked it up to the general counsel's office, accompanied by a handwritten marginal note from his assistant: "We've already forwarded NSC info on Tamraz. FYI: he is a U.S. citizen, so I've asked DO/LGL to O.K. passage of file info to NSC."

Cohen wasn't the only one running for cover. On November 13, 1995, Paul Redmond, the deputy director for counterintelligence, sent the October memo to George Tenet, then deputy director and soon to be number one. Although it said right on the cover sheet in black and white that Tamraz was in touch with Fowler and Heslin, as well as a bunch of other politicians, Tenet wrote in the margin, "Have not fully read. Please pay careful attention here." Tenet doesn't have the time to read a two-page memo concerning financial ties between the president of the United States and an indicted middleman? Frankly, if I'd been in Tenet's position, I would have checked out for the day and pretended I hadn't seen the memo at all. There was no way to win on that one.

The general counsel's office apparently was oblivious to the executive jitters on the seventh floor. In that narrow legal view of the world, it didn't matter whether Tamraz was in contact with Osama bin Laden or Jesus Christ. The rule was simple, and never mind any competing findings: The CIA did not send derogatory information on American citizens to other government agencies, including the White House. Accordingly, the Office of General Counsel duly removed every negative comment about Tamraz and sent it back to Cohen. Now absolved of any responsibility, Cohen then faxed it to Heslin on December 26,1995. Requested in June, the follow-up memo arrived nearly seven months late and didn't say a bad thing about Roger. Little wonder that Heslin, in her complete ignorance about the CIA, believed she'd stumbled onto an evil and venal CIA conspiracy.

★

IF ONLY that had been the end of it. On December 6 I met Roger Tamraz for lunch, at his request. We sat at one of those semicircular booths at the Four Seasons, overlooking the C&O Canal. Businessmen preferred these tables because they could lean head to head and whisper without being overheard.

"Well, I did it," Roger said, very proud of himself. "I met the president."

"How'd you manage to do that, Roger?" I asked, although I knew the moment the words left my mouth that they shouldn't have.

"It was easy. Fowler gave me a price list of what I could get for campaign donations, from a night in the Lincoln Bedroom to a one-on-one with the president in the Oval Office."

I must have looked like I'd just swallowed my napkin ring.

"I started out small—a coffee," Tamraz said, proud of his frugality. "I got to mention my Armenian route to Bill. He was intrigued and wanted to talk more about it."

"Heslin's going to love this," I thought out loud. In truth, I, too, was a little alarmed that the president of the United States had become plain old "Bill" to Roger. Tamraz wasn't a man you wanted to let too far into your good graces.

"No, no," he went on. "It's gone much further than that. Tomorrow I have my one-on-one in the Oval Office. Bill and I are going to work out a strategy for the whole area. I've opened a channel to Russia."

A channel to Russia? The last time Tamraz was involved in a diplomatic channel, he ended up losing a bank.

"In fact, I just got back from a meeting with the Russians in Milan. I saw Alexander Korzhakov and Pavel Borodin."

On the upside, Korzhakov and Borodin ran Russia during those many days and nights when Boris Yeltsin was too drunk to find the hotline. On the downside, Korzhakov and Borodin also doubled as Yeltsin's bagmen. Borodin would be arrested on a Swiss money-laundering charge in January 2001 in New York, on his way to George W. Bush's inauguration.

"They told me Yeltsin would like to help Clinton's reelection campaign. You know . . . with money."

By now I was almost out of my seat. Roger obviously had lost his mind. I wished desperately that we had taken a larger table, one with more space between the two of us.

"And here's the best part for our project."

I really wished he'd stop calling it "our" project.

"Yeltsin will sign off on the Armenian route, but in

return he'll want some money for his campaign. It will be no problem. We talked about a ballpark figure of a hundred million. The Chinese promised all the money I need. Yeltsin even agreed to let a little money leak into Bill's campaign. Everyone walks away from this a winner. I can't wait to see the president and tell him."

I raced back to Langley after we had finished and told Roger's story to Bill Lofgren, the tough and irascible Central Eurasian Division chief.

"That's utter and complete bullshit," Bill responded. "I don't believe him."

Just to be certain, he picked up the telephone and asked his secretary to get Rome on the line. He wanted to find out if Borodin and Korzhakov really had been in Milan on December 1 and 2, as Tamraz claimed. Always start with the facts you can establish.

The following day, after we learned that the two Russians really had been where Roger said they were, I brought Lofgren to see Tamraz so he could get the story straight from the horse's mouth. Roger repeated it almost verbatim. He was still planning to see Clinton that afternoon. The only new twist was that Roger now had on display an official White House photograph of himself talking to Clinton over coffee.

When we got back to headquarters, Lofgren called then director John Deutch and told him the story. Deutch's assistant called back the same afternoon. He said the president was going to Paris shortly and had no plans to meet Tamraz. "I think you have a problem with your source. Apparently he's a liar," the assistant told Lofgren.

★

FOUR DAYS LATER, Fowler called. "Son, have you changed your mind about that memo?"

Unaware that the October memo was still being scrubbed and polished by the deputy director of operations and the general counsel's office, I told Fowler again that if any CIA paper on Tamraz existed, it was with Sheila Heslin. He could get it from her.

"That damn broad won't give me anything," Fowler grumbled.

With that, I decided to throw caution to the winds. If anyone was going to know just how deeply the major oil companies were into the NSC, it was going to be Don Fowler.

"Mr. Fowler, I believe your problem is with the big boys, and the biggest bully seems to be Amoco. It doesn't appreciate an interloper like Roger poaching in its preserve. That's why he's been frozen out of the White House."

"You're goddamned right. I know exactly what Amoco is doing, and Amoco's ambassador at the NSC, Heslin."

"Well, it seems she's got you pretty well trumped."

"We'll see about that," Fowler said as he hung up the phone.

★

IF IT HAD BEEN JUST a matter of money or even political corruption, I might have been able to walk away from all I had learned about big oil, the White House, and the NSC. Elective politics always breed a certain amount of nastiness. What I couldn't get around, though, was this: Every time I turned over a new rock, there was something even nastier underneath. Finally I got to the ugliest rock of all, the one that lives were waiting under, to be saved or lost. That, I guess, is when I snapped.

A little background first: After Iran released the last of the American hostages in 1991, the White House kept its fingers crossed that Iran was finally out of the terrorism business. By December, however, it was becoming apparent that Iran had simply switched battlefields. The CIA picked up information that several leaders of the Saudi Hizballah had traveled to Tehran. Obviously something was brewing. After the meeting, the Iranian Pasdaran opened a training base in the Biqa' for Saudi Hizballah terrorist cadres. It issued the terrorists false passports and provided all the funding they needed, and in July 1995, the Iranian-trained networks started to watch American facilities in Saudi Arabia, including the consulate in Jeddah. When a cleric in Qum, Iran's most holy city, issued a fatwa, or religious finding, to conduct attacks in Saudi Arabia, the White House braced itself for the worst. The first attack came against the Saudi National Guard facility in Riyadh in November 1995, killing five Americans. The Khobar barracks were hit on June 25, 1996, killing nineteen Americans.

Just as ominously, the CIA was learning about the first tentative contacts between Osama bin Laden and Iran. In December 1995 one of bin Laden's Egyptian associates visited Tehran and met with several officers from the Ministry of Intelligence and Security. The U.S. wasn't sure bin Laden had reached an agreement with the Iranians on a strategic relationship, but we in the intelligence community suspected he had. Bin Laden desperately needed the terrorist expertise Iran possessed. Our fears were confirmed, as I've mentioned, when bin Laden met an Iranian intelligence officer in Afghanistan in July 1996 to hammer out a strategic relationship. The possibility of a grand terrorist alliance aimed against the U.S. was staggering. It wasn't something we could just ignore.

By then I was a group chief and could instruct my stations to do essentially what I wanted, so I leaned on our offices in the Caspian and Central Asia to concentrate on the Iranian target. Early in 1996 one place came up with a plan to bug a clandestine Pasdaran facility. At that point we had no idea what the Pasdaran was doing in the Caspian, but the possibility always existed that it intended to open a third front, in addition to Saudi Arabia. Any information would have been helpful.

I knew the routine and called Sheila Heslin for her permission to go ahead. I described what we intended to do, what we expected the take to be, and what the benefit would be to U.S. interests in the region. I could feel a frigid Arctic air coming over the telephone line.

Less than twenty minutes later, my green phone rang—the superencrypted communications line used for discussing sensitive information. Rand Beers was on the other end. "What's this about the Iranian Pasdaran and some audio operation?" he asked.

"Yeah, what's the problem?"

"Well, Heslin's worried about the blowback."

"The *blowback*?"

"She's afraid the Iranians will take revenge on Amoco's people in Azerbaijan."

Even though Beers had just handed me a gem about how the NSC worked, I was furious. "Do you mean to tell me we have to stop an operation against a terrorist group—one perhaps responsible for killing five Americans in Saudi Arabia—to protect Amoco's balance sheets?"

"Well, I wouldn't put it that way," Beers said.

"Fine, I'll call Congress and tell them that Sheila Heslin, Amoco's ambassador to the NSC, no longer wants us to target the Iranian Pasdaran because we're worried about Amoco's profits."

Like a good bureaucrat, I fired off what is called a spot report to the deputy director of operations, Dave Cohen, about my conversation with Beers. I never got a response, but Beers called back that same day to tell me the NSC had had a change of mind and decided not to object to South Group's targeting the Pasdaran. Congress and Iran had a certain resonance in the White House.

I remember thinking that it should have been a big moment. After all the bureaucratic infighting, all those internal and external battles within the intelligence community, I had finally won one. For a moment, at least, the battle against terrorism had trumped the battle for oil money. But I was just so tired of it all. We were talking about lives, for God's sake. The fight shouldn't have been so difficult.

"This is the way the world ends," T. S. Eliot wrote

in "The Hollow Men." "Not with a bang but a whimper."

★

ROGER TAMRAZ DISAPPEARED from my life as suddenly as he had appeared. He never called again after the December 7 meeting when he told his story to Bill Lofgren. Although I ran into him several times in 1996, our conversations were stiff and formal. There wasn't a word about campaign financing or Roger's plans to fund Yeltsin's campaign. He had obviously heard that I'd ratted him out. *Another bureaucrat without vision*, he must have thought.

Lofgren asked me to put on paper everything Roger had told me, from my first official meeting in May to our last one on December 7. I wrote it all up, from the White House price list to Fowler's call. I even devoted a full page to the Milan meeting and the possibility that Tamraz might be planning to channel Russian money into the 1996 U.S. presidential campaign. My memo was duly logged out of South Group on December 28, 1995. A copy was put in the group's chronological file. I wouldn't hear about it again until I found reference to it splashed across the American press two years later.

21

IN MARCH 1997, I called Bill Lofgren, who had by now retired, and told him that I'd seen enough of what was going on in the White House and intended to blow the whistle. Bill didn't say anything for a moment. I could almost hear his brain crunching through the possible consequences.

"Do it," he finally said, all doubt banished.

It wasn't easy advice for Bill to give. For starters, he knew as well as I did that whistle-blowers are among the least popular subspecies in Washington, where everyone who counts seems to feed off the same two or three teats. Why ruin a good thing by calling attention to the truth?

Bill also had a personal stake in my keeping silent. After he retired from the CIA, he hung out his shingle as a consultant on the former Soviet Union. One of the first clients to call was Roger Tamraz, who still had problems in Azerbaijan and wanted Bill's advice on how to solve them. It was only a small contract, but it at least paid the telephone bills in the early going. When we kidded Bill about working for a wanted felon, he laughed and noted the fancy pedigrees he had joined. If Senator Kennedy's wife could work for Tamraz, why couldn't he? And wasn't it Tamraz who had helped foot the bill for Clinton's fiftieth-birthday gala in New York and attended the White House showing of *Independence Day*? If Roger had rehabilitated himself enough to befriend the president of the United States, Lofgren didn't see why he couldn't do a little honest work for him.

Deciding to blow the whistle was hard enough. Finding someone to blow it to proved damn near impossible. First I tried calling the office of Alabama Democrat-turned-Republican senator Richard Shelby. A member of the Senate Select Committee on Intelligence (SSCI), Shelby had fired the opening shot in the Clinton campaign-finance scandal when he asked the NSC for its records on suspicious campaign donors. I figured he needed all the help he could get, but obviously I was wrong.

When Shelby's office didn't return my call, I tried an end run to him through John Millis, chief of staff on the House intelligence committee. Millis was a former CIA case officer who had quit to work for Congress. I'd replaced him in Rabat and knew that even though he held a highly charged political job, he was discreet and lived by a strict code of integrity. He wouldn't dime me out to the CIA.

Millis laughed when I told him the story. "Do you have any idea what you're doing?"

I considered telling him about all my suspicions and then left it by telling him about Tamraz's buying access to the president.

"They'll come after you. You'll find yourself a very lonely man in this town. Anyhow, I'll pass the word to Shelby," Millis said as he hung up.

I don't know if he did pass the word, but I didn't hear anything more from Millis or Shelby, so I called the Justice Department task force investigating campaign financing and volunteered to come downtown and share what I knew. When I alerted my boss to what I had done, alarm bells went off all over Langley's seventh floor. The general counsel's office immediately called the task force to cancel my meeting. "We're sorry he [Baer] went out of channels," the task force was told. The CIA would do its own investigation and get back to Justice when the inquiry was complete.

In theory that all sounded just fine. The CIA had picked up the aroma of questionable campaign financing long before Congress and the press had. It had even started doing its own damage assessment, trying to root out the skeletons in the closet. But all the trails seemed to end up going cold.

There was the case of Larry Wallace, for instance. An old business crony of former White House chief of staff Mack McLarty, Wallace held an open day pass to the White House and a letter naming him an ex-officio representative of the president. Basically, thanks to McLarty, he could come and go as he pleased, and he certainly did. Wallace used the letter to drum up business overseas, including with Yasir Arafat. He eventually hit a speed bump in Belgrade when he made the mistake of letting Slobodan Milosevic make a copy of the letter. Our office in

Belgrade got ahold of a copy and faxed it back to headquarters, which prompted the Central European Division to open a file on Wallace. (The CIA can collect information on Americans if there is good evidence they are spies or making common purpose with the enemy.) But Wallace's file was lost before it could be turned over to congressional and Justice investigators.

Then there was the case of Lieutenant Colonel Liu Chao Ying, of Chinese military intelligence. It was Liu who gave Johnny Chung the famous $300,000 to put into Bill Clinton's campaign. Chung must have had other things on his mind, because he forwarded only $20,000 to the DNC, but what wasn't known was that one of our case officers had been in touch with Liu while this was all going on. It was particularly embarrassing because the CIA had neglected to tell Justice about her.

In fact, as the case officer found out, the less headquarters heard about Liu, the better. When she sent a cable asking if Chung had some White House appointment—his business card sported an embossed presidential seal in the corner—headquarters never responded. Nor did it want to think too hard about a company Liu had ties to: China National Aero-Technology Import and Export Corporation, which was secretly negotiating with Iran to exchange sophisticated arms, many of U.S. design, for oil.

The CIA did eventually send the Justice task force a set of Tamraz documents, but they had been cherry-picked to make certain nothing would see the light of day that suggested the agency had dropped the ball. In the meantime, someone leaked the administration's spin on Roger Tamraz to *Wall Street Journal* reporter Michael Frisby.

It was only when Shelby got word of Frisby's story that he decided I was worth his time. The CIA bundled me up in a van and sent me downtown to the Hart Office Building and the offices of the SSCI. Six of us were in attendance. Shelby and his aide sat on my left. The CIAs general counsel, Mike O'Neil, and the head of congressional affairs, John Moseman, sat across the table. Senator Bob Kerrey wasn't there, as I had hoped. A Vietnam combat veteran, Kerrey not only had guts, he understood how the political sands shift in Washington. But I was happy to see that his SSCI staffer Chris Straub had filled in for him. Straub and I and another congressional staffer had spent three days in northern Iraq, traveling around and talking about the CIA and what it was trying to do there. I liked him, and I think he felt he could trust me.

Whatever hopes I had for the meeting, though, were dashed when it quickly became clear that it was precooked. Like the Justice task force, Shelby was shown only the documents the CIA wanted him to see. He hadn't even heard about the possibility that Tamraz might have funneled Russian money into the DNC, nor am I certain he would have much cared if he had. All Shelby was after was more ammo to shoot down Tony Lake's nomination as CIA director. Shelby had never gotten over Lake's giving Iran a wink and a nod to go into Bosnia.

I was determined to tell my story whether the

senator wanted to hear it or not, so at a pause in the conversation, I asked Shelby: "Senator, do you know how Roger Tamraz found his way into the White House? It was through Senator Kennedy."

"Sir, we are not here to talk about my esteemed colleague," Shelby cut me off, much faster than I thought he was capable of responding.

Now annoyed, he stood up and announced that the meeting was over. He'd gotten whatever he needed to use against Lake, and he had no intention of sticking around to hear my thoughts on big oil, campaign financing, or the ethics of his colleagues.

I was about to give up on ever telling more of the story when Straub pulled me aside as we were walking out. "What the hell is going on?" he asked.

"A lot. And if you put me up in front of a full committee hearing, I'll spell it out."

I told him about Amoco, and about Heslin's opposition to the Iranian Pasdaran bugging.

"Is it really that bad?"

"Yes, Chris, I think it is."

Straub talked to Kerrey that afternoon. The following Saturday, Kerrey called President Clinton to let him know he could no longer support Lake's nomination for CIA director. Lake withdrew his nomination the next day. It should have been a triumphant moment, but there was no time to celebrate.

KGB DEFECTOR YURI NOSENKO should have served as example enough of what happens to someone who's off message at the CIA. When Nosenko offered a version of Lee Harvey Oswald and the Kennedy assassination that didn't fit with the agency's corporate view, he was sent to solitary confinement at the Farm for three years. I don't know why I thought I'd be treated any differently.

At eight-thirty A.M. on March 18, 1997, I presented myself to the CIA inspector general exactly as ordered. I was shown into a room without any windows. A mahogany conference table separated me from the two men sitting directly across from me. With their bloodless, pinched faces and identical Dacron suits, they could have passed for twins. Neither of them offered his name.

Before I could even sit down, the nastier of the two fired the first shot: "Did you keep a record of the documents you destroyed?"

I didn't say anything as I took on board what was happening. Destroying official documents is a crime, a felony. Soon they had let loose a withering enfilade of questions about the December 28 memo, the one Bill Lofgren had asked me to prepare in which I had set down everything that had passed with Roger Tamraz.

"Look," I finally said. "Is it logical to frame myself by writing a memo that details someone else's crime, file it away in the chrons for all the world to see, and then destroy it? Anyhow, go ask Paul Redmond how it ended up in his safe. That's proof enough I didn't destroy it."

I, in fact, had no idea how my memo had ended up in the safe of the deputy director for counterintelligence, but its mere existence there seemed to me proof enough that I had papered the executive suites of the CIA with the damn thing. It was almost as if I hadn't said anything at all. "Just tell us why you destroyed the December 28 memo," one of the twins said. "You might get off easy."

After an hour, even they got tired of asking the same question over and over. "How much did Tamraz pay you to clean up the October memo?" one of them asked.

They ignored me when I countered that the cover sheets proved that the general counsel's office had done the scrubbing, not me.

The questioning shifted again. "Why did you badger Sheila Heslin to take Tamraz's name off the Secret Service blacklist?"

I exploded. "It's not true. No officer in my position would dare cross an NSC staffer and survive to tell about it." If that was the story Heslin was telling, I thought, she had obviously gone around the bend.

"That's not what she says," one of them came back at me. "She says you pressured her to remove Tamraz's name from the White House blacklist. She says you called her at least a dozen times with the same demand. You scared her."

I considered telling them about a dinner I had hosted for an Azeri delegation six months earlier, on September 15, at La Chaumiere in Georgetown. I'd included several government officials, including Heslin. Not only had she lobbied for the invite, she even cadged a ride home from me afterward, at a time when I supposedly had her scared half to death. Go figure, but I knew my new pals wouldn't be interested. Instead I used my last trump card—Heslin's internal White House e-mails. You had to read only a few of them to conclude she had lost her grip on reality.

"Take a look at Heslin's e-mails," I said, and offered to make copies. "She seriously believes the CIA is behind a conspiracy to take over the world."

They weren't interested in looking at them, either. "We're investigating you, not Heslin," one of my interrogators said.

"By the way," I finally asked, "how long have you guys worked for the agency?" Although they both were wearing blue CIA staffer badges, something didn't smell right.

They looked at each other and nodded. Apparently, they had no choice but to tell me. "We're from the Secret Service."

Lovely, I thought. Two outsiders had been put in charge of an internal CIA investigation.

★

THE NEXT MORNING six men in black and a woman in a puce dress buttoned up to the neck descended on South Group like Ostrogoths sacking Rome. They barred everyone from leaving; then, without saying a word, they started rifling through safes, ripping apart files, and throwing them onto the floor. It looked like a typhoon had hit the place.

Soon they were interviewing my employees behind closed doors. Invariably the first question was: "Do you have an attorney? If not, you might consider retaining one." It was pure intimidation. With only one or two exceptions, no one had been working there in 1995 at the time I was meeting Tamraz. But just in case the message didn't sink in, notifications began flashing across monitors that afternoon that the inspector general was in the process of auditing their computers. This wasn't a particularly subtle threat: Misusing a computer in the CIA got you fired. Before long I found myself sitting alone in South Group. Everyone who could found a job elsewhere.

In mid-May I took a routine medical exam. A computer-generated notice landed on my desk on May 30 informing me that I'd passed, but a few days later, as I was making preparations for a short European trip, I got a new notice that there had been a "problem" with my physical. A staff doctor had not signed it, I was told, and I would have to take another one. When that turned out to be a load of baloney, I was told I needed a "routine" psychological exam. That wasn't true, either: The CIA doesn't require psychological exams unless an employee is going to a hardship post like Moscow or Peking. Clearly, my employer was trying to send a message: I needed to shut my mouth or risk going to the loony bin. I'm sure someone up on the seventh floor wondered if Yuri Nosenko's cell was available.

As the Clinton campaign-finance scandal moved forward in the courts and toward a showdown in Congress, it became apparent to me that the Justice Department task force, like the CIA, wasn't looking for the truth, the whole truth, or anything like the truth.

In a pre-grand jury session on June 5, I told Laura Ingersol, the head of the Justice task force, about my dealings with Tamraz. Her deputy and an FBI agent attended the meetings. Ingersol listened patiently, took notes, read the Tamraz documents—she had a complete set—and asked some very good, pertinent questions.

I zeroed in on the fact that Tamraz didn't have a penny in his name, at least any accounts we knew about. OCL, Delaware was a phantom company with something like $250 in its Citibank account and no employees or other assets. It was the same thing with OCL, Panama: no assets, no money. The company was run out of a lawyer's office. Since Roger appeared to be broke, wasn't there a strong possibility that the money he shelled out to the Clinton people had come from some other source? Maybe even the KGB? Yes, Ingersol allowed, that might be so.

In front of the grand jury, though, the source of Roger's money was the last thing on Ingersol's mind. When I tried to bring up the evidence that Russian money might be going into the campaign, she called a recess. After we returned and I tried to raise the subject again, she cut me off cold. When I asked her if she wanted to know the truth or continue with her pointless questions, she threatened me with contempt. Ingersol avoided the Russian angle and the Milan meetings altogether. She didn't have a single question about Tamraz's claims that he'd bought access to the White House. Nothing about Don

Fowler's price list. Nothing about his hiring Ted
Kennedy's wife. Nothing about Secretary of State
Warren Christopher's son being on his payroll.
Nothing about the other political figures—Democratic senator Tom Harkin of Iowa among them—
who appeared to have solicited donations from the
always affable, always generous Tamraz. Nothing at
all. It was as if I somehow had accidentally found my
way into the wrong grand-jury hearing.

But it wasn't until her very last question that I
understood where she intended to take the grand
jury. "Did Tamraz ever offer you a job?" she asked,
looking around the room to make sure the jurors
understood the serious implications of her question.

There it was, in all its beauty: the one question
solely meant to discredit everything I had managed to
get in about Russia and the DNC. Like every good
prosecutor, Ingersol already knew the answer. She'd
talked to enough of Tamraz's acquaintances to know
he offered *everyone* he met a job, from the waiter at
the Four Seasons to two congressional staffers who
flew out to Geneva to interview him. He'd probably
even offered one to Heslin. The grand jury, though,
knew none of that. In the version of events Ingersol
had scripted for them, the whole Tamraz affair boiled
down to a venal CIA officer playing the system—a
perfect red herring to draw attention away from his
DNC donations and the Russians. Obviously Laura
Ingersol knew who signed the paychecks at Justice.

The Senate's televised hearings on campaign
financing were no different. No one wanted to touch
the Russian-money question. The only thing anyone

seemed to care about were the titillating rumors about the CIA. And why not? A CIA officer who fronted for a shady oilman of Middle Eastern descent satisfied everyone's interests. Senators Kennedy, Harkin, and others certainly didn't want to linger long over Roger Tamraz's largesse. The Republicans also knew that the National Republican Senatorial Committee had solicited Roger's money, as had the Reagan administration. And of course Democrats were understandably squeamish about the possibility that KGB rubles perhaps had purchased some first-rate face time with the commander in chief. Roger might not have been called at all if it weren't for his entertainment value. Sitting alone without a lawyer as he promised to double his contributions to $600,000 the next time around, Roger provided a brilliant coup de théâtre with which to bring the curtain down on the whole sham operation.

As for me, I made it into the hearings as a sound bite, most notably when Illinois Democratic senator Dick Durbin, who had clearly bought in to Heslin's version of events, said of me: "What does this guy do for a living? It sounds like he worked for the Chamber of Commerce." But I couldn't help noticing that I was the only witness to be disinvited from appearing in person. Senator Fred Thompson had probably heard that once I started to open up my fat mouth about foreign money oozing around American politics, there'd be no way to close it. Instead of an appearance, the CIA wrote up a one-page stipulation of fact that said basically nothing.

★

How DO YOU CALL an end to a career that has taken you so far into the heart of darkness and shown you so many of the secrets that lie there? I didn't want to go out bitter, but I didn't want to just slink away, either. I'd spent a quarter century building up a body of knowledge and a set of instincts about some of the worst people and most dangerous organizations on the planet. I decided to find out, really find out to the best of my knowledge, what the truth was behind Iranian-sponsored terrorism.

Maybe, I thought, the search would lead me to what I considered the biggest secret of all, the one that had been gnawing at me for more than thirteen years: Who bombed the U.S. embassy in Beirut, and why had they never been brought to justice? I wanted to tie up loose ends, especially after being pulled off the trail to spend time in Tajikistan and northern Iraq, and the embassy bombing was the loosest end of my career as far as I was concerned. But there was more to it than just satisfying myself. Whoever bombed the embassy was clearly someone to be reckoned with. He—or it or they—had the will, the experience, and the determination to do enormous damage. If we couldn't identify who had done it, if we couldn't even learn what kind of explosives had been used, chances are it would all happen again, maybe at a far greater magnitude. I didn't want that on my conscience if I could avoid it, and by now it had become obvious to me that the new, politically correct CIA was neither up to nor interested in the challenge.

There was one more advantage to tackling Iranian

terrorism for an encore: Not only was it familiar territory, but I was also convinced it was the last issue Washington politicians would try to manipulate to their personal benefit. Sure, I'd seen Sheila Heslin try to block our operation against the Iranian Pasdaran to help an oil company, but she was one person and was eventually overruled. I'd also heard rumors that the Clinton administration was putting the brakes on the investigation into the Khobar barracks bombing. But I figured that had to be an exaggeration: Even the White House wouldn't dare cover up a terrorist attack in which nineteen servicemen were killed.

I started out by running a computer search for intelligence we knew to be factual on the hostages in Lebanon. The first thing I noticed was that, by the time Iran made the decision to release the hostages in March 1991, it had given up any attempt to hide its hand. Two senior Pasdaran officials, Feridoun Mehdi-Nezhad and Hossein Mosleh, directly supervised the releases. Then, on April 28, 1991, both men flew to Damascus to see 'Imad Mughniyah. Their message was clear: Iran was getting out of the hostage business, and so was the super-shadowy Islamic Jihad Organization. The orders, they said, came directly from Iran's spiritual leader, Ayatollah Khameini. Mughniyah left the same day for Beirut and started making preparations to carry out Iran's orders. By September 1991 Mehdi-Nezhad and Mosleh were in Beirut pretty much full time, closing down safe houses, paying off guards, and preparing communiqués, as well as reassuring the IJO that Iran wasn't getting out of the terrorism business entirely.

There was still work for the IJO.

Once I was sure I had that trail down, I went back to the 1987 release of French hostages, looking for comparables. In fact, the process played out much the same way. After then prime minister Jacques Chirac agreed to give Iran everything it wanted, we watched Mehdi-Nezhad and Mosleh roll into action, handing down orders to the Iranian Pasdaran office in Lebanon and the IJO. On November 26, 1987, the Pasdaran office at the Shaykh Abdallah barracks composed and translated into Arabic a communiqué related to the two hostages, Roger Auque and Jean-Louis Normandin. The next day, the communiqué and the Frenchmen went free.

The deeper into the files, the more I was struck by the fact Mehdi-Nezhad and Mosleh were at the center of every major Pasdaran terrorist operation. Their involvement went back to the early eighties, when the two were assigned to Balabakk after the Israeli invasion. They were also there when our own American hostages were incarcerated in the married officers' quarters, and they kept showing up at the edge of other events as well. Mehdi-Nezhad met with Mughniyah's deputy halfway through the hijacking of TWA Flight 847. As the hijacking drama was playing itself out on the tarmac at Beirut International Airport, Mosleh could be seen talking to Mughniyah at planeside. We didn't know the subject, but it had to be something important for Mughniyah to take time out of his busy, murderous day.

Mehdi-Nezhad, especially, seemed to be involved in more than just Lebanese-based terrorism. In 1989 he personally led an Iranian hit team that assassinated a Kurdish leader in Vienna. One of his Lebanese agents, Talal Hamiyah, was involved in two attacks in Buenos Aires. He was implicated in the Al-Khobar barracks attack in Saudi Arabia. Mehdi-Nezhad, you will recall, showed up in the Pan Am 103 chronicles: in January 1988 in Tripoli, Libya, and again in July 1988 in Frankfurt—six months before Pan Am 103 exploded over Lockerbie. Was he the Pasdaran officer who met Muhammad Hafiz Dalqamuni in the Biqa' Valley and instructed him to blow up an American airplane? It was circumstantial at best, but the man did have a track record.

THE PHANTOM I kept running up against in my investigation was the IJO. It seemed to pop into existence whenever some new horror was inflicted in the Middle East and elsewhere, and then it seemed to slip completely back into the shadows again. We knew it had deep ties to the Iranian Pasdaran, but we knew next to nothing about its command structure, its recruiting methods, its personnel, its training bases, or anything else. How was it possible? More to the point, how could you ever begin to solve the embassy bombing and other outrages if you could never penetrate the group that took credit for so many of them?

And then it occurred to me, as clearly as it had been hidden the moment before: The IJO had never existed. It was only a name the Pasdaran used for communiqués to claim terrorist operations. What's more, the CIA knew the IJO was merely a front for the Iranians. It was clear from the documents I dredged up that, by at least 1997, the CIA knew the Pasdaran's command structure inside and out, just as it knew that Ayatollah Ali Khameini and President Rafsanjani approved every terrorist operation to come out of Iran. As I looked at the evidence in front of me, the conclusion was unavoidable: The Islamic Republic of Iran had declared a secret war against the United States, and the United States had chosen to ignore it.

I had to be missing something, I felt, so I went to see an analyst who had followed Iran since the 1979 revolution. I'll call him Jim. A maverick, Jim made a lot of people in the bureaucracy uncomfortable. He stuck to the facts and wouldn't budge no matter how hot it got. The only solution was to take him off a sensitive account like Iran, but like me, Jim kept his own files.

I laid out for Jim what I'd found. I showed him the pile of documents I'd assembled, the important parts underlined in yellow. "Who do Mehdi-Nezhad and Mosleh work for?" I asked.

"That's a question I once struggled with myself," Jim said, pushing the papers back to me. He'd already seen them. "Mosleh was the interesting case. Early on, in 1983, we came across his name. At first he was referred to only as Shaykh Hossein from Khurasan. We didn't have a full name for him or a title, and no one paid much attention to him. The assumption was that he was a rogue operator and had no position in the Iranian government.

"I didn't ignore him, though. He seemed to be
everywhere there was trouble. He often met
Mughniyah. It wasn't until later, after the Algerians
fingered Mughniyah, that a member of the IJO put it
together and identified him by his full name, Hossein
Mosleh. Using a little regressive analysis, I determined that Mosleh had organized the IJO. He had
good connections with Fatah, and he organized the
IJO along the lines of Fatah's Black September—no
identifiable leaders, no office, no logo. In other words,
no return address for its terrorist operations. And yes,
you're right. The IJO is a fiction, meant only to hide
the Iranian hand in its operations."

"I'd already more or less figured that out," I said.
"But how long ago did the CIA know it?"

"I'm trying to tell you. Right from the beginning. It
was there in black and white, at least if you looked at
the evidence objectively."

Jim pulled out a stack of files and leafed through
them, pulling out the best reports to show me.

"Why didn't I know this when I was in Beirut?" I
asked, my jaw slack.

"Because all the good stuff was squirreled away in
the Hostage Task Force."

Made up of a half-dozen analysts who convened
privately from time to time to discuss hostage issues,
the Hostage Task Force kept no minutes, produced
no disseminated assessments, and maintained no
computer databases. Under normal circumstances, it
would have prepared what is called a National
Intelligence Estimate (NIE) on the hostages and
Iranian terrorism. But this didn't happen. The raw

reporting on Iran was simply buried, all to keep it out of the hands of Congress and the press. Incidentally, the same thing happened with Saudi Arabia. The CIA was not allowed to produce an NIE on the growing fundamentalist threat there. Had it leaked, it would have offended the Saudi royal family. All this I should have worked out before now.

I had one last question. "What did we know about Iran and the 1983 embassy bombing?"

Jim sucked in some air and reached in the back of his safe to pull out a three-page paper. "Take a look at this puppy."

It was an intelligence report from March 1982—a full thirteen months before the embassy bombing—stating that Iran was in touch with a network capable of destroying the U.S. embassy in Beirut. A subsequent report even specified a date the operation should be carried out. The source was firsthand and its reliability rock solid.

Another lingering question I wanted to answer before I gave up on my research: I'd always had my suspicions about what became known as the "second channel" in the Iran-contra affair—the one that opened up after the go-between Ghorbanifar proved such a bust. Ali Hashemi-Bahramani, President Rafsanjani's nephew, had been the primary person in the second channel, but a second Iranian had appeared with Bahramani near the end of the affair, at a meeting held on October 29, 1986, in Mainz, Germany, with Ollie North and George Cave. At the time, I couldn't figure out who he was or why he had come; now I rifled through the Iran-contra files until

I found what I was looking for. About halfway through the meeting, a mysterious Iranian who called himself Ayyub Mozzafari showed up. And what was his true name? I can't reveal the evidence here, but the answer was beyond challenge: Feridoun Mehdi-Nezhad. In seekmg the release of the hostages, the American government was doing business with Iran's master terrorist. But almost as good, I found out that Mehdi-Nezhad is now in Iranian president Mohammad Khatami's camp—the same Khatami official Washington looks at as the hope for better relations between the U.S. and Iran.

There was one final thing I decided to look into: the relationship between Mughniyah and Osama bin Laden. If there was one, which two pieces of fragmentary evidence suggested, it would be America's worst nightmare. We suspected strongly and immediately that bin Laden had a hand in the November 1995 bombing of the Egyptian embassy in Islamabad, Pakistan; his fingerprints were all over it. Shortly afterward we learned that Mughniyah's deputy had provided a stolen Lebanese passport to one of the planners of the bombing. Six months later we found out that one of bin Laden's most dangerous associates was calling one of Mughniyah's offices in Beirut. Neither piece of evidence amounts to a smoking gun, but both should scare anyone who knows how terrorism works.

As for me, both items added to a growing rage that I was having more and more trouble containing. Whether it was Osama bin Laden, Yasir Arafat, Iranian terrorism, Saddam Hussein, or any of the other evils that so threaten the world, the Clinton administration seemed determined to sweep them all under the carpet. Ronald Reagan and George Bush before Clinton were not much better. The mantra at 1600 Pennsylvania Avenue seemed to be: Get through the term. Keep the bad news from the newspapers. Dump the naysayers. Gather money for the next election—gobs and gobs of it—and let some other administration down the line deal with it all. Worst of all, my CIA had decided to go along for the ride. Now that such horrendous neglect has come home to roost in such misery-provoking ways, I take no pleasure whatsoever in having been right.

As my research drew to an end in late November 1997, I began thinking seriously about resigning from the CIA. The FBI and our own inspector-general investigations had told me what I needed to know about the agency. Politics had seeped down to its lowest levels, into operations, where I worked. I'd always assumed the DO was immune. I was wrong.

I'd joined the CIA hoping to get at a slice of truth not available to everyone. I'd even succeeded, in a sense. In my last months there, I unraveled the Beirut embassy bombing, at least to my satisfaction: Iran ordered it, and a Fatah network carried it out. Along the way, I'd also gotten to see the underbelly of a collapsing superpower, and I'd spent my days and too many nights with a cast of characters that no novelist could create. For all its ups and downs, it had been a good run, and now it was time to go. I also knew I had used up my goodwill chits. The CIA I'd spent twenty-one years serving was changing a lot faster than I could adapt. Maybe I should have tried to move up into management and change it from the top, but that wasn't me.

One Friday afternoon I walked up the seven flights of stairs to the office of the director of operations, Jack Downing, and handed my letter of resignation to his assistant. "This cowboy is hanging up his spurs," I said, my voice trembling slightly. Downing immediately asked to see me. He tried for twenty minutes to convince me that the CIA was going to go back to the way it was and there was a place for me. I could see, though, that he knew it wasn't the truth. The agency had become an ocean liner; turning it would take decades, assuming the powers that be even wanted to alter its course.

"I'm sorry to see you go," Downing finally said. "I promise you'll get a medal for your remarkable career."

True to his word, he arranged for me to be awarded the Career Intelligence Medal on March 11, 1998, officially signed by my old Georgetown classmate George Tenet. The medal turned out to be one secret the CIA was willing to keep. I didn't learn about it until two years later, when some friends finally called and told me. Still, I love it, especially the part of the citation that reads: *He repeatedly put himself in personal danger, working the hardest targets, in service to his country.*

Maybe, after all, someone had noticed.

EPILOGUE

WHEN THE WORLD as most of us knew it began to fall apart on the morning of September 11, 2001, I was at my home in Washington, D.C., not many blocks from the United States Capitol. If United Airlines Flight 93 had been allowed by its passengers to fly on to its intended destination, I would have heard it crash into the White House. If the target had been the Capitol, and it might have been, I would have felt the crash as well.

For me, the irony of the situation was hard to miss. After two decades in some of earth's true hellholes, I had returned only recently to the heart of the most powerful nation on earth, protected by a military force such as the world has never known, watched over by domestic and foreign security services that number in the hundreds of thousands. And what had saved the city I was living in? Not the CIA. Not the FBI. Not the air force or navy or marines or army. But the raw courage and determination of a fistful of average Americans. As I said at the beginning of this book, the lapse made me furious to think about. All of us have a right to expect more from those in whom we vest such power.

But there's one more thing I felt in the immediate aftermath of the attacks, as I watched the deaths unfold on TV and the horror mount both in New York

and across the Potomac River in Virginia. If it weren't
for personal commitments, I would have gotten the
hell out of Dodge, and in a big hurry. The people who
planned this attack are good. Very good. I'd found
out too much about their capabilities, from sophisticated chemical warheads to portable nuclear
weapons. I also knew they wouldn't be discouraged if
Osama bin Laden were captured and paraded down
the streets of Lower Manhattan in a cage or if
Afghanistan were bombed back into the Stone Age.

WERE THE ATTACKS of September 11 conceived in the
fertile imagination of Osama bin Laden? I don't know
for certain, and I'm not sure anyone ever will. But I
am absolutely sure that it's in Osama bin Laden's
best interests for us to believe that is so. Terrorist
campaigns aren't directed just against the enemy.
They are campaigns of recruitment as well, and by
demonizing bin Laden, by holding him up as the
mastermind of the attacks and as the archenemy, we
have assured that the disillusioned, the angry, the
desperate young men of the Muslim world will flock
to his cause, whether he's dead or alive to lead it. And
yes, there are more men like that than we could ever
count.

Did Osama bin Laden act alone, through his own
Al Qaeda network, in launching the attacks? About
that I'm far more certain and emphatic: no.

Even before I left the CIA in late 1997, we had
learned that bin Laden had suggested to the Iranians
that they drop their efforts to undermine central

Asian governments and instead join him in a campaign against the United States. We knew, too, that in July 1996 bin Laden's allies, the Egyptian Gama'at, had been in touch with 'Imad Mughniyah, whom my own research had shown to be behind the 1983 bombing of the American embassy in Beirut. Throw in bin Laden's connections to the Egyptian fundamentalists, and what we have is the most formidable terrorist coalition in history.

We also have to keep in mind that the Islamic terrorists we're up against are not hampered by self-protective bureaucracies. They don't care about institutions and egos. In the pursuit of their goals, they form ad hoc networks that dissolve as soon as the mission is accomplished, only to be reconstituted later in some new permutation or combination. And Osama bin Laden had all the right connections to put together perhaps the most dangerous ad hoc network ever. Once he set up shop in Afghanistan, opened his training camps there, and sent out word that he was ready to take violence across the ocean, it was only a matter of time until he and his colleagues struck. The questions were always how and how big, what and where, and when, not if.

IN THE AFTERMATH of the attacks, I had my own little piece of the puzzle to add.

After resigning from the agency, I moved to Beirut and set up shop with another ex-CIA officer as a consultant. It was territory I knew and understood, far better than I understood official Washington. It was also where I had my best contacts, including some I wasn't very keen on. At the height of the Internet-bubble stock market, for instance, one of Mughniyah's former associates proposed forming a dot-com company with me.

But, more interesting, among the clients we attracted (and I use the word advisedly) was a member of a Gulf royal family who was then living in Damascus, having tried unsuccessfully to overthrow his cousin, who was the emir. We would meet him irregularly at a desert location between our office and his home, and one night in December 1997, as we sat huddled by a fire to hold off the night cold, he told us this story:

When he'd been working as chief of police in his government, he had become aware that his government was harboring an Osama bin Laden cell. The two main members of the cell, he said, were Shawqi Islambuli, whose brother had assassinated Anwar Sadat in 1981, and Khalid Shaykh Muhammad, whose area of expertise was airplane hijackings. The prince went on to tell us that when the FBI attempted to arrest Muhammad and Islambuli, his government had equipped them with alias passports and spirited them out of the country; both eventually settled in Prague.

Getting out of the spy business proved a lot harder than I thought it would be. As if I'd never left, I passed everything I had learned from the ex-police chief back to the CIA in early 1998. Not surprisingly, there was no follow-up. No response. No indication that my message even got to anyone who bothered to read it. It was just like the coup in Iraq.

It wasn't until three years later, in the early summer of 2001, that an associate of my prince, a military officer still working for his government, informed me he was aware of a spectacular operation about to occur. He also claimed to possess the name of Osama bin Laden operatives in Yemen and Saudi Arabia. He provided us with a computer record of hundreds of secret bin Laden operatives in the Gulf. In August 2001, at the military officer's request, I met with an aide to the Saudi defense minister; Prince Sultan bin 'Abd-al-'Aziz. The aide refused to look at the list or to pass them on to Sultan. Apparently, Saudi Arabia was following the same see-no-evil operating manual the CIA uses.

IT ALL COMES DOWN TO the point that we have to start listening to people again, no matter how unpleasant the message is. The CIA doesn't have a choice but once again to go out and start talking to people— people who can go where it can't, see what it can't, and hear what it can't. That's the CIA I joined in 1976, not one enamored of satellite technology and scared of its own shadow, but one with the guts to walk into the wilderness and deal with what it finds there. That's the CIA we need today. And until we have that CIA—one with thousands of human ears and eyes, out listening where the ones who will do us harm hatch their evil schemes—I don't think any of us should feel safe again.

We are at war in America and throughout the

Western world, at war with an enemy with no infrastructure to attack, with no planes to shoot out of the sky, with no boats to sink to the bottom of the sea and precious few tanks to blow up for the amusement of the viewers of CNN. The only way to defeat such an enemy is by intelligence, by knowing what they plan to do next, and by being ready for them when they arrive. And the only way to gather such intelligence is by having the political will to let those who know how to learn secrets perform their jobs, no matter how murky the swamp is. I wish I had the confidence that we were willing to walk down that path and stay on it.

GLOSSARY.

Abu Nidal Organization: Sabri Al-Banna. Heads Fatah breakaway faction. Responsible for a series of terrorist attacks in the eighties. The Abu Nidal Organization is believed to be dormant.

AK-47: Soviet-era automatic assault rifle.

Amal: A Lebanese political party and militia. It is the rival of Hizballah for control over the Lebanese Shi'a.

'Asal, Munir Shafiq: Headed the Islamic wing of Fatah. He was a follower of Sayyid Qutub.

ASALA: Armenian Secret Army for the Liberation of Armenia. A terrorist group that has attacked mainly Turkish targets.

'Ayn Al-Dilbah: A small neighborhood in Beirut's southern suburbs where a large number of Hizballah terrorists lived.

'Azzam, 'Abdallah: A Palestinian cleric who first indoctrinated Osama bin Laden in Jihad.

Case officer: A CIA employee who recruits and runs foreign agents.

Committee of 77: A secret organization organized by Yasir Arafat to recruit Islamic fundamentalists.

DI: Directorate of Intelligence. A CIA component responsible for producing finished intelligence.

DO: Directorate of Operations. A CIA component responsible for running foreign agents.

DST: Direction de la surveillance du territoire. France's counterpart to the FBI.

Fadlallah, Muhammad Husayn: A Lebanese Shi'a leader. Fadlallah is popularly believed to have had a hand in the hostage taking in Lebanon in the 1980s; however, this is not true.

Fatah: A Palestinian organization founded by Yasir Arafat in Kuwait in the fifties.

Force 17: A Palestinian security organization under the control of Yasir Arafat.

Al-Gama'at Al-Islamiyah: A radical offshoot of the Egyptian Muslim Brotherhood. In 1988 it secretly established ties with Iranian intelligence.

Green Line: Confrontation line between Christian East Beirut and Muslim West Beirut.

Hamas: A Palestinian fundamentalist organization founded in 1988. It has close links to the Muslim Brotherhood.

Hamiyah, Talal Husni: Deputy to 'Imad Mughniyah. Probably coordinated most of the IJO's operations outside of Lebanon, including the hijacking of TWA-847.

Hammadah, Muhammad: TWA-847 hijacker. Arrested at the Frankfurt airport on January 13, 1987, carrying a highly volatile explosive, probably intended for use in attacks in France.

Hizballah: A Lebanon-based organization officially founded on February 16, 1985.

Hizballah of the Hijaz: Saudi Hizballah. Probably organized in 1991, it was funded and its members were trained by Iran's Islamic Revolutionary Guard Corps.

Hyperbaric switch: A switch sensitive to changes in altitude. It has been used by the PFLP/GC to blow up airplanes in flight.

IJO: Islamic Jihad Organization. A cover name used by Iran's Islamic Revolutionary Guard Corps to conduct terrorist operations around the world.

IRGC: Islamic Revolutionary Guard Corps, founded on May 5, 1979, shortly after the Islamic revolution in Iran.

KDP: Kurdish Democratic Party. A Kurdish-Iraqi political party and militia headed by Masud Barzani.

Lebanese Forces: A Lebanese Christian militia. In 1987 it secretly allied with Hizballah in Hizballah's war against Amal.

LST-5: A satellite transceiver.

Microdot: A reverse photographic negative small enough to be buried in a piece of paper.

Mughniyah, 'Imad: Head of Special Security, an organization loosely tied to Lebanon's Hizballah. Special Security used the cover name Islamic Jihad Organization for some terrorist operations.

Al-Musawi, Husayn: Founded Islamic Amal in 1982.

Muslim Brotherhood: An Islamic reform movement dedicated to instituting Islamic law and ending Western colonialism in all Islamic countries. It was founded in Egypt by Hasan Al-Banna in 1929.

NIE: National Intelligence Estimate, a special analytical assessment.

PFLP/GC: Popular Front for the Liberation of Palestine/General Command. Based in Syria, it is headed by Ahmad Jabril.

PETN: Pentaeryhritol tetranitrate, an explosive used to make military plastique.

PLO: Palestine Liberation Organization, a Palestinian umbrella group founded in 1964. It is headed byYasir Arafat.

PUK: Patriotic Union of Kurdistan, a Kurdish-Iraqi political party and militia headed by Jalal Talabani.

RPG: Rocket-propelled grenade. Soviet-era weapon used in many parts of the world.

Safe house: An ordinary apartment or house used to meet agents. The lease (or title) is never in the name of the spy organization using it.

Shaykh Abdallah barracks: A Lebanese gendarmerie barracks in the Biqa' Valley, occupied by Iran's Islamic Revolutionary Guard Corps in November 1982.

Al-Sugayr, Azmi: Aka Abu Al-'Abd. Headed Fatah stay-behind unit in Beirut during the early eighties.

T-72: A Soviet-era main battle tank in the inventory of most former Soviet countries and many states in the Middle East.

UAZ: A Soviet-era jeep.

INDEX